Economic Statistics
1900~1983

United Kingdom, United States of America, France, Germany, Italy, Japan

Economic Statistics
1900~1983

United Kingdom, United States of America, France, Germany, Italy, Japan

Compiled and written by **Thelma Liesner**

Facts On File Publications
New York, New York ● Oxford, England

Published in the United States by
Facts On File, Inc.
460 Park Avenue South
New York, N.Y. 10016

Library of Congress Cataloging in Publication Data
Liesner, Thelma.
   Economic statistics, 1900–1983.

   1. United States – Economic conditions – Statistics.
2. Europe – Economic conditions – Statistics.   3. Japan –
Economic conditions – Statistics.   I. Title.
HC106.L68 1985   330.973'09'021   85–10141
ISBN 0–8160–1299–7

Charts by Richard Natkiel

Typeset and Printed by the Pindar Group of Companies,
Scarborough, North Yorkshire, UK

CONTENTS

LIST OF CHARTS

ACKNOWLEDGEMENTS

The data presented in this volume are drawn very largely from official publications. For the earlier periods, however, I also used estimates made and data collected by academic researchers, in particular Professor C H Feinstein, Professor J W Kendrick, Professor Simon Kuznets and Dr B R Mitchell. Their work has been an essential input to the volume.

I have inevitably made demands on the staff of a number of libraries. I would like to thank in particular Stephanie Kenna of the British Library (Official Publications section), Mr Donald Ross of the British Library of Political and Economic Science, and Mrs Olga Peppercorn of the Department of Applied Economics library at the University of Cambridge. I am also grateful for the help given to me by Mr C G E Bryant at the Central Statistical Office and Mr C T Taylor at the Bank of England. Mr Stanley Millward kindly checked a number of calculations for me.

My warmest thanks, however, go to my husband for his help and encouragement throughout.

Thelma Liesner
November 1984

GENERAL NOTES

Sources

For the UK and the USA, national official statistics have been used as far as possible in compiling the tables. For France, Germany, Italy and Japan, the data have been taken primarily from the statistics produced by international organisations, but national official statistics have also been used. Sources and explanatory notes are given at the end of each set of tables. Obvious discontinuities in the series are pointed out in these notes, but for further information about the data reference should be made to the sources.

Figures in italics for 1983 are author's estimates.

Index numbers

Index numbers are shown with 1980 = 100 for all countries as far as possible. The original base year will vary considerably and reference should be made to the original source for details. Indices have been linked to obtain a continuous series.

Boundary changes

Changes of boundaries affect the figures for most of the countries; the problem is particularly serious for Germany. This will clearly affect the interpretation of a number of tables.

Decimal places

Many of the series are given to one decimal place, sometimes more. This is not intended to indicate a high degree of accuracy but merely to show the movement in the series. If the figures were always rounded, many of the series would show no movement at all in the early years and this would be inaccurate.

Units of measurement

Metric measurements have been used throughout. For example, where tons are shown, the measurement is in metric tons.

Billion = 1,000 mn

Symbols used

. . .	no data available
—	nil or negligible
Heavy horizontal bar:	significant break in series
Light horizontal bar:	minor break in series
Figures in brackets:	approximate figures obtained by extrapolation or other indirect means or not wholly in accord with the column heading.

Timing

This volume was completed at the end of October 1984. Revised statistics published subsequently have not in general been incorporated.

Part I

Introduction

CONTENTS

Introduction

The general slowdown in economic growth during the 1970s and the depth and duration of the post-1979 recession have revived interest in economic experience in the earlier decades of the century and especially in the interwar period. Examination of that period presupposes the availability of consistent statistics. The purpose of this book is to bring together from a wide variety of sources basic economic statistics for the main industrial countries from 1900, and to make them as consistent as possible.

The main emphasis is on the UK and the USA, and for these two countries the principal components of economic activity have been covered. Part II gives basic data on national output and expenditure, personal income and profits, employment and earnings, trade, finance and prices for the UK and the USA. Some of the more important series for France, Germany, Italy and Japan have also been included although the coverage for these countries is less comprehensive than for the UK and the USA. The data for these four countries are in Part III.

For both the UK and the USA, nearly 150 series are presented, most of which cover the period 1900–83. Two main factors were borne in mind in selecting a particular series for inclusion:

(a) its usefulness as an economic indicator;
(b) the availability of reasonably consistent data over a long period of time.

At the time the manuscript was completed, the data were as up to date as possible; readers may wish to add later statistics as these become available. For this reason, the form of the tables has generally followed the presentation of official statistics, which can thus readily be used to update the information. Details of the sources are shown in the notes following the tables for each country.

The choice of 1980 as the base year for the constant price and index number series for the UK was dictated by current UK official statistics. For the USA, the constant price series for gross national product and its components are given in 1972 dollars. For the other four industrialised countries, the constant price base is 1975. Index numbers have, however, in all cases been converted arithmetically to a 1980 base to make comparison with UK data easier. Physical quantities have been converted, where necessary, to metric measurements.

Certain series which have been important historically in the development of the UK or the USA but are now no longer major contributors to total output have been included in the tables; an obvious example is woven cotton cloth production in the UK.

In addition to tables covering basic data for each of the six countries, 16 analytical tables are set out in Part IV, summarising the main data and bringing out some of the more interesting trends.

The tables and charts in this book will indicate quite clearly the trends in the pattern of overall economic activity over the last 80 years. No attempt has been made, however, to analyse the underlying causes of the changes which have occurred; that would not be appropriate for a volume of this kind. The main purpose is to provide the statistics, which can then be used for economic analysis.

The narrative sections which follow are intended to highlight the main features of statistical tables for the UK, the USA and the other four industrialised countries. They are divided into eleven sections, covering:

(a) trends and cycles in the total economy;
(b) growth of output by sector and by commodity;
(c) capital formation;
(d) income and expenditure;
(e) prices;
(f) earnings and productivity;
(g) employment and unemployment;
(h) population;
(i) trade;
(j) finance;
(k) transport and energy.

Trends and cycles in the total economy

The general trend in the growth of gross domestic/national product in the twentieth century is shown in Chart I.1, which is based on the data in Tables UK.1, US.1, F.1[1], G.1, It.1 and J.1. Two main features are evident from this chart.

(a) The rate of growth of gross domestic/national product has been very much faster in the period after the Second World War than it was in the previous 50 years. The 1950s–1970s might be called the 'golden age' of each of the six countries.
(b) Over the 80 years since 1900, four countries – France, Germany,[2] Italy and the USA – have, in the main, experienced a similar pattern and rate of growth. The countries which stand out are the UK and Japan: the UK as the country with the slowest rate of growth and Japan as the fastest growing economy (data available only since 1930).

Comparing rates of growth is inevitably a tricky exercise. The first problem is the selection of appropriate periods for comparison. Before the Second World War the periods are more or less self selecting (although there is a data restraint for Germany and Japan). In the post-war period, cyclically comparable years have been chosen as far as possible, but the cycles of economic activity do not always coincide for the six countries. The periods used in Table IV.1, which shows the annual average rates of growth for each country from 1900 (as far as possible), seem reasonably comparable; in addition, two long run periods (1900–38 and 1950–83) have been given.

For the UK, the annual average rate of growth in the 1950s was nearly double that of the period before the First World War and 50 per cent higher than in the period 1920–29. It is interesting to note, however, that the rate of growth was higher in the UK in the period 1929–38 than in 1900–13 despite the world recession. This can also be seen in Chart I.1. Over the period 1950–83 the annual average rate of growth of nearly 2·5 per cent compares favourably with that for the period 1900–38 of just over 1 per cent.

In the USA, the rate of growth over the 1930s reflects the large decline in activity in the early years of the decade. For the other four industrialised countries, the fall in activity between 1929 and 1938 is marked only in France, where the rate of growth of output declined even more rapidly than in the USA (see chart), after reaching a peak in 1929 and having sustained an average annual rate of growth of nearly 6 per cent in the period 1920–29. For Germany, incomplete data are available for 1920–29; from 1929–38 the annual average rate of growth was about the same as in the period before the First World War. Experience in Italy was similar to that in France, but growth in the 1920s was a good deal less, and that in the 1930s higher than, in France. Data for Japan are available

---

[1] Figures for gross domestic product and its components for France are not given in Table F.1 until 1930 because insufficient data were available. The chart for the period 1900–29 is based on an index of Revenue Nationale in constant prices given in *Annuaire Statistique*, 1983.

[2] The figures for Germany in the chart have been roughly adjusted to what is now the Federal Republic of Germany.

3

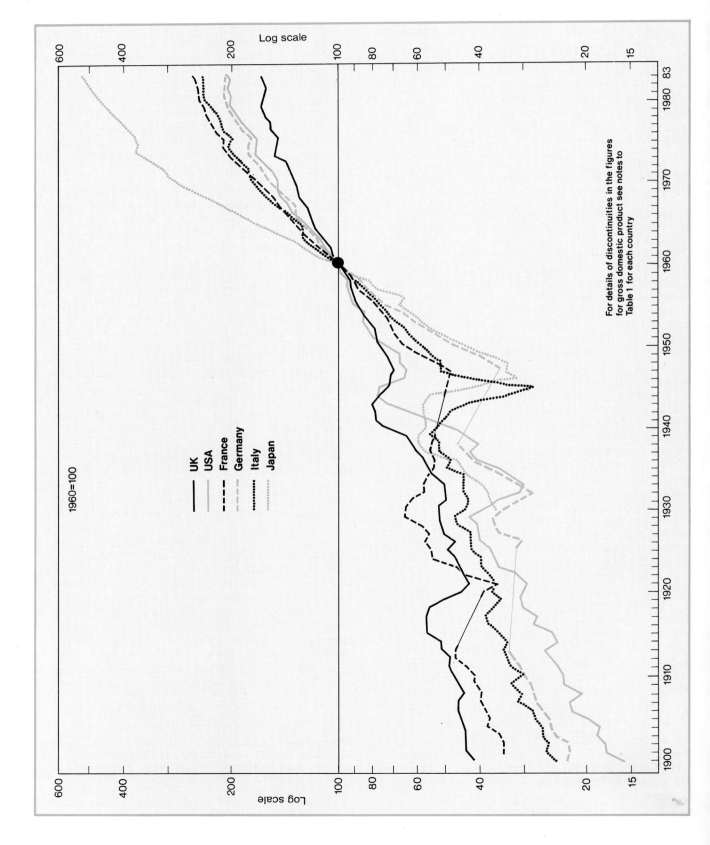

Chart I.1 Gross domestic product, six countries, 1900–83

Log scale

1960=100

UK
USA
France
Germany
Italy
Japan

For details of discontinuities in the figures
for gross domestic product see notes to
Table 1 for each country

4

from 1930 only; in the period 1930–38 Japan had an average annual rate of growth of over 6 per cent, higher even than the German rate and well above that in the other four countries.

In the postwar period, a number of features stand out:

(a) the German 'economic miracle' in the period 1950–60 (annual average rate of growth of nearly 8 per cent);

(b) the relatively high annual average rates of growth in France and Italy in the periods 1950–60 and 1960–73;

(c) the effect of the 1973 oil crisis on annual average rates of growth in all six countries and particularly in Japan;

(d) the relatively slow rate of growth in the UK (even in the 1950–70 period) compared with other European countries.

Over the long period of 1950–83, the difference between rates of growth in Japan and the UK on the one hand and the other four countries on the other is even more marked, with the UK well below the average rate of growth of the other four countries (with the possible exception of the USA) and Japan well above. The factors responsible for these divergencies have, of course, been the subject of much discussion.

Growth of output by sector and by commodity

For the UK and the USA, output data are shown in two forms: by broad industrial group or sector (Tables UK.2 and US.2), and with reference to actual commodities such as coal and steel (Tables UK.3 and US.3). For the other four countries the data are mainly for commodity output, but an industrial production index is also given in Tables F.2, G.2, It.2 and J.2.

Table UK.2 shows the breakdown of total UK output by seven main sectors from 1900 to 1983 in index number form. In the case of the USA, the range of data available is much narrower. Table US.2 thus shows output in three broad sectors from 1909, and a supplementary table shows output by sector in a similar form to that given in Table UK.2, but from 1947 only.

Shifts in each sector's contribution to total output can be broadly deduced by comparing the rates of growth of different sectors with those of total output. Table I.1 shows the percentage change in output of three of the main industrial sectors and of total output for five different periods from 1900 for the UK and from 1950 for the USA. For the UK, the most striking feature is the shift in the period 1973–83 from the manufacturing and distribution sectors to the services sector. In the USA, also, there appear to have been shifts towards the services sector in 1950–60 and 1973–83 with a less marked shift between 1960 and 1973.

For the other four countries, consistent statistics for sectoral output at constant prices are not available. However, the percentage contribution of different sectors to total output can be obtained from current price data. Accordingly, Table I.2 shows the contribution of three main sectors to total output at ten year intervals from 1900. The decreasing importance of the agricultural sector in each of the four countries is shown clearly in this table, along with the growing contribution of the industrial sector.

Table I.1 Changes in output, UK and USA, selected periods, 1900–83

	Mfg		Distribution		Services		Total output	
	UK	USA	UK	USA	UK	USA	UK	USA
	% changes in output							
1900–13	28·9	...	28·6	...	27·0	...	25·5	66·2[a]
1920–38	57·5	...	25·7	...	13·2	...	35·4	38·6
1950–60	35·9	30·7	34·9	34·3	15·6	50·6	28·2	37·7
1960–73	47·8	89·6	39·0	79·5	42·2	73·1	44·2	70·2
1973–83	− 16·0	8·9	− 2·4	26·5	27·6	43·0	8·4	22·2

a From the expenditure side.

Table I.2 Output by sector of origin, France, Germany, Italy and Japan, selected periods, 1900–80

	France			Germany			Italy			Japan		
	Agriculture	Mfg	Commerce	Agriculture	Mfg	Commerce	Agriculture	Mfg	Commerce	Agriculture	Mfg	Commerce
	% total output											
1900	37[a]	34[a]	7[a]	30	40	9	51	17[d]	16	34	11	46[g]
1910	35[b]	36[b]	7[b]	25	43	9	42	22[d]	17	30	15	42[g]
1920	...	...	...	...	...	...	48	27[d]	14	27	18	40[g]
1930	...	...	...	18	45	...	31	25	19[f]	22	25	30[g]
1940	22[c]	36[c]	14[c]	...	...	...	30	28	18[f]	24	33	31[g]
1950	15	38	12	11	36	13	29	31	9	26	25	16
1960	9	37	12	6	40	15	13	31	13	13	33	17
1970	6	29	13	3	41	12	8	35[e]	16	6	36	14
1980	4	26	12	2	36	9	6	35	15	4	34	12

a 1898.   b Average of 3 year period centred on 1909.
c 1938; figure is the percentage of net domestic product in 1938 prices.   d Includes construction up to 1920.
e Includes mining and quarrying and public utilities.   f Includes some services.
g All other activities except transport and communication and construction.

Notes: Manufacturing in the years before 1950 includes other industrial activity in some instances. Commerce covers wholesale and retail trade and restaurants and hotels.

Sources: UN *Year Book of National Accounts*; B R Mitchell, *European Historical Statistics 1750–1975*, 2nd rev. edn. Macmillan, London, 1980; B R Mitchell, *International Historical Statistics Africa and Asia*, New York University Press, 1982.

The changing importance of the basic materials used by the industrial sector is shown in the output figures for coal and steel. Tables UK.3 and US.3 give data on UK and US coal and steel output as well as some information on finished products such as cars and commercial vehicles output. Similar information is given for France, Germany, Italy and Japan.

One of the problems in selecting items for long run series is that many products will, because of technical developments, change quite markedly over time. For inputs such as coal and steel there are no great difficulties, but with chemicals and motor vehicles there are many ambiguities. Chemicals output has been shown in index number form for the UK and USA (but the composition of the index will have changed over the period) while motor vehicle output has been given in thousands. It hardly needs to be said that a motor vehicle in the 1980s is not the same as a motor vehicle made in 1910. Nevertheless, the series given in the tables in Parts II and III indicate some of the changes which have taken place in the output of a number of basic industrial inputs and outputs over the last 80 years. Table IV.4 shows some of the information contained in these tables in relation to total population: an indication of the growth of real income, although it is a partial assessment only.

To complete the picture, some mention ought also to be made of agricultural output. The selection of commodities to represent agricultural output as a whole is even more difficult than for industrial output, and the years chosen for comparison are equally hazardous. Table I.3 uses corn crops for the USA and European countries and the rice crop for Japan as an indicator; data are given at ten year intervals. The most noticeable feature of this table is the growth in output in the UK from 1950. The UK is now, in fact, self sufficient in certain types of cereals, and exports of cereals and cereal products have increased rapidly in the last ten years or so (see p. 9). Output of corn crops in France and Germany also grew rapidly between 1950 and 1980 but much less than in the UK.

Table I.3 Agricultural output, six countries, selected periods, 1900–80

	UK[b]	USA	France	Germany[a]	Italy	Japan
	Index nos., 1950 = 100					
1900	103·4	86·6	116·9	237·8	52·1	64·4
1910	105·6	92·8	104·5	264·8	54·8	72·5
1920	92·3	99·9	94·0	145·8	49·3	98·2
1930	55·4	67·6	91·0	226·9	71·8	103·9
1940	64·4	79·9	73·9	204·8	91·8	94·6
1950	100·0	100·0	100·0	100·0	100·0	100·0
1960	188·9	140·3	150·8	146·7	86·1	133·2
1970	290·7	135·0	181·6	173·9	130·1	170·9
1980	470·3	216·1	292·7	232·2	132·2	126·3

a Federal Republic of Germany from 1950.   b Including Southern Ireland up to 1920.

Notes: For all countries except Japan, corn crops have been used (corn crops include wheat, rye, barley and oats); for Japan, output of rice has been used.

Capital formation

A basic requirement for the growth in output is the provision of plant and machinery, buildings and infrastructure, while investment in housing and other social provision such as hospitals and schools will be necessary for general development within a country. In addition, capital formation is an important component of aggregate demand in developed countries.

Data on capital formation by asset and by industry are given for the UK and, as far as possible, for the USA in Tables UK.4 and US.4. Figures for total capital formation only are given for the other four countries in Tables F.1, G.1, It.1 and J.1. Table I.4 sets out the proportion of capital formation in gross domestic/national product for the six industrial countries over the last 80 years (as far as possible). Chart I.1 shows the dramatic fall in capital formation in 1914–18 and 1939–45 for the UK and the USA.

A breakdown of capital formation by industry in the UK is given in Table UK.4; information in a similar form is not available for the USA. Capital formation by type of asset is, however, shown for both countries in Tables UK.4 and US.4. The information given in these tables is summarised in Table I.5. This table shows that construction (buildings and works and dwellings) was the major component of investment in both the UK and the USA in the early years of the century, and still accounts for about half of total investment in both countries. Residential building has formed 20–30 per cent of this for most of the period.

Table I.4 Fixed capital formation as a proportion of gross domestic (national) product, six countries, selected periods, 1900–80[a]

	UK	USA[b]	France	Germany	Italy	Japan[e]
	%					
1900	11·4	20·6	...	...	...	...
1910	7·6	20·5	...	...	...	...
1920	8·9	13·4	...	...	...	...
1930	12·5	13·7	...	...	18·5	...
1940	8·8	11·1	13·0[c]	16·6[d]	19·1	21·0
1950	13·0	15·5	17·2	20·7	17·6	17·5
1960	16·6	13·7	19·3	24·3	26·0	23·1
1970	21·0	14·3	23·8	24·2	24·4	34·6
1980	18·1	14·4	22·0	21·6	20·0	32·1

a Fixed capital formation and gross domestic product at constant market prices.   b Excluding government enterprises.
c 1938 figure; calculated from original data.   d 1936 figure.   e Including stocks before 1960.

Table I.5 Capital formation, in constant prices, by type of asset, UK and USA, selected periods, 1900–80

	Buildings & works		Dwellings		Plant & machinery	
	UK	USA[a]	UK	USA	UK	USA
	% total capital expenditure					
1900	46·7	61·2	23·4	22·8	17·6	18·3[b]
1910	42·3	59·9	22·1	24·1	21·7	20·6[b]
1920	44·3	51·5	15·9	20·8	20·9	38·2[b]
1930	35·7	58·0	31·7	20·7	22·2	19·2
1940	45·5[c]	47·3	[d]	32·4	46·6	24·0
1950	33·4	34·6	22·5	39·4	30·8	23·7
1960	37·4	43·9	21·3	33·3	28·6	25·3
1970	39·9	41·1	21·7	25·8	29·7	31·2
1980	32·6	31·3	20·2	21·2	36·2	38·1

a Including government expenditure on buildings and works.   b All producers' durable goods including transport equipment.
c Including dwellings.   d Included with buildings and works.

Income and expenditure

In this section, personal income and expenditure are briefly examined. Tables UK.5 and US.5 give data on personal income and profits; Tables UK.6 and US.6 give more detailed information on consumers' expenditure. For the other four countries, wages and salaries (compensation of employees) and national income data are given in Tables F.3, G.3, It.3 and J.3; consumers' expenditure in total is given in Tables F.1, G.1, It.1 and J.1.

If the crude figures for personal disposable income are used for comparison, it will be seen that income rose at a much faster rate in the UK than in the USA, particularly at certain periods. This reflects, in part, different rates of inflation in the two countries. Table I.6 therefore sets out the growth of real personal disposable income (that is, abstracting from price changes); in times of relatively high rates of inflation this is a more meaningful measure. Not surprisingly, the table shows a faster rate of growth of real disposable income in the USA than in the UK from 1938/39 to 1983.

From the point of view of the distribution of the 'national cake', the share of wages and salaries and of rental and other property income is of interest. More reliable data are available on wages and salaries than on property income, and the share of wages and salaries in national income is shown in Table I.7 for all six countries for selected years. (Data are not available for all the countries for the whole period.) The table indicates that the share of wages and salaries in national income has been rising quite sharply over the postwar period except in the UK and the USA, where it has been at the relatively high level of over 60 per cent on average right through the century.

Table I.6 Real personal disposable income, UK and USA, selected periods, 1922–83

	UK	USA
	Index nos., 1980 = 100	
1922	28·0	—
1938	39·8	22·5 (1939)
1950	43·1	35·5
1960	58·7	47·9
1973	76·2	73·6
1980	100·0	100·0
1983	100·1	107·1

On the expenditure side, the growth in total consumers' expenditure in real terms is shown in Table I.8 for each of the six countries. At least two points emerge clearly from this table:

(a) the very fast rise in private consumption in Japan in the postwar period;
(b) the relatively slow rate of growth of personal consumption in the UK.

The figures are perhaps not so surprising in view of the overall rates of growth of gross domestic product, of which private consumption is a major component, in all six countries.

In addition to data on total consumers' expenditure, a breakdown of the total by categories is given for the UK and the USA. There are certain breaks in the series in these tables partly because the classification of particular items has changed over the period (see notes on pp. 37 and 67). An analysis of expenditure per head on certain items in constant prices is set out in Table IV.5.

Table I.7 Proportion of wages and salaries[a] in national income, six countries, selected periods, 1900–80

	UK	USA	France	Germany	Italy	Japan
	% share					
1900	53·5	58·0	...	...	...	...
1920	67·1	67·3	...	59·9[b]	...	...
1938	59·4	63·3	50·0	54·9	...	...
1950	62·5	59·7	44·6	50·0	41·9[c]	41·8
1960	63·8	65·2	48·5	51·2	46·1	45·3
1970	65·3	69·0	54·1	59·1	52·3	49·3
1980	68·4	70·2	62·0	64·1	60·0	62·6

a From 1950 (1960 in the case of the UK), OECD figures of compensation of employees have been used. The figures therefore include payments other than wages and salaries; see notes on p. 83.   b 1925.   c 1951.

Notes: National income figures for UK and USA are not given in main tables; they can be obtained from 1950 from **15, 26** and **37** in UK references and **14, 15** and **19** in US references. The figures for Germany before 1950 have been taken from *Statistiches Jahrbuch*, 1974, and are for the whole of Germany.

***Table* I.8** Total consumers' expenditure by volume, six countries, selected periods, 1900–80

	UK	USA	France	Germany	Italy	Japan
	\multicolumn{6}{c}{Index nos., 1960 = 100}					
1900	48	16	...	...	...	...
1910	52	25	...	...	...	...
1920	53	32	...	...	...	...
1930	61	44	...	...	51	46
1940	64	51	62a	...	56	41
1950	78	75	63	47	63	42
1960	100	100	100	100	100	100
1970	126	149	169	163	186	254
1980	156	206	256	223	251	401

a 1938.

Prices

Consumer and wholesale price indices have been calculated for many years, but the levels of sophistication have been variable. Price indices currently constructed are far more comprehensive than those available for the early part of the period. As the later indices have been linked to the earlier series, this point should be borne in mind when the tables are consulted. Tables UK.7, US.7, F.3, G.3, It.3 and J.3 give long run data for both wholesale and consumer prices from 1900, and Table IV.10 sets out comparative data on the rate of rise of prices.

The main feature to emerge from the latter table is the stability of consumer prices in the UK and France before the First World War and the rather surprising rate of increase in Germany during the same period. In the post-war period, prices have risen at a much faster rate, with the exception of Germany. The effect of the oil price rises in the 1970s is clearly reflected in the price indices for all countries.

Earnings and productivity

There is, of course, a broad relationship between prices and earnings over the long period, although there is much controversy over the exact form that this relationship takes. Tables UK.10 and US.10 give data on average earnings for manufacturing production workers in the USA and for male manual workers in manufacturing and certain other industries in the UK. (A large amount of data on earnings or wage rates is available in both the UK and the USA, but it is often for single industries or occupations and covers relatively short or broken periods.) Data for earnings in manufacturing industry in Germany, Italy and Japan and for wage rates in France are given in Tables F.6, G.6, It.6 and J.6.

Table IV.11 shows the average rate of rise in earnings (mainly in manufacturing) in the postwar period. For 1950–83, the average rate of increase in earnings was nearly 10 per cent per year in the UK and 10 per cent or more in France, Italy and Japan. Increases in earnings in Germany were somewhat lower, at just under 8 per cent per year, and in the USA manufacturing workers' earnings rose at an annual rate of 5·5 per cent over the period.

Two series on productivity are also given in Tables UK.10 and US.10: a series on output per person employed in the whole economy (UK) and on output per manhour in the private economy (USA), and a series on output per man (UK) and output per manhour (USA) in manufacturing industry. Table IV.2 shows the annual average rates of growth for each of these series; it can be seen that the rate of growth of output per man in the UK was not very different from the rate of growth of output per manhour in the USA in the periods 1950–60 and 1960–73 and was higher in the UK in the period 1973–83.

Long period data for the other four countries on a consistent basis are not readily available before 1950 or 1954, and no productivity series are given in the tables for the other four countries. Figures in Tables F.1, G.1, It.1 and J.1 and F.5, G.5, It.5 and J.5 have been used, however, to construct the annual average rates of growth of productivity shown for these four countries in Table IV.2. Not unexpectedly, the table shows Japan as the country in which productivity (on this simple measure) has grown fastest over the period, with France, Germany and Italy experiencing roughly the same annual average increases. In all four countries, however, the annual average increase in productivity was higher (in some cases much higher) than in either the UK or the USA.

Employment and unemployment

In section 2 of this introduction, the distribution of activity as measured by output data has already been considered (see pp. 5 and 6). The same issue can also be examined from the employment side. Tables UK.9 and US.9, together with Tables F.5, G.5, It.5 and J.5, show numbers in employment by industry group; and Tables IV.6–IV.8 set out the changes that have taken place in the distribution of employment. (For the UK and the USA the figures refer, in the main, to employees in employment, but for the other four countries they usually include the self employed.)

The single most noticeable feature is the decline in employment in the agricultural sector; this is particularly remarkable in the case of Japan. The second common feature is the rise in employment in distribution and services. No clear picture emerges with respect to the long run trend in employment in industry/manufacturing.

In view of the recent sharp increases in unemployment in nearly all countries, particular interest attaches to the course of unemployment over the century. Unfortunately, although data are available for most countries back to the 1920s, there are various problems. The method of collection and coverage of statistics on unemployment vary from country to country, and the figures given in Tables UK.10, US.10, F.6, G.6, It.6 and J.6 should not be crudely compared without referring to the notes to these tables. For instance, in some countries, such as the USA and Japan, the percentage of unemployed is calculated using the civilian labour force as the denominator; the percentage figure will on that account be lower than if the number of employees in employment (including the unemployed themselves) is used as the denominator, as in the UK and Germany. Similarly, statistics are collected in different ways; in the USA and Italy, data are collected by means of labour force sample surveys, whereas in Germany and the UK it is the numbers registering or claiming benefit at unemployment offices that are counted. Each method has advantages and disadvantages, and countries have changed their coverage and definition of unemployment from time to time, particularly in the 1970s and 1980s.[3]

Nevertheless, it is worth drawing attention to the unemployment figures of the 1930s for each country, and again from 1975 onwards, compared with rates in the 'golden era' of the 1950s and 1960s.

Population

From a crude examination of the unemployment figures, it might appear that Japan is the one country of the six which, in the early 1980s, need not be too concerned about the level of unemployment. On the other hand, it is conceivable that Japan's population growth over the last 80 years could present problems of a different kind. Population data are shown in Tables UK.8, US.8, F.4, G.4, It.4 and J.4 and an analysis of total population trends and age distribution is given in Table IV.9.

Total population in Japan has grown nearly 170 per cent since 1900[4] compared with under 40 per cent in France, 73 per cent in Italy and 37 per cent in the UK. Japan is geographically about the same size as the UK but its population is nearly twice as large. The United States's population grew faster than that of Japan in the period 1900–82 but the geographical area is, of course, much larger.

Changes in population are brought about by natural increase and by migration. The last 80 years have seen a number of migration 'waves' including one from the European continent, especially Germany and Italy, to the American continent in the early years of the century and, in more recent times, from Commonwealth countries to the UK. Both the age distribution and the population of areas within a country will be affected by these migratory movements.

Table IV.9 shows the changes in the age composition of the population. The 15–64 years age group currently averages around two thirds of the total population, and this has not varied in any of the six countries to a great extent over the period. The proportions in the under 15 and in the 65 years and over age groups have, however, changed considerably. Although the extent of the shift has varied in the six countries examined, there has been a general decline in the proportion of the population under 15 years of age and a corresponding increase in the 65 and over age group which, in part, reflects common factors such as advances in medical care.

The geographical distribution of the population shown for the UK and USA is a broad one and can indicate only rather general trends. In the UK, there have been changes in the composition of the South East region (see notes on p. 38), and this makes comparison over the long period rather hazardous. What is clear, however, is that the population in England and Wales has grown at a faster rate than that of either Scotland or Northern Ireland betwen 1911 (the first year for which separate figures are available for Northern Ireland) and 1982.

In the USA over the long period, the greatest growth has been in the West, where population increased five-fold between 1910 and 1982, at least in part, as a result of migratory factors within the USA. In the last ten years or so, the rate of growth of population in the West and South of the country has been fairly rapid compared with the East and North/Central regions, where the population has been stable or has grown only slowly.

Trade

The tables concerned with trade present data on the commodity composition of imports and exports for the UK and USA and details of trade by area for all six countries. The figures in these tables are in current values and not volume; volume data would be much more difficult to obtain on a consistent basis back to 1900. For many purposes, for example the examination of the share of different commodities in total trade or the shares of different countries, current value data are not inappropriate.

Before considering trade in detail, Table I.9 shows the changes that have taken place in the dependence on trade in each of the six countries. (The ratio of imports of goods and services to gross domestic product at market prices is used as the measure.) This table shows rather clearly the increasing dependence on trade in five of the six countries. The UK has always been a major importer and exporter, but it is interesting to note that it is only in recent years that the ratio of imports to gross domestic product has surpassed the 1930 level.

Tables UK.11, US.11, UK.12 and US.12 show the composition of this trade for the UK and the USA by broad categories. Tables IV.12 and IV.13 illustrate how the percentage of total imports and exports in each broad category has altered over the period. For the USA, the most noticeable change is in the percentage of petrol and petroleum products in the total value of imports after 1973. In the UK the change in the composition of trade that has occasioned most comment in recent years is the relatively high proportion of finished manufactures in total imports: from 5 per cent in 1920, the proportion rose to 36 per cent of all imports in 1980. Basic materials, on the other hand, have become less important in total imports in recent years.

The broad categories shown in the table, however, mask the developments that have taken place within the categories. The importance of oil in UK exports in recent years is well known, but during the 1970s the proportion of dairy products in total UK food exports doubled and the proportion of cereals and cereal preparations increased from 10 to 30 per cent between 1972 and 1982. There are other examples of this kind in both the UK and the USA.

The country or area of origin and destination is of interest as well as the composition of trade. In the light of the trading blocs which have emerged in the postwar period, it is instructive to ask what difference these blocs appear to have made to the pattern of trade which existed before they were formed. The question cannot, of course, be answered unequivocally, but Tables UK.13, US.13, F.7, G.7, It.7 and J.7 present imports and exports by country or by area and Tables IV.14–IV.16 provide some additional analysis for the UK and the USA in the form of percentage shares in selected years.

Visible trade is only one aspect of exchange among countries. Others include trade in services such as shipping, financial services, insurance and tourism. Broad categories are shown in Tables UK.14 and US.14 together with the current account balance in the balance of payments.

Features of the figures for the UK are the substantial current account surpluses in 1979–82 (larger than at any time since 1900) and the very large fluctuations which occur in the current balance, particularly in the postwar period. It is also interesting to note that, apart from the years 1940–50 (war years and their aftermath) and 1963–65, services have for the most part contributed a surplus to the current account, and this surplus has been growing substantially during the 1970s and 1980s.

For the USA, fluctuations in the balance on current account are, if anything, greater than in the UK. But

---

[3]Articles in the *British Labour Statistics Year Book*, 1976, and the *Employment Gazette*, August 1980 set out the differences in the unemployment statistics of the six countries included here as well as other countries.

[4]For details of geographical changes see notes on p. 122.

Table I.9 Trade dependence, selected periods, 1900–80

	UK	USA	France	Germany	Italy	Japan
	Imports of goods and services as % of GDP in current prices					
1900	27·4	...	...	...	...	...
1910	30·6	...	...	...	...	...
1920	34·0	...	...	...	...	...
1930	23·5	4·9	...	...	...	...
1940	20·6	3·6	...	...	...	...
1950	23·6	4·0	16·3	12·7	13·2	11·4
1960	21·6	4·4	12·9	16·5	14·3	10·6
1970	21·4	5·5	15·8	19·1	17·2	9·5
1980	25·0	11·0	24·0	27·6	28·0	14·9

Sources: OECD National Accounts; UK National Accounts, 1984; C H Feinstein, *National Income, Output and Expenditure 1860–1965*; National Income and Product Accounts of the USA, 1929–76.

while continuing deficits on the UK current account are a serious matter because of the consequential effects on interest rates and exchange rates, a deficit on the US current account does not have quite the same serious implications for the US economy. Although the ratio of US trade in goods and services to gross national product is now above 10 per cent (more than twice the 1930 ratio), it is still far smaller than in the UK. Nevertheless, there has been some concern in the rest of the world in recent years over the size of the American deficits, particularly in 1977, 1978 and 1983.

The fluctuations in the balance on current account for both countries are illustrated in Charts UK.14 and US.14. These charts show the current account balance as a percentage of gross domestic (national) product indicating the proportion of national income which the two countries have invested (or disinvested) abroad at different periods over the last 80 years.

Finance

Tables UK.15 and US.15 present data on share prices and selected interest rates for the UK and the USA and also foreign exchange rates in terms of sterling. Two other monetary indicators are given: money supply and consumer credit. There are a number of measures of money supply, and the one given in the tables is perhaps the simplest: M1 (see notes to tables for definition). The consumer credit figures include not only hire purchase by individual consumers but also the purchase of machinery and equipment by businesses on credit terms.

Transport and energy

The final tables presented for the UK and the USA (Tables UK.16 and US.16) cover transport and energy consumption. The main features which these tables show are:

(a) the shift away from rail transport towards road transport for both freight and passengers;
(b) the increase in air passenger travel;
(c) the increasing importance of petroleum and natural gas relative to coal as a primary fuel input.

The first point can be illustrated only very broadly because the statistics on road traffic are shown in the form of vehicle registrations (USA) or current licences (UK) and therefore are a proxy for passenger km. The increase in these proxy indicators is shown in Table I.10 together with the movement in passenger km and freight ton km on the railways.

Over the period since 1920, the growth in passenger car use appears to have been more rapid in the UK than in the USA. However, the USA started from a much higher base; by 1920 private car vehicle registrations in the USA already numbered over 8 mn, while in the UK the number of current licences in that year was 187,000.

The decline in railway passenger traffic has been more severe in the USA than in the UK. On the other hand, in the period from 1960, the US railways have increased their freight traffic, while in the UK freight traffic on the railways continued the decline which first became noticeable in the 1920s. The number of licensed (or registered) goods vehicles has continued to increase in both countries, albeit more slowly since 1973.

The growth of air passenger traffic in the postwar period has been very rapid in both countries. In absolute numbers of passenger km, however, the UK is well behind the USA.

With respect to the consumption of primary fuel, the energy statistics point to two distinct periods in the UK. Coal was the most important single item in total fuel consumption for the first 60 years of the century. Its importance began to decline in the early 1960s until, in 1970, petroleum and natural gas together became more important than coal in total fuel consumption. The shift away from coal has continued; by 1983, consumption of coal had declined by over 50 per cent from 1960. In the USA, crude petroleum and natural gas together overtook coal as the most important fuel input in the late 1940s, and the trend has continued. Coal is now the least significant of these fuels in energy consumption in the USA.

There are many trends and other interesting relationships that have not been touched on in this brief summary of the data given in the following tables. The main aim of the volume, however, is to provide a comprehensive series of statistics.

Table I.10 Changes in road and rail transport, UK and USA, selected periods, 1920–79

	Road transport				Rail transport			
	Private cars		Goods vehicles		Passenger km		Freight ton · km	
	UK	USA	UK	USA	UK	USA	UK	USA
	% changes							
1920–30	465	183	244	236	− 5	− 43	− 7	− 7
1930–39	97	14	44	30	4c	− 16	− 9c	− 13
1950–60	145	53	56	39	7	− 33	− 16	− 3
1960–73	147a	65	26a	94	− 14	− 56	− 25	50
1973–79	8b	16	2b	41	7	20	− 12	6

a 1960–74. b 1974–79. c 1930–38.

Part II

**Statistical tables for
the United Kingdom and
the United States of America**

UNITED KINGDOM

CONTENTS

Table UK.1 Gross domestic product at constant prices, 1900–83

	Consumers' expenditure	General govt final consumption	Gross domestic fixed capital formation	Value of physical increase in stocks & w.i.p.	Exports of goods & services	Imports of goods & services	Gross domestic product at market prices	Adjustment to factor cost	Gross domestic product at factor cost
	£ bn, 1980 prices								
1900	41·8	9·0	6·9	—	11·9	−11·6	60·3	−9·7	51·4
1901	42·6	10·1	7·2	0·6	12·2	−12·1	62·7	−9·9	53·5
1902	42·8	9·6	7·6	0·2	12·7	−12·1	62·9	−9·9	53·7
1903	43·0	8·5	7·7	—	13·3	−12·1	62·9	−9·8	53·8
1904	43·6	8·2	7·3	0·1	13·5	−12·2	63·3	−9·8	54·1
1905	43·8	8·1	7·1	0·2	14·7	−12·6	64·4	−9·9	55·0
1906	44·6	8·0	6·8	0·5	15·6	−13·0	65·8	−10·0	56·3
1907	45·2	7·9	5·7	0·2	16·6	−13·2	65·9	−10·2	56·4
1908	45·0	8·1	5·0	−0·6	15·4	−12·6	63·6	−10·0	54·3
1909	45·3	8·4	5·1	0·3	16·3	−13·1	65·7	−9·8	56·3
1910	46·0	8·7	5·2	0·6	17·5	−13·5	68·0	−9·9	58·3
1911	47·4	9·0	4·9	0·6	18·0	−13·9	69·6	−10·2	59·7
1912	47·7	9·1	4·8	0·3	18·9	−14·9	69·4	−10·3	59·5
1913	49·4	9·3	5·5	0·9	19·6	−15·4	73·0	−10·6	62·6
1914	49·6	13·4	5·6	0·9	16·2	−14·5	73·6	−10·5	63·2
1915	50·7	40·1	3·7	−3·4	13·5	−15·3	80·9	−10·7	70·2
1916	46·5	45·6	2·6	−4·0	15·6	−14·2	80·8	−10·0	70·7
1917	42·9	49·9	2·9	−1·1	11·1	−12·1	81·2	−8·6	72·1
1918	42·5	47·7	2·9	0·9	8·7	−12·3	79·8	−8·4	70·8
1919	48·6	20·9	3·5	0·9	12·7	−13·9	72·8	−9·8	63·0
1920	48·7	12·0	6·0	−0·7	13·6	−13·8	67·9	−10·7	57·7
	46·6	11·2	5·8		14·2	−14·2	65·1	−10·2	55·4
1921	43·8	11·4	6·6	−0·8	11·3	−12·5	61·3	−9·5	52·2
1922	45·4	10·7	6·1	−0·7	14·3	−14·3	63·5	−9·4	54·4
1923	46·7	10·1	6·1	−0·5	15·6	−15·4	65·4	−9·5	56·1
1924	47·8	10·2	7·3	−0·05	16·1	−16·9	67·4	−9·8	57·8
1925	48·9	10·5	8·3	1·0	16·1	−17·3	70·7	−10·0	60·9
1926	48·7	10·7	8·1	0·1	14·7	−18·0	67·5	−9·9	57·9
1927	50·6	10·8	9·0	0·4	16·6	−18·3	72·2	−10·3	62·1
1928	51·4	11·0	8·9	0·1	16·7	−17·8	73·4	−10·4	63·2
1929	52·5	11·2	9·4	0·4	17·2	−18·7	75·1	−10·6	64·7
1930	53·3	11·5	9·4	0·9	14·8	−18·4	75·1	−10·6	64·6
1931	53·9	11·8	9·2	−0·03	11·9	−19·1	71·2	−10·4	61·1
1932	53·5	11·8	8·0	0·01	11·7	−17·0	71·4	−10·1	61·5
1933	54·9	11·9	8·3	−0·8	11·8	−17·1	72·3	−10·4	62·1
1934	56·5	12·2	10·1	0·4	12·3	−17·8	77·1	−10·7	66·5
1935	58·0	13·0	10·5	0·1	13·9	−18·7	80·0	−11·2	69·0
1936	59·7	14·2	11·5	−0·1	13·5	−19·2	82·5	−11·6	71·1
1937	60·7	15·8	11·8	0·6	14·2	−19·9	86·0	−11·6	74·2
1938	61·2	18·9	12·0	1·0	13·2	−19·4	88·6	−12·2	76·5
1939	61·6	28·6	10·8	1·1	12·2	−21·2	92·1	−12·5	79·7
1940	55·8	66·7	9·3	1·7	8·4	−21·5	105·3	−12·2	92·7
1941	53·5	83·6	7·5	0·7	7·2	−18·8	111·7	−12·7	98·5
1942	52·9	87·7	6·5	−0·6	6·5	−15·9	112·8	−12·6	99·6
1943	52·3	90·6	4·5	0·7	7·2	−15·7	114·9	−12·7	101·5
1944	53·9	84·8	3·4	−1·4	9·1	−17·5	109·7	−12·8	96·5
1945	57·3	68·9	3·9	−1·4	7·3	−16·7	102·9	−13·1	89·7
1946	63·2	37·8	9·7	0·8	12·4	−16·7	102·3	−13·4	88·9
1947	65·2	26·7	11·4	1·6	12·4	−16·8	99·8	−13·2	86·6
1948	65·7	25·6	12·3	0·9	15·1	−16·4	102·4	−13·2	89·1
1949	66·7	27·1	13·4	0·3	16·8	−17·7	105·5	−13·4	92·0
1950	68·5	27·0	14·2	−1·0	19·2	−17·8	109·4	−13·8	95·5
1951	67·6	29·0	14·3	2·3	19·0	−19·1	111·8	−14·3	97·4
1952	67·6	31·9	14·5	0·2	18·6	−17·7	113·0	−14·0	98·9
1953	70·6	32·7	16·1	0·5	19·4	−19·1	118·1	−14·6	103·3
1954	73·5	32·6	17·5	0·2	20·5	−19·8	122·8	−15·3	107·3
1955	76·6	31·7	18·5	1·4	21·7	−21·7	127·0	−15·9	110·9
1956	77·3	31·4	19·4	1·1	22·7	−21·8	129·1	−15·8	113·0
1957	78·9	30·9	20·4	1·1	23·2	−22·4	131·6	−16·2	115·2
1958	80·8	30·1	20·6	0·5	22·9	−22·6	131·9	−17·0	114·8
1959	84·3	30·6	22·2	0·9	23·5	−24·1	137·2	−18·4	118·8
1960	87·5	31·2	24·2	2·8	24·9	−26·9	143·6	−19·3	124·2
1961	89·5	32·3	26·5	1·4	25·7	−26·7	148·3	−19·7	128·6
1962	91·5	33·3	26·7	0·04	26·1	−27·3	149·9	−19·7	130·1
1963	95·7	34·0	27·1	0·8	27·4	−28·6	156·2	−20·5	135·6
1964	98·6	34·6	31·6	3·4	28·4	−31·5	164·4	−21·5	142·9
1965	100·1	35·5	33·1	2·2	29·8	−31·8	168·1	−21·5	146·6
1966	101·9	36·4	33·9	1·4	31·2	−32·6	171·4	−21·9	149·5
1967	104·4	38·4	36·9	1·1	31·4	−34·9	176·2	−22·6	153·6
1968	107·3	38·6	39·2	1·7	35·4	−37·5	183·6	−23·1	160·6
1969	107·9	37·8	38·9	1·9	38·9	−38·7	186·0	−23·0	163·2
1970	110·8	38·4	39·9	1·4	41·0	−40·7	190·2	−23·9	166·4
1971	114·2	39·6	40·7	0·4	43·8	−42·8	195·3	−24·8	170·6
1972	121·2	41·2	40·6	−0·1	44·3	−47·1	199·8	−26·7	173·0
1973	127·4	43·2	43·5	5·0	49·5	−52·7	215·6	−28·4	187·0
1974	125·6	43·9	41·7	2·8	53·1	−53·4	213·3	−27·5	185·5
1975	124·7	46·3	41·8	−3·0	51·7	−49·6	211·8	−27·2	184·3
1976	125·2	46·9	42·4	1·0	56·3	−51·6	220·1	−28·2	191·5
1977	124·6	46·1	41·3	2·6	59·9	−52·3	222·2	−28·2	193·6
1978	131·4	47·1	42·9	2·1	61·1	−54·3	230·3	−30·9	199·4
1979	137·3	48·1	43·9	2·5	63·4	−59·9	235·2	−32·2	203·1
1980	136·8	48·8	41·6	−2·9	63·3	−57·4	230·2	−30·9	199·3
1981	136·7	48·8	38·1	−2·7	62·1	−55·4	227·6	−30·1	197·5
1982	138·1	49·2	40·6	−1·2	62·7	−57·6	231·9	−31·6	200·3
1983	144·0	50·5	42·3	0·2	63·3	−60·8	239·6	−32·5	207·2

13

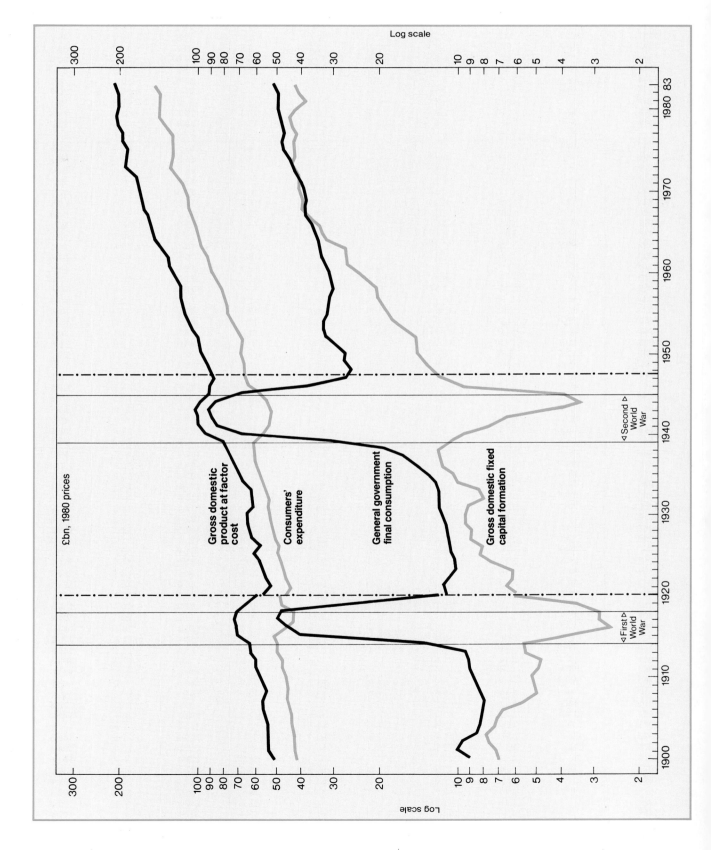

Chart UK.1 Gross domestic product at constant prices, 1900–83

£bn, 1980 prices

Gross domestic product at factor cost

Consumers' expenditure

General government final consumption

Gross domestic fixed capital formation

◁First◁ World War

◁Second ◁ World War

Log scale

14

	Total output	Agriculture, forestry & fishing	Production & construction	*of which:* Mfg	Transport & communication	Distributive trades	Services	*of which:* Public admin. & defence
				Index nos., 1980 = 100				
1900	27·1	44·4	20·3	20·1	17·3	38·5	28·9	36
1901	27·5	45·1	20·3	20·0	17·6	39·1	30·2	40
1902	28·0	46·7	20·7	20·1	18·0	39·8	30·8	41
1903	27·6	42·8	20·3	19·6	18·2	39·3	30·5	38
1904	28·1	45·1	20·5	19·7	18·8	39·9	30·4	36
1905	29·2	45·8	21·7	21·4	19·4	41·5	31·1	37
1906	29·9	42·8	22·6	22·4	20·0	42·7	31·6	38
1907	30·7	46·4	23·0	23·0	20·8	44·0	32·3	39
1908	29·7	47·7	21·2	21·1	20·3	42·1	33·2	44
1909	30·2	48·7	21·3	21·3	20·9	42·9	33·7	41
1910	30·7	48·0	21·6	21·6	21·5	43·6	34·5	43
1911	31·9	47·1	23·2	23·4	22·3	45·4	35·3	44
1912	32·8	46·4	23·8	24·4	23·3	47·6	35·7	45
1913	34·0	46·4	25·3	25·9	24·3	49·5	36·7	46
1914	...	...	23·7	24·2	...	...	...	...
1920	33·2	43·1	25·1	26·3	23·8	47·8	38·3	74
1921	31·9	33·2	24·8	25·9	23·1	45·9	37·0	53
1922	28·0	33·8	20·2	20·1	20·8	40·3	34·2	58
1923	30·1	34·2	23·3	23·4	24·2	44·5	33·4	52
1924	31·1	34·7	24·7	25·1	26·5	45·2	33·3	49
1925	32·7	33·7	27·4	27·6	27·4	46·4	33·9	48
1926	33·6	36·3	28·5	28·5	27·8	47·6	34·4	49
1927	32·9	37·3	27·0	27·6	26·6	46·2	35·0	48
1928	35·7	37·4	31·1	30·5	29·3	49·2	35·9	48
1929	35·7	39·6	30·3	30·4	29·7	49·3	36·7	48
1930	36·6	39·7	31·8	31·7	30·9	50·4	36·5	49
1931	36·1	40·7	30·4	30·3	30·7	49·9	36·9	50
1932	34·8	37·1	28·4	28·2	29·2	50·6	35·8	51
1933	34·9	38·8	28·3	28·4	28·1	50·4	37·0	51
1934	36·3	41·6	30·2	30·5	28·7	52·1	37·7	51
1935	38·3	42·1	33·2	33·3	29·6	54·2	38·5	51
1936	40·0	41·0	35·7	36·3	30·5	56·0	39·4	53
1937	42·2	40·4	39·0	39·7	32·0	58·2	40·4	54
1938	43·8	40·2	41·3	42·1	33·5	59·1	41·3	57
	43·2	39·7	40·2	40·8	33·4	57·7	41·9	62
1946	45·4	44·0	41·2	42·7	38·1	47·1	60·8	148
1947	45·9	42·2	43·4	45·2	39·8	51·0	52·5	108
1948	48·0	45·4	47·1	49·3	42·8	53·0	50·1	95
1949	49·7	48·6	50·2	52·8	45·0	55·3	50·4	92
1950	51·5	49·3	53·2	56·8	46·4	56·8	50·7	89
1951	52·4	50·6	54·4	58·5	48·5	56·2	51·6	94
1952	52·1	51·9	52·8	55·6	49·9	55·3	51·8	96
1953	54·2	52·9	56·2	59·6	51·5	59·1	52·2	97
1954	56·5	53·5	59·0	62·8	52·7	62·2	52·9	96
1955	58·4	53·1	61·8	66·7	54·0	65·2	53·6	93
1956	59·0	56·1	62·3	66·6	54·9	65·9	53·6	92
1957	60·0	57·3	63·5	68·2	54·8	67·5	56·4	90
1958	59·9	56·1	63·0	67·5	54·3	69·1	55·6	87
1959	62·7	58·3	66·1	71·4	56·7	73·0	57·2	85
1960	66·0	62·1	70·7	77·2	59·6	76·6	58·6	84
1961	67·2	62·4	71·6	77·4	60·9	78·1	60·3	84
1962	68·2	64·5	72·3	77·5	61·4	78·7	61·4	84
1963	70·4	67·0	74·4	80·3	63·5	81·8	63·2	86
1964	74·7	69·6	80·7	87·6	67·5	85·4	65·2	86
1965	76·8	71·5	83·1	90·0	69·0	87·1	66·9	87
1966	78·1	71·8	84·4	91·7	70·9	87·8	68·8	89
1967	79·5	74·1	85·4	92·2	71·8	88·6	71·1	92
1968	82·9	74·0	90·8	99·3	74·7	91·2	73·3	92
1969	84·5	73·8	93·3	102·0	77·7	91·7	74·3	90
1970	86·0	78·4	93·4	103·3	81·0	94·3	76·1	91
1971	87·2	82·5	93·1	102·2	83·1	96·4	78·3	93
1972	90·0	85·2	95·0	104·4	87·1	101·7	80·7	96
1973	95·2	87·8	102·6	114·1	93·7	106·5	83·3	99
1974	93·8	88·8	98·8	112·7	94·0	102·3	84·9	98
1975	92·0	81·9	93·5	104·9	92·8	98·6	88·1	100
1976	93·9	75·3	95·8	106·9	92·3	99·6	91·2	101
1977	96·5	85·1	99·8	108·9	94·9	99·0	92·8	100
1978	99·9	91·5	103·4	109·6	97·3	104·8	94·9	99
1979	103·0	90·6	106·9	109·3	101·6	107·9	97·6	99
1980	100·0	100·0	100·0	100·0	100·0	100·0	100·0	100
1981	98·3	103·1	95·4	93·7	98·9	98·3	101·3	99
1982	100·3	111·9	97·1	93·7	99·0	100·2	103·6	98
1983	103·2	107·2	100·4	96·0	102·4	104·0	106·3	97

Table UK.3 Industrial production, selected series, 1900–83

	Coal	Crude steel	Cars & commercial vehicles	Chemicals & allied industries	Cotton cloth	Manmade fibres & mixtures	Woollen & worsted woven fabrics	Electricity
	mn tons	mn tons ingot equiv.	'000	Index nos., 1980 = 100	mn linear m		mn sq. m	bn KWh
1900	228·8	4·98	...	4·9	...	...	...	0·1
1901	222·5	4·98	...	4·9	...	...	...	...
1902	230·7	4·99	...	5·1	...	...	...	...
1903	234·0	5·11	...	5·2	...	...	...	...
1904	236·1	5·11	...	5·5	...	...	...	...
1905	239·9	5·90	...	6·1	...	...	...	...
1906	255·1	6·56	...	6·7	...	...	...	...
1907	272·1	6·62	12	7·1	(6,483)	...	(535)	...
1908	265·7	5·37	11	6·3	...	...	...	...
1909	268·0	5·97	11	6·9	...	...	...	...
1910	268·6	6·47	14	7·7	...	...	...	...
1911	276·3	6·56	19	7·7	...	...	...	...
1912	264·6	6·91	23	7·9	7,361	...	604	...
1913	292·0	7·78	34	8·3	...	...	...	1·3
1914	270·0	7·97	...	8·0	...	...	...	...
1915	257·3	8·69	...	8·2	...	...	...	...
1916	260·5	9·13	...	8·5	...	...	...	...
1917	252·5	9·88	...	8·5	...	...	...	...
1918	231·3	9·69	...	8·6	...	...	...	...
1919	233·5	8·02	...	8·7	...	...	...	...
1920	233·2	9·22	...	9·3	...	...	...	4·3
1921	165·9	3·76	...	6·7	...	...	...	3·9
1922	253·6	5·97	73	7·9	...	...	...	4·6
1923	280·4	8·62	95	8·7	...	...	...	5·3
1924	271·4	8·33	147	9·2	5,111	37	394	6·1
1925	247·1	7·51	167	8·9	...	...	...	6·7
1926	128·3	3·66	198	8·2	...	...	...	7·1
1927	255·2	9·25	212	9·4	...	...	...	8·5
1928	241·3	8·66	212	9·8	...	...	...	9·4
1929	262·0	9·79	239	10·3	...	...	(343)	10·5
1930	247·8	7·45	237	9·8	2,907	138	288	11·0
1931	223·0	5·28	226	9·4	...	...	(272)	11·5
1932	212·0	5·34	233	10·0	...	...	(289)	12·3
1933	210·4	7·13	286	10·5	2,911	274	345	13·7
1934	214·0	8·99	342	11·4	2,849	294	352	15·6
1935	225·8	10·02	417	12·3	2,822	316	367	17·7
1936	232·1	11·97	482	12·9	...	...	(393)	20·4
1937	244·2	13·19	508	13·7	3,328	423	397	23·1
1938	230·6	10·57	445	13·0	...	...	...	24·6
1939	235·0	13·43	402	...	...	...	...	26·7
1940	227·9	13·19	134	...	...	...	...	29·0
1941	209·6	12·51	145	...	1,966	276	...	32·7
1942	208·2	12·90	161	...	1,620	258	...	36·0
1943	202·1	13·24	149	...	1,608	257	306	37·4
1944	195·9	12·33	133	...	1,507	266	251	38·8
1945	185·7	12·01	139	...	1,407	282	250	37·7
1946	193·1	12·90	366	19·5	1,487	318	289	41·7
1947	200·7	12·68	442	19·8	1,484	356	298	43·1
1948	212·9	15·12	512	21·4	1,734	455	347	47·0
1949	218·6	15·80	631	22·2	1,833	537	367	49·7
1950	219·8	16·55	784	25·2	1,941	647	376	55·6
1951	226·5	15·89	734	26·4	2,013	694	349	60·7
1952	228·2	16·37	689	25·1	1,546	550	316	62·8
1953	226·9	17·89	835	28·1	1,672	690	344	66·4
1954	227·2	18·82	1,038	31·6	1,823	714	346	73·9
1955	225·1	20·11	1,237	33·5	1,629	638	343	81·2
1956	225·6	20·90	1,004	34·9	1,474	642	332	88·3
1957	227·2	22·05	1,148	36·3	1,489	604	329	92·2
1958	219·3	19·51	1,364	36·3	1,307	550	292	99·8
1959	209·4	20·51	1,561	40·2	1,223	540	305	106·6
1960	196·7	24·70	1,811	44·5	1,183	564	307	120·5
1961	193·5	22·44	1,464	45·1	1,129	555	294	129·4
1962	200·6	20·82	1,674	46·9	957	517	274	143·6
1963	198·9	22·88	2,011	50·4	927	512	272	156·0
1964	196·7	26·19	2,332	55·5	946	558	272	164·6
1965	190·5	27·42	2,177	59·3	928	572	270	177·4
1966	177·4	24·69	2,042	62·7	837	564	253	184·1
1967	175·0	24·26	1,937	66·3	681	484	246	191·1
1968	166·7	26·26	2,225	71·9	668	507	246	204·4
1969	153·0	26·82	2,183	75·9	661	538	239	218·4
1970	144·6	27·79	2,098	80·0	627	484	215	228·2
1971	147·1	24·15	2,198	81·6	559	480	186	235·7
1972	119·5	25·29	2,329	86·2	513	470	183	242·7
1973	130·2	26·59	2,164	96·4	454	502	192	258·8
1974	109·3	22·32	1,936	101·6	409	505	175	250·5
1975	127·8	20·10	1,649	91·0	405	503	151	251·3
1976	122·2	22·27	1,705	102·8	375	493	143	254·9
1977	120·6	20·41	1,714	106·3	368	497	150	262·0
1978	121·7	20·31	1,608	107·5	380	458	144	266·8
1979	120·7	21·46	1,479	110·5	365	467	138	279·5
1980	128·2	11·28	1,313	100·0	314	350	118	266·4
1981	125·3	15·57	1,185	100·2	278	273	97	259·7
1982	121·5	13·70	1,157	100·8	261	251	100	255·4
1983	116·4	14·99	1,289	107·0	255	228	94	260·4

16

Chart UK.3 Industrial production, selected series, 1900–83

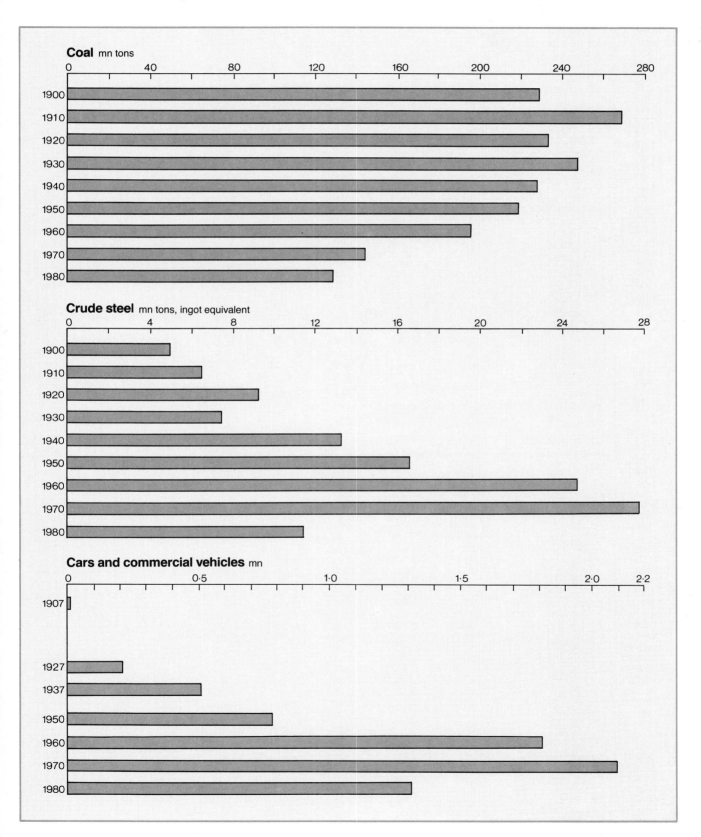

Coal mn tons

Crude steel mn tons, ingot equivalent

Cars and commercial vehicles mn

Table UK.4 Gross domestic fixed capital formation by industry group and by type of asset, 1900–83

	Agriculture, forestry & fishing	Mfg & construction	Energy & water supply	Distribution & business services	Transport & communication	Other services	Dwellings	Other new buildings & works, etc	Vehicles, ships & aircraft	Plant & machinery
	£ mn, 1980 prices									
1900		2,693			2,238	693	1,718	3,425	903	1,289
1901		2,693			2,476	832	1,668	3,829	938	1,273
1902		2,730			2,619	935	1,818	4,020	938	1,336
1903		3,065			2,429	797	1,843	4,139	764	1,480
1904		2,675			2,667	797	1,718	3,782	903	1,368
1905		2,489			2,810	728	1,569	3,378	1,094	1,320
1906		2,359			2,857	624	1,544	3,163	1,129	1,241
1907		1,987			2,381	554	1,444	2,640	955	1,066
1908		1,839			1,572	554	1,320	2,355	608	955
1909		1,950			1,572	554	1,320	2,046	677	1,161
1910		2,043			1,619	589	1,170	2,236	747	1,130
1911		1,950			1,714	520	996	2,141	834	1,034
1912		1,857			1,857	554	822	2,283	938	923
1913		2,266			2,143	589	722	2,450	1,060	1,225
1914		2,526			2,093	515	623	2,569	955	1,368
1915		1,876			1,256	258	398	1,570	591	1,050
1916		1,430			837	184	224	951	504	827
1917		1,226			1,798	18	100	809	1,094	684
1918		1,096			1,970	37	50	737	1,233	620
1919		1,579			1,822	166	100	1,665	1,112	541
1920	149	1,616	589	658	1,748	258	921	2,569	1,094	1,209
1921	127	1,754	763	543	1,576	331	1,892	2,164	834	1,766
1922	85	1,261	916	357	1,872	405	1,668	2,022	1,042	1,384
1923	85	1,123	1,046	586	1,699	515	1,519	2,355	921	1,511
1924	64	1,143	1,199	629	1,921	626	2,166	2,474	1,181	1,591
1925	64	1,596	1,286	500	2,044	736	2,714	2,830	1,164	1,830
1926	64	1,399	1,155	515	1,453	699	3,411	2,450	869	1,702
1927	64	1,399	1,330	529	1,896	791	3,735	2,474	1,147	1,941
1928	64	1,517	1,177	772	2,290	736	2,913	2,450	1,425	2,164
1929	64	1,517	1,439	729	1,995	920	3,312	2,902	1,372	2,020
1930	85	1,379	1,635	844	1,773	1,086	3,088	3,473	1,077	2,084
1931	64	1,143	1,744	801	1,453	1,251	3,237	2,902	764	2,514
1932	42	1,123	1,569	615	1,034	902	3,262	2,402	452	2,195
1933	42	1,123	1,504	586	690	736	4,283	2,236	382	1,925
1934	64	1,714	1,548	772	1,108	828	4,806	2,616	799	2,370
1935	85	1,675	1,657	872	1,478	883	4,582	2,878	1,025	2,450
1936	106	1,951	1,787	758	2,044	1,104	4,557	3,235	1,425	2,609
1937	127	2,423	1,569	772	2,143	1,306	4,258	3,948	1,407	2,641
1938	106	2,147	1,635	971	2,315	1,325	4,208	3,806	1,390	2,911
1939	...	...	...	...	...	...	2,739	4,281	1,042	2,864
1940	...	...	...	...	...	...	4,039		695	4,136
1941	...	...	...	...	...	...	3,029		869	3,182
1942	...	...	...	...	...	...	2,272		1,042	2,705
1943	...	...	...	...	...	...	1,515		1,042	1,591
1944	...	...	...	...	...	...	1,010		1,042	1,114
1945	...	...	...	...	...	...	1,767		869	1,114
1946	...	...	...	...	...	...	6,563		1,564	2,068
1947	...	...	...	...	...	...	3,540	3,092	1,911	2,864
1948	871	3,035	1,461	815	2,044	920	3,288	3,330	1,911	3,500
1949	858	3,429	1,786	1,006	2,099	1,123	3,220	4,088	2,005	3,866
1950	820	3,911	1,938	1,093	1,964	1,340	3,152	4,672	1,849	4,310
1951	749	4,207	1,926	1,089	1,723	1,482	3,100	4,597	1,641	4,694
1952	698	4,010	1,990	1,080	1,581	1,407	3,735	4,721	1,457	4,461
1953	679	3,905	2,234	1,163	1,920	1,489	4,849	5,058	1,717	4,511
1954	724	4,190	2,630	1,411	2,007	1,529	5,004	5,601	1,844	5,014
1955	781	4,650	2,811	1,734	1,988	1,651	4,639	6,235	2,038	5,435
1956	692	5,379	2,665	1,690	2,433	1,854	4,440	6,957	2,218	5,659
1957	749	5,675	2,752	1,773	2,958	1,996	4,277	7,370	2,450	6,053
1958	858	5,390	2,863	1,991	2,890	2,213	4,072	7,700	2,506	6,076
1959	967	5,116	3,189	2,365	3,075	2,497	4,645	8,209	2,757	6,478
1960	1,006	5,960	3,043	2,744	3,285	2,639	5,162	9,049	3,088	6,908
1961	1,057	7,011	3,200	3,067	3,038	3,153	5,517	10,363	2,875	7,892
1962	1,006	6,414	3,468	3,102	2,624	3,708	5,924	10,790	2,478	7,810
1963	1,076	5,866	4,050	3,298	2,488	3,897	5,983	10,604	2,587	8,125
1964	1,082	6,666	4,632	3,842	2,939	4,628	7,380	12,331	3,050	9,132
1965	1,149	7,318	4,853	3,877	2,970	4,804	7,846	12,882	2,970	9,749
1966	1,108	7,287	5,584	3,727	2,904	4,950	8,105	12,996	2,627	10,407
1967	1,163	7,009	6,162	4,054	3,437	5,749	9,146	14,388	2,970	10,851
1968	1,304	7,519	5,156	4,460	4,149	6,338	9,877	15,133	3,692	11,077
1969	1,249	8,074	4,352	4,760	4,076	6,450	9,539	15,326	3,627	11,035
1970	1,308	8,621	3,983	5,087	4,469	6,905	8,655	15,903	3,886	11,847
1971	1,386	7,811	3,847	5,681	4,600	7,116	9,433	16,165	4,043	11,618
1972	1,523	6,898	3,475	5,886	4,837	7,318	9,701	15,804	4,567	11,164
1973	1,635	7,559	3,328	6,819	5,331	8,028	9,476	16,604	5,146	12,593
1974	1,411	8,196	4,145	6,595	4,794	6,964	8,497	15,618	4,903	12,908
1975	1,247	7,399	5,734	5,572	4,361	6,382	9,681	15,790	4,297	12,230
1976	1,238	7,085	6,603	5,845	3,983	6,419	9,831	15,815	4,168	12,758
1977	1,234	7,361	6,032	6,563	4,050	5,552	8,990	14,822	4,730	12,913
1978	1,312	7,849	5,985	7,527	4,116	5,138	9,209	14,617	5,208	13,904
1979	1,159	8,168	5,529	8,765	4,060	5,224	9,295	14,204	5,460	14,966
1980	1,033	6,938	5,640	8,976	3,870	5,078	8,419	13,573	4,571	15,065
1981	894	5,262	6,007	9,027	3,067	4,739	7,294	13,103	3,614	14,064
1982	1,090	5,143	6,122	9,844	2,831	5,428	8,147	14,376	3,714	14,408
1983	1,172	5,066	5,929	10,164	3,183	5,690	8,937	14,577	3,925	14,909

Chart UK.4 Gross domestic fixed capital formation by type of asset and industry, 1900–83

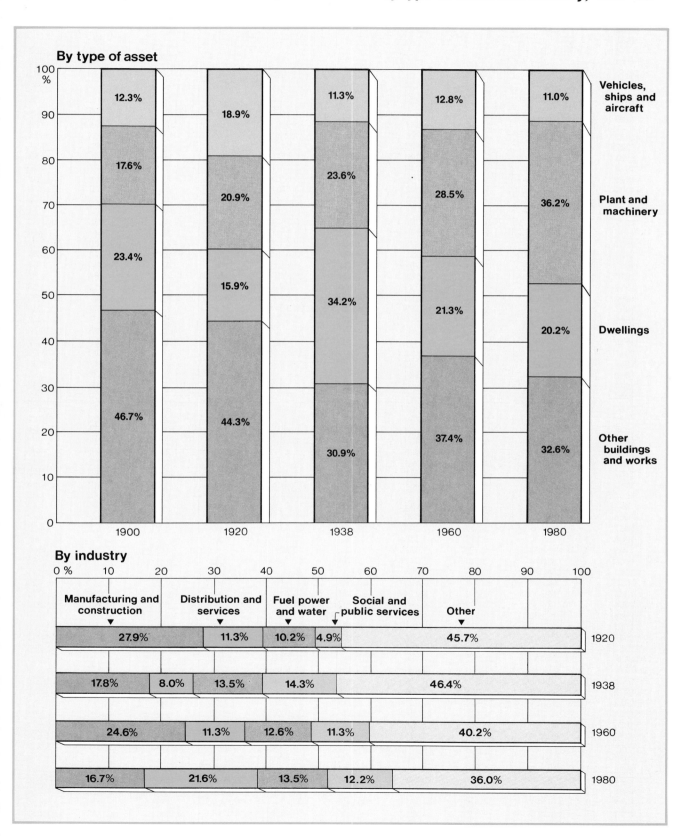

By type of asset

	1900	1920	1938	1960	1980
Vehicles, ships and aircraft	12.3%	18.9%	11.3%	12.8%	11.0%
Plant and machinery	17.6%	20.9%	23.6%	28.5%	36.2%
Dwellings	23.4%	15.9%	34.2%	21.3%	20.2%
Other buildings and works	46.7%	44.3%	30.9%	37.4%	32.6%

By industry

	Manufacturing and construction	Distribution and services	Fuel power and water	Social and public services	Other	
1920	27.9%	11.3%	10.2%	4.9%	45.7%	
1938	17.8%	8.0%	13.5%	14.3%	46.4%	
1960	24.6%	11.3%	12.6%	11.3%	40.2%	
1980	16.7%	21.6%	13.5%	12.2%	36.0%	

19

Table UK.5 Personal and company income, 1900–83

	Wages & salaries	Other income	Taxes etc	Personal disposable income	Consumers' expenditure	Personal saving	Savings ratio	Gross trading profits of companies	Gross trading surplus of public corporations & gen. govt enterprises
	£ mn						%	£ mn	
1900	899	...	...	...	...	...	...	230	8
1901	898	...	...	...	...	...	...	216	8
1902	889	...	...	...	...	...	...	223	10
1903	897	...	...	...	...	...	...	208	11
1904	882	...	...	...	...	...	...	204	14
1905	902	...	...	...	...	...	...	228	13
1906	940	...	...	...	...	...	...	258	14
1907	996	...	...	...	...	...	...	271	15
1908	963	...	...	...	...	...	...	242	15
1909	974	...	...	...	...	...	...	245	17
1910	1,014	...	...	...	...	...	...	261	17
1911	1,051	...	...	...	...	...	...	272	18
1912	1,095	...	...	...	...	...	...	308	21
1913	1,136	...	...	...	...	...	...	326	20
1919	3,040	...	...	...	...	...	...	...	36
1920	3,470 / 3,394	1,894	331	4,957	5,020	−63	—	621	20
1921	2,767	1,823	322	4,268	4,315	−47	—	343	25
1922	2,333	1,788	320	3,801	3,842	−41	—	437	44
1923	2,338	1,772	307	3,703	3,717	−14	—	456	44
1924	2,293	1,844	313	3,824	3,777	47	1·2	477	40
1925	2,335	1,907	294	3,948	3,878	70	1·8	468	42
1926	2,245	1,948	303	3,890	3,833	57	1·5	420	40
1927	2,410	1,955	300	4,065	3,887	178	4·4	478	48
1928	2,401	2,008	313	4,096	3,939	157	3·8	474	51
1929	2,447	2,032	306	4,173	3,983	190	4·6	485	52
1930	2,385	2,041	343	4,083	3,932	151	3·7	411	54
1931	2,281	1,977	328	3,930	3,805	125	3·2	360	55
1932	2,252	1,920	345	3,827	3,683	144	3·8	321	59
1933	2,296	1,924	336	3,884	3,696	188	4·8	380	62
1934	2,398	1,922	326	3,994	3,802	192	4·8	464	67
1935	2,482	2,011	339	4,154	3,935	219	5·3	514	68
1936	2,623	2,107	358	4,372	4,080	292	6·7	627	69
1937	2,784	2,125	392	4,517	4,289	228	5·0	717	71
1938	2,863	2,180	418	4,625	4,392	233	5·0	687	72
1939	3,080	...	...	...	...	...	...	865	76
1940	3,695	...	...	...	...	...	...	1,109	77
1941	4,370	...	...	...	...	...	...	1,238	90
1942	4,860	...	...	...	...	...	...	1,377	136
1943	5,280	...	...	...	...	...	...	1,405	149
1944	5,550	...	...	...	...	...	...	1,388	134
1945	5,680	...	...	...	...	...	...	1,350	119
1946	5,527	3,271	1,203	7,595	7,280	315	4·1	1,476	110
1947	5,935	3,477	1,229	8,183	8,036	147	1·8	1,694	159
1948	6,428	3,584	1,317	8,695	8,617	78	0·9	1,793	224
1949	6,823	3,742	1,430	9,135	8,980	155	1·7	1,843	263
1950	7,172	3,928	1,425	9,675	9,479	196	2·0	2,126	339
1951	8,008	4,041	1,594	10,455	10,238	217	2·1	2,483	381
1952	8,572	4,290	1,634	11,228	10,785	443	3·9	2,180	322
1953	9,049	4,603	1,627	12,025	11,510	515	4·3	2,313	388
1954	9,673	4,708	1,737	12,644	12,210	434	3·4	2,576	466
1955	10,566	5,043	1,901	13,708	13,177	531	3·9	2,886	431
1956	11,521	5,263	2,088	14,696	13,888	808	5·5	2,928	472
1957	12,157	5,536	2,254	15,439	14,659	780	5·1	3,075	458
1958	12,530	6,135	2,513	16,152	15,472	680	4·2	2,983	501
1959	13,114	6,659	2,622	17,151	16,306	845	4·9	3,317	560
1960	14,114	7,210	2,848	18,476	17,124	1,352	7·3	3,717	723
1961	15,229	7,838	3,256	19,811	18,020	1,791	9·0	3,625	747
1962	16,033	8,341	3,603	20,771	19,110	1,661	8·0	3,581	829
1963	16,809	9,078	3,774	22,113	20,319	1,794	8·1	4,094	932
1964	18,226	9,731	4,190	23,767	21,693	2,074	8·7	4,541	1,028
1965	19,596	10,985	4,974	25,607	23,110	2,497	9·8	4,742	1,100
1966	20,940	11,778	5,494	27,224	24,462	2,762	10·1	4,597	1,148
1967	21,735	12,623	6,021	28,337	25,704	2,633	9·3	4,637	1,242
1968	23,153	13,877	6,820	30,210	27,679	2,531	8·4	5,276	1,495
1969	24,799	14,862	7,494	32,167	29,379	2,788	8·7	5,705	1,604
1970	27,760	16,093	8,439	35,414	31,935	3,479	9·8	6,083	1,599
1971	30,394	17,889	9,329	38,954	35,748	3,206	8·2	7,114	1,700
1972	34,207	20,846	10,000	45,053	40,411	4,642	10·3	8,142	1,817
1973	39,456	24,520	11,741	52,235	46,004	6,231	11·9	10,389	2,187
1974	46,707	29,435	15,518	60,624	53,072	7,552	12·5	11,429	2,661
1975	60,465	36,774	21,998	75,241	65,216	10,025	13·3	11,741	3,174
1976	67,888	44,513	25,819	86,582	75,712	10,870	12·6	14,693	4,594
1977	75,079	50,494	27,657	97,916	86,537	11,379	11·6	19,967	5,217
1978	85,881	58,257	29,640	114,498	99,486	15,012	13·1	22,599	5,534
1979	100,486	70,119	33,308	137,297	117,912	19,385	14·1	28,942	5,689
1980	118,741	82,377	39,754	161,364	136,789	24,575	15·2	29,008	6,218
1981	127,492	93,420	44,984	175,928	152,125	23,803	13·5	29,957	7,835
1982	136,432	104,436	49,782	191,086	166,477	24,609	12·9	33,886	9,204
1983	146,469	111,891	53,676	204,684	182,427	22,257	10·9	41,530	9,552

Table UK.6   Consumers' expenditure at constant prices, selected commodities, 1900–83

	Food	Alcoholic drink & tobacco	Clothing & footwear	Energy products	Durable goods	of which: Cars, motor cycles, etc	Other goods	Rent, rates & water charges	Other services
					£ mn, 1980 prices				
1900	10,268	11,679	3,170	2,539	1,576	32	1,499	3,544	13,412
1901	10,388	11,560	3,309	2,539	1,613	32	1,522	3,624	13,819
1902	10,402	11,441	3,142	2,632	1,613	32	1,569	3,690	13,819
1903	10,616	11,135	3,022	2,595	1,563	32	1,592	3,757	13,819
1904	10,790	10,914	3,068	2,595	1,651	32	1,638	3,823	13,751
1905	10,790	10,775	3,012	2,465	1,613	32	1,697	3,876	13,904
1906	10,897	10,727	3,040	2,465	1,626	32	1,755	3,929	14,057
1907	10,830	10,795	3,022	2,651	1,713	32	1,801	3,996	14,209
1908	10,790	10,336	3,133	2,595	1,688	32	1,743	4,036	14,531
1909	10,897	11,101	3,244	2,595	1,601	32	1,743	4,089	14,633
1910	10,816	9,571	3,272	2,651	1,638	64	1,813	4,129	14,820
1911	11,217	9,945	3,504	2,743	1,676	64	1,871	4,182	14,955
1912	11,177	9,911	3,513	2,484	1,751	95	1,929	4,235	15,159
1913	11,244	10,285	3,624	2,725	1,951	127	2,022	4,275	15,396
1914	11,097	10,149	3,114	2,669	1,889	95	2,010	4,341	16,990
1915	11,244	9,962	3,365	2,817	1,738	32	2,080	4,367	17,770
1916	10,843	9,112	2,345	2,780	1,376	—	2,057	4,367	16,600
1917	10,108	6,681	2,187	2,688	1,301	—	1,987	4,381	15,922
1918	9,894	6,494	2,095	2,428	1,401	32	2,045	4,407	15,871
1919	11,231	9,435	3,420	2,651	1,926	191	2,115	4,460	15,362
1920	11,725	9,588	3,689	2,854	1,313	206	3,742	4,726	12,158
1920	11,164	9,129	3,550	2,725	1,276	206	3,591	4,500	11,717
1921	11,592	8,126	2,929	2,391	1,113	111	3,137	4,514	11,089
1922	12,367	7,310	3,309	2,706	1,326	175	3,347	4,553	11,174
1923	13,210	7,310	3,346	2,817	1,463	238	3,428	4,593	11,191
1924	13,236	7,616	3,392	3,021	1,551	333	3,474	4,633	11,530
1925	13,450	7,735	3,457	3,095	1,701	429	3,614	4,673	12,005
1926	13,517	7,497	3,467	2,762	1,751	413	3,521	4,766	12,191
1927	13,731	7,548	3,661	3,392	1,901	444	3,730	4,872	12,581
1928	13,998	7,446	3,680	3,355	1,976	444	3,823	4,978	12,971
1929	14,092	7,531	3,754	3,522	2,064	444	3,962	5,045	13,344
1930	14,466	7,412	3,708	3,540	2,101	429	3,997	5,151	13,785
1931	14,948	6,970	3,782	3,522	2,126	365	3,986	5,230	14,074
1932	14,961	6,324	3,624	3,466	2,301	397	3,951	5,297	14,362
1933	14,961	6,613	3,763	3,522	2,414	460	4,125	5,376	14,921
1934	15,162	6,885	3,800	3,670	2,689	572	4,346	5,469	15,311
1935	15,095	7,191	3,939	3,855	2,914	683	4,555	5,615	15,769
1936	15,295	7,514	4,069	4,059	3,039	762	4,694	5,761	16,278
1937	15,416	7,888	4,051	4,226	2,952	778	4,822	5,907	16,600
1938	15,469	7,990	4,060	4,300	2,714	683	4,764	6,040	17,177
1939	15,736	8,143	4,143	4,393		7,214		6,717	16,719
1940	13,530	7,752	3,485	4,041		5,781		6,810	16,210
1941	12,715	8,279	2,595	4,041		4,669		6,770	17,176
1942	13,049	8,092	2,586	3,781		3,904		6,784	17,533
1943	12,474	8,109	2,354	3,540		3,768		6,863	18,211
1944	13,143	8,291	2,642	3,559		3,805		7,022	18,380
1945	13,343	8,976	2,688	3,763		4,311		7,195	20,313
1946	16,231	8,823	3,198	4,393	1,413	254	4,392	7,859	19,245
1947	17,421	8,432	3,606	4,708	1,788	300	4,648	8,124	18,279
1948	17,796	8,092	3,995	4,504	1,876	254	4,776	8,350	17,770
1949	18,469	7,843	4,314	4,471	2,236	325	5,124	8,329	16,902
1950	19,336	7,923	4,468	4,664	2,496	336	5,310	8,490	16,550
1951	18,994	8,176	4,048	4,808	2,466	321	5,232	8,405	16,417
1952	16,720	8,218	3,985	4,761	2,400	443	5,276	8,468	19,506
1953	17,684	8,349	4,085	4,800	3,102	768	5,707	8,635	19,537
1954	18,052	8,425	4,378	5,001	3,700	968	6,114	8,866	20,028
1955	18,692	8,687	4,698	5,095	4,071	1,264	6,580	9,116	20,500
1956	18,994	8,842	4,884	5,288	3,592	1,007	6,722	9,291	20,688
1957	19,278	9,034	5,019	5,167	4,019	1,161	6,855	9,411	20,883
1958	19,511	9,100	5,040	5,520	4,669	1,518	7,252	9,589	20,657
1959	19,885	9,479	5,311	5,443	5,554	1,864	7,746	9,850	21,344
1960	20,313	9,899	5,719	5,920	5,711	2,143	8,279	10,116	21,812
1961	20,649	10,324	5,845	6,011	5,496	1,950	8,675	10,322	22,478
1962	20,856	10,164	5,820	6,602	5,758	2,214	8,930	10,671	23,245
1963	21,081	10,589	6,066	7,093	6,699	3,182	9,399	11,101	24,166
1964	21,343	10,860	6,320	7,235	7,238	3,660	9,777	11,303	24,986
1965	21,329	10,616	6,560	7,733	7,203	3,535	10,036	11,593	25,603
1966	21,566	10,998	6,555	8,077	7,086	3,527	10,347	11,866	26,026
1967	21,922	11,262	6,653	8,247	7,533	3,868	10,736	12,192	26,416
1968	22,037	11,562	7,014	8,717	8,047	4,121	11,107	12,569	26,756
1969	22,065	11,622	7,125	9,057	7,546	3,684	11,093	12,898	27,130
1970	22,152	12,066	7,436	9,243	8,164	4,205	11,229	13,216	27,833
1971	22,093	12,342	7,562	9,302	9,668	5,554	11,562	13,506	28,631
1972	21,947	13,177	7,970	9,918	11,748	6,653	12,721	13,811	30,174
1973	22,442	14,545	8,336	10,394	12,408	6,365	13,895	14,121	31,388
1974	22,122	14,701	8,237	10,353	10,886	4,855	14,203	14,387	30,874
1975	22,001	14,356	8,350	10,127	11,067	5,152	13,603	14,655	30,673
1976	22,159	14,273	8,407	10,347	11,613	5,325	13,573	14,941	29,917
1977	21,883	14,083	8,526	10,533	10,809	4,725	13,629	15,232	29,927
1978	22,501	14,912	9,333	10,759	12,284	5,804	14,603	15,516	31,465
1979	22,893	15,342	9,996	11,114	13,963	6,668	14,872	15,790	33,286
1980	22,873	14,776	9,863	10,957	13,320	6,307	14,369	16,044	34,587
1981	22,676	14,082	10,170	10,992	13,486	6,366	14,420	16,279	34,609
1982	22,587	13,511	10,734	11,038	14,193	6,510	14,626	16,530	34,916
1983	22,858	13,812	11,683	11,129	16,459	7,909	14,934	16,764	36,369

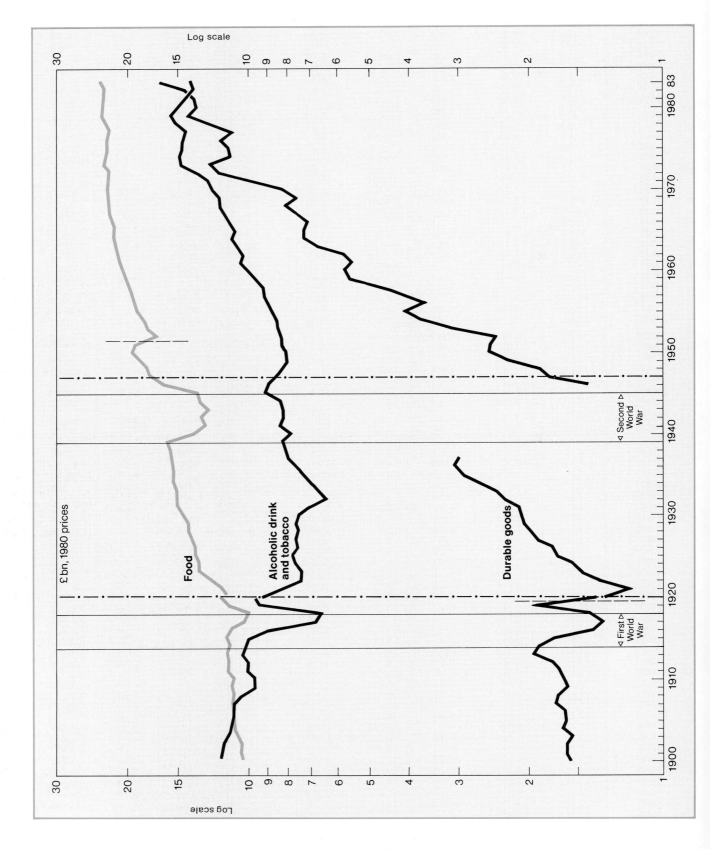

Chart UK.6   Consumer's expenditure at constant prices, selected commodities, 1900–83

Log scale

£ bn, 1980 prices

Food

Alcoholic drink and tobacco

Durable goods

◁ First ▷ War World

◁ Second ▷ World War

30
20
15
10
9
8
7
6
5
4
3
2
1

1900   1910   1920   1930   1940   1950   1960   1970   1980 83

Log scale

22

	Producer prices		Consumer prices					Average values		Terms of trade
	Materials & fuel purchased by mfg industry	Output of mfd products	All items	Food	Durable[a] goods	Clothing[a] & footwear	Housing[a]	Exports	Imports	
	Index nos., 1980 = 100									
1900	3·5		3·9	3·8	4·3	4·8	3·8	3·4	4·6	73·9
1901	3·3		3·9	3·8	4·3	4·9	3·2	3·2	4·3	74·4
1902	3·3		3·9	3·8	4·3	4·9	3·9	3·0	4·3	69·8
1903	3·3		3·9	3·9	4·4	4·9	3·9	3·0	4·3	69·8
1904	3·5		3·9	3·9	4·4	5·0	4·0	3·2	4·3	74·4
1905	3·3		3·9	3·9	4·5	5·2	4·0	3·2	4·3	74·4
1906	3·5		3·9	3·9	4·5	5·3	4·0	3·2	4·8	66·7
1907	3·6		4·1	3·9	4·6	5·4	4·0	3·4	5·0	68·0
1908	3·6		4·1	4·1	4·6	5·4	4·0	3·2	4·6	69·6
1909	3·6		4·1	4·1	4·5	5·4	4·1	3·2	4·8	66·7
1910	3·8		4·1	4·1	4·7	5·4	4·1	3·4	5·0	68·0
1911	3·8		4·3	4·1	4·8	5·6	4·0	3·4	5·0	68·0
1912	4·0		4·3	4·3	5·0	5·7	4·0	3·4	5·2	65·4
1913	4·1		4·3	4·3	5·1	5·8	4·1	3·6	5·0	72·0
1914	4·1		4·3	4·5	4·9	5·5	4·1	...	...	...
1915	4·9		5·4	5·8	5·5	5·7	4·1	...	...	...
1916	6·5		6·2	7·0	6·5	7·2	4·1	...	...	...
1917	8·4		7·7	8·6	8·8	9·7	4·2	...	...	...
1918	9·3		8·7	9·4	11·2	17·4	4·3	...	...	...
1919	10·4		9·5	9·6	14·2	19·6	4·5	9·7	12·0	80·8
1920	12·5		10·8	11·3	15·6	22·4	4·8	12·7	14·3	88·8
1921	7·9		9·7	10·2	13·4	16·5	5·6	9·5	9·5	100·0
1922	6·5		7·9	7·7	11·2	13·1	5·8	7·2	7·7	93·5
1923	6·5		7·7	7·5	10·2	12·2	5·6	7·0	7·7	90·9
1924	6·8		7·7	7·5	10·2	12·3	5·5	7·0	8·1	86·4
1925	6·5		7·7	7·5	10·5	12·5	5·5	7·0	7·9	88·6
1926	6·0		7·5	7·3	9·9	12·0	5·6	6·5	7·5	86·7
1927	5·7		7·2	7·1	9·4	11·6	5·7	6·1	7·0	87·1
1928	5·7		7·2	7·0	8·7	11·8	5·7	6·1	7·2	84·7
1929	5·5		7·2	6·8	8·8	11·7	5·8	5·9	7·0	84·3
1930	4·7		6·8	6·4	8·6	11·3	5·8	5·7	6·0	95·0
1931	4·3		6·4	5·8	8·2	10·4	5·8	5·1	5·0	102·0
1932	4·1		6·2	5·6	7·4	10·0	5·8	4·8	4·6	104·3
1933	4·1		6·2	5·3	7·5	9·7	5·8	4·6	4·3	107·0
1934	4·3		6·2	5·5	7·6	9·8	5·9	4·8	4·6	104·3
1935	4·3		6·2	5·6	7·6	9·8	5·9	4·6	4·8	95·8
1936	4·6		6·4	5·8	7·7	9·9	6·0	4·8	5·0	96·0
1937	5·2		6·6	6·0	8·3	10·5	6·0	5·3	5·6	94·6
1938	4·7		6·8	6·2	8·7	10·8	6·0	5·5	5·4	101·8
1939	4·9		7·0	6·2	...	11·1	6·2	5·5	5·4	101·8
1940	6·6		7·9	7·3	...	14·4	6·3	6·3	7·5	84·0
1941	7·4		8·7	7·7	...	17·7	6·3	7·8	8·3	94·0
1942	7·6		9·3	7·9	...	19·3	6·4	8·4	8·9	94·4
1943	7·7		9·7	7·9	...	18·7	6·5	9·7	10·4	93·3
1944	7·9		9·7	8·1	...	19·4	6·6	10·3	10·1	102·0
1945	8·1		10·1	8·3	...	19·9	6·9	9·9	10·4	95·2
1946	8·4		10·6	8·3	17·9	20·0	7·1	10·8	11·0	98·2
1947	9·2	10·6	11·2	8·8	19·3	20·4	7·5	12·2	13·7	89·1
1948	(11)	(13)	11·8	9·4	20·6	22·6	7·6	13·1	15·1	86·7
1949	(11)	(14)	12·2	9·9	20·3	23·5	7·8	13·5	15·5	87·1
1950	14·4	14·9	12·5	10·6	21·1	23·8	8·0	14·3	17·6	92·4
1951	19·5	16·8	13·6	11·8	24·2	27·6	8·4	17·3	23·4	73·9
1952	16·9	17·7	14·9	13·7	26·0	27·5	8·8	18·6	22·8	81·6
1953	15·5	17·6	15·4	14·5	24·8	27·3	9·3	18·1	20·3	89·2
1954	15·4	17·6	15·6	14·8	24·4	27·5	9·5	17·9	20·3	88·2
1955	15·8	18·0	16·4	15·9	24·7	27·6	9·7	17·9	20·7	86·5
1956	16·4	18·8	17·2	16·7	26·5	28·2	10·1	18·8	21·3	88·3
1957	16·5	19·4	17·8	17·1	26·8	28·7	10·9	19·6	21·9	89·5
1958	15·5	19·5	18·4	17·5	26·9	28·9	12·3	19·6	20·1	97·5
1959	15·6	19·6	18·5	17·6	26·5	28·7	13·0	20·0	20·3	98·5
1960	15·6	19·9	18·7	17·5	26·4	29·1	13·3	20·3	20·5	99·0
1961	15·5	20·4	19·3	17·8	26·5	29·6	13·9	20·5	20·3	101·0
1962	15·5	20·9	20·1	18·4	26·6	30·4	14·8	20·7	20·1	103·0
1963	15·8	21·1	20·5	18·9	25·5	30·9	15·9	21·1	20·7	101·9
1964	16·5	21·7	21·2	19·4	25·8	31·2	17·1	21·6	21·3	101·4
1965	16·7	22·5	22·2	20·1	26·3	32·0	18·6	22·0	21·5	102·3
1966	17·1	23·1	23·1	20·8	26·6	32·9	19·9	22·7	21·7	104·6
1967	17·0	23·4	23·6	21·4	26·9	33·3	20·8	22·8	21·9	104·1
1968	18·5	24·3	24·7	22·2	28·3	33·8	21·8	24·7	24·3	101·6
1969	19·3	25·2	26·1	23·6	29·5	35·1	23·3	25·4	25·1	101·2
1970	20·3	27·0	27·7	25·3	31·5	37·0	25·2	27·2	26·2	103·8
1971	21·2	29·5	30·3	28·1	34·0	39·5	27·9	28·6	27·2	105·1
1972	22·1	31·0	32·5	30·5	35·1	42·3	31·3	29·9	27·9	107·2
1973	29·3	33·3	35·5	35·2	36·6	46·3	35·4	33·2	34·9	95·1
1974	43·2	40·9								
	49·1	42·6	41·2	41·5	42·3	54·6	42·0	42·9	51·2	83·8
1975	54·9	52·4	51·1	52·1	52·4	62·3	50·7	52·4	58·2	90·0
1976	68·4	60·9	59·5	62·5	59·4	69·0	58·4	62·2	70·4	88·4
1977	78·9	72·0	69·0	74·4	70·8	77·8	65·5	72·6	81·4	89·2
1978	81·6	79·1	74·7	79·7	80·7	84·0	73·0	78·1	82·4	94·8
1979	92·2	87·7	84·8	89·3	91·3	91·8	84·6	86·5	89·5	96·6
1980	100·0	100·0	100·0	100·0	100·0	100·0	100·0	100·0	100·0	100·0
1981	109·2	109·5	111·9	108·5	103·0	100·9	119·6	108·2	107·0	101·1
1982	117·2	118·0	121·5	117·0	106·8	101·7	135·3	115·5	114·3	101·0
1983	125·3	124·4	127·1	120·7	111·2	103·7	139·4	125·0	122·9	101·7

a Average value indices.

23

	Total home pop. mid year	Births	Age distribution 0–14	15–34	35–64	65 & over	England & Wales	of which: South East	Scotland	N. Ireland
	mn	'000	mid year estimates				mn			
1900	41·16	1,160	13·38	14·67	11·16	1·99	32·25	...	4·44	...
1901	41·54	1,163	13·41	14·80	11·30	2·03	32·61	...	4·48	...
1902	41·89	1,175	13·49	14·87	11·49	2·08	32·95	...	4·51	...
1903	42·25	1,183	13·50	14·94	11·68	2·13	33·29	...	4·54	...
1904	42·61	1,181	13·57	15·07	11·90	2·19	33·64	...	4·56	...
1905	42·98	1,163	13·57	15·11	12·07	2·23	33·99	...	4·59	...
1906	43·36	1,171	13·62	15·19	12·27	2·30	34·34	...	4·62	...
1907	43·74	1,149	13·67	15·25	12·46	2·35	34·70	...	4·65	...
1908	44·12	1,173	13·75	15·36	12·69	2·41	35·06	...	4·68	...
1909	44·52	1,146	13·78	15·41	12·88	2·48	35·42	...	4·71	...
1910	44·92	1,123	13·85	15·48	13·06	2.52	35·79	...	4·74	...
1911	45·27	1,105	13·95	15·47	13·25	2·60	36·14	...	4·75	1·25
1912	45·44	1,097	13·89	15·44	13·49	2·63	36·33	...	4·74	1·25
1913	45·65	1,103	13·88	15·42	13·71	2·66	36·57	...	4·73	1·24
1914	46·05	1,102	13·90	15·54	14·23	2·69	36·97	...	4·75	1·24
1915	46·34	1,025	13·90	15·52	14·47	2·72	35·28	...	4·77	1·21
1916	46·51	987	13·80	15·51	13·96	2·73	34·64	...	4·80	1·21
1917	46·61	852	13·69	15·47	14·69	2·77	34·20	...	4·81	1·21
1918	46·58	849	13·46	15·41	14·87	2·81	34·02	...	4·81	1·21
1919	46·53	888	13·20	15·32	15·07	2·86	35·43	...	4·82	1·25
1920	43·72	1,127	12·34	14·37	14·40	2·63	37·25	...	4·86	1·26
1921	44·07	1,002	12·32	14·44	14·59	2·67	37·89	10·48	4·88	1·26
1922	44·37	925	12·29	14·56	14·75	2·72	38·16	10·54	4·90	1·27
1923	44·60	900	12·17	14·65	14·91	2·79	38·40	10·61	4·89	1·26
1924	44·92	865	12·08	14·84	15·11	2·83	38·75	10·70	4·86	1·26
1925	45·06	843	11·96	14·94	15·25	2·88	38·89	10·75	4·87	1·26
1926	45·23	826	11·84	14·97	15·42	2·98	39·07	10·83	4·86	1·25
1927	45·39	777	11·73	15·06	15·58	3·04	39·29	10·83	4·85	1·25
1928	45·58	783	11·57	15·14	15·72	3·12	39·48	10·89	4·85	1·25
1929	45·67	762	11·39	15·25	15·87	3·16	39·61	10·92	4·83	1·24
1930	45·87	769	11·25	15·34	16·03	3·25	39·81	10·93	4·83	1·24
1931	46·07	750	11·19	15·34	16·11	3·44	39·99	13·42	4·84	1·24
1932	46·34	730	11·17	15·36	16·29	3·52	40·20	13·64	4·88	1·25
1933	46·52	691	11·19	15·28	16·45	3·60	40·35	13·76	4·91	1·26
1934	46·67	712	11·19	15·17	16·61	3·69	40·47	13·86	4·93	1·27
1935	46·87	712	10·90	15·34	16·83	3·79	40·65	14·01	4·95	1·27
1936	47·08	720	10·69	15·44	17·07	3·88	40·84	14·19	4·97	1·28
1937	47·29	724	10·53	15·49	17·28	3·99	41·03	14·37	4·98	1·28
1938	47·49	735	10·42	15·47	17·50	4·09	41·22	14·49	4·99	1·29
1939	47·76	727	10·30	15·62	17·59	4·25	41·46	14·60	5·01	1·29
1940	48·23	702	10·23	33·64		4·35	41·86	13·26	5·06	1·30
1941	48·22	696	10·14	15·58	18·08	4·42	41·75	12·06	5·16	1·31
1942	48·40	772	10·11	15·42	18·31	4·56	41·90	12·12	5·17	1·33
1943	48·79	811	10·17	15·33	18·57	4·72	42·26	12·12	5·19	1·34
1944	49·02	878	10·26	15·13	18·77	4·85	42·45	11·98	5·21	1·36
1945	49·18	796	10·34	14·91	18·96	4·97	42·64	12·38	5·19	1·36
1946	49·22	955	10·36	14·87	18·94	5·05	42·70	12·56	5·17	1·35
1947	49·52	1,025	10·68	14·65	19·09	5·15	43·05	12·46	5·12	1·35
1948	50·01	905	10·97	14·54	19·28	5·28	43·50	13·26	5·15	1·36
1949	50·31	855	11·16	14·39	19·46	5·35	43·79	13·58	5·16	1·37
1950	50·57	818	11·31	14·26	19·62	5·43	44·02	13·63	5·17	1·38
1951	50·29	797	11·38	13·84	19·59	5·45	43·82	13·62	5·10	1·37
1952	50·43	793	11·45	13·78	19·63	5·57	43·96	13·69	5·10	1·37
1953	50·59	804	11·53	13·86	19·59	5·63	44·11	13·71	5·10	1·38
1954	50·77	795	11·62	13·91	19·54	5·72	44·27	13·73	5·10	1·39
1955	50·95	789	11·70	13·70	19·80	5·77	44·44	13·76	5·11	1·39
1956	51·18	825	11·86	13·52	20·00	5·84	44·67	13·82	5·12	1·40
1957	51·43	851	11·96	13·40	20·16	5·94	44·91	13·89	5·13	1·40
1958	51·65	871	12·05	13·40	20·26	5·99	45·11	13·92	5·14	1·40
1959	51·96	879	12·11	13·47	20·36	6·04	45·39	13·76	5·16	1·41
1960	52·37	918	12·22	13·56	20·46	6·14	45·78	13·86	5·18	1·42
1961	52·81	944	12·33	13·67	20·56	6·21	46·20	13·93	5·18	1·43
1962	53·27	976	12·35	14·12	20·60	6·28	46·64	14·07	5·20	1·44
1963	53·55	990	12·40	14·36	20·60	6·32	46·90	14·16	5·21	1·45
1964	53·89	1,015	12·53	14·32	20·59	6·45	47·22	14·31	5·21	1·46
1965	54·22	997	12·69	14·39	20·55	6·59	47·54	14·39 / 16·95	5·21	1·47
1966	54·50	980	12·84	14·51	20·48	6·67	47·82	17·01	5·20	1·48
1967	54·80	962	13·00	14·57	20·40	6·83	48·11	17·12	5·20	1·49
1968	55·05	947	13·17	14·66	20·32	6·95	48·35	17·23	5·20	1·50
1969	55·26	920	13·29	14·75	20·14	7·09	48·54	17·30	5·21	1·51
1970	55·42	904	13·37	14·85	20·00	7·21	48·68	17·32	5·21	1·53
1971	55·61	902	13·41	14·97	19·88	7·35	48·85	16·99	5·22	1·54
1972	55·78	834	13·43	15·11	19·77	7·47	49·03	17·01	5·21	1·55
1973	56·22	780	13·38	15·28	19·66	7·59	49·15	17·00	5·21	1·55
1974	56·23	737	13·24	15·42	19·54	7·72	49·16	16·93	5·22	1·55
1975	56·21	698	13·07	15·59	19·42	7·83	49·16	16·89	5·21	1·54
1976	56·20	676	12·84	15·86	19·26	7·93	49·14	16·86	5·21	1·54
1977	56·17	657	12·56	16·10	19·17	8·02	49·12	16·83	5·20	1·54
1978	56·16	687	12·29	16·29	19·13	8·13	49·12	16·83	5·18	1·54
1979	56·22	735	12·05	16·48	19·12	8·23	49·17	16·86	5·17	1·54
1980	56·30	754	11·83	16·68	19·10	8·33	49·24	16·89	5·15	1·55
1981	56·35	731	11·61	17·02	19·26	8·46	49·63	17·01	5·18	1·56
1982	56·33	719	11·37	16·95	19·55	8·47	49·60	17·01	5·17	1·57
1983	56·38	721	11·17	16·97	19·82	8·42	49·65	17·04	5·15	1·57

Table UK.9 Labour market: employment, 1900–83

	Employed labour force	Employment by sector									
		Agriculture, forestry & fishing	Mining & quarrying	Mfg	Construction	Gas, electricity & water	Transport & communication	Distributive trades	Services	Public administration & defence	Self employed
		'000									
1900	18,020	...	...	...	...	...	...	...	...	...	...
1901	18,080	2,420	1,020	5,990	1,090	100	1,450	1,990	3,590	880	...
1902	18,110	...	...	...	...	...	...	...	...	...	...
1903	18,140	...	...	...	...	...	...	...	...	...	...
1904	18,050	...	...	...	...	...	...	...	...	...	...
1905	18,400	...	...	...	...	...	...	...	...	...	...
1906	18,830	...	...	...	...	...	...	...	...	...	...
1907	18,980	...	...	...	...	...	...	...	...	...	...
1908	18,340	...	...	...	...	...	...	...	...	...	...
1909	18,530	...	...	...	...	...	...	...	...	...	...
1910	19,280	...	...	...	...	...	...	...	...	...	...
1911	19,790	2,400	1,290	6,550	1,030	120	1,580	2,460	3,890	840	...
1912	19,890	...	...	...	...	...	...	...	...	...	...
1913	20,310	...	...	...	...	...	...	...	...	...	...
1914	20,250	...	...	...	...	...	...	...	...	...	...
1915	20,890	...	...	...	...	...	...	...	...	...	...
1916	21,200	...	...	...	...	...	...	...	...	...	...
1917	21,350	...	...	...	...	...	...	...	...	...	...
1918	21,490	...	...	...	...	...	...	...	...	...	...
1919	21,160	...	...	...	...	...	...	...	...	...	...
1920	21,570										
1920	20,297	1,741	1,325	7,208	927	185	1,641	2,352	3,521	637	...
1921	17,908	1,669	1,210	5,665	888	185	1,544	2,189	3,433	634	...
1922	17,875	1,620	1,200	5,927	808	185	1,504	2,194	3,447	598	...
1923	18,106	1,571	1,280	6,083	831	190	1,532	2,199	3,483	589	...
1924	18,378	1,582	1,295	6,187	863	194	1,555	2,211	3,552	593	...
1925	18,588	1,576	1,205	6,227	924	199	1,558	2,320	3,630	599	...
1926	18,593	1,552	1,204	6,054	950	205	1,562	2,406	3,701	610	...
1927	19,136	1,523	1,123	6,434	1,009	210	1,592	2,516	3,776	606	...
1928	19,204	1,511	1,045	6,428	1,010	216	1,600	2,591	3,852	615	...
1929	19,479	1,502	1,055	6,522	1,011	224	1,601	2,669	3,925	637	...
1930	19,115	1,460	1,034	6,066	1,035	230	1,595	2,724	3,980	664	...
1931	18,665	1,425	958	5,659	1,008	238	1,558	2,778	4,031	685	...
1932	18,753	1,413	902	5,744	930	242	1,537	2,850	4,125	687	...
1933	19,136	1,413	873	5,963	983	244	1,524	2,905	4,218	690	...
1934	19,685	1,394	883	6,235	1,079	251	1,548	2,949	4,323	698	...
1935	20,037	1,370	870	6,387	1,141	263	1,579	2,965	4,411	718	...
1936	20,670	1,335	873	6,737	1,213	272	1,620	3,023	4,511	737	...
1937	21,364	1,313	901	7,077	1,263	284	1,678	3,086	4,620	765	...
1938	21,418	1,272	904	6,970	1,266	291	1,692	3,090	4,700	801	...
1939	23,300	...	...	...	...	...	...	...	...	...	...
1940	23,100	...	...	...	...	...	...	...	...	...	...
1941	24,000	...	...	...	...	...	...	...	...	...	...
1942	24,800	...	...	...	...	...	...	...	...	...	...
1943	25,000	...	...	...	...	...	...	...	...	...	...
1944	24,700	...	...	...	...	...	...	...	...	...	...
1945	24,200	...	...	...	...	...	...	...	...	...	...
1946	23,000	...	...	...	...	...	...	...	...	...	...
1947	23,100	...	...	...	...	...	...	...	...	...	...
1948	23,064	1,203	881	8,294	1,475	327	1,840	2,581	4,102	1,421	...
1948		842	879	8,128	1,334	327	1,771	2,045	3,588	1,413	...
1949	23,090	821	880	8,295	1,322	339	1,760	2,114	3,511	1,428	...
1950	23,257	806	857	8,520	1,325	360	1,769	2,130	3,573	1,402	1,802
1951	23,603	772	860	8,746	1,331	369	1,741	2,162	3,584	1,387	1,798
1952	23,590	724	877	8,669	1,324	379	1,756	2,187	3,606	1,376	1,794
1953	23,703	709	881	8,747	1,338	379	1,727	2,237	3,635	1,362	1,791
1954	24,038	702	872	8,975	1,359	379	1,714	2,314	3,706	1,368	1,789
1955	24,298	692	867	9,222	1,385	384	1,708	2,378	3,755	1,331	1,787
1956	24,514	661	862	9,293	1,431	384	1,720	2,440	3,818	1,342	1,782
1957	24,543	647	873	9,285	1,412	386	1,715	2,511	3,859	1,343	1,778
1958	24,278	625	860	9,183	1,371	383	1,696	2,502	3,898	1,342	1,774
1959	24,348	630	831	9,122	1,403	381	1,674	2,558	3,989	1,347	1,770
1959	23,760	768	803	8,071	1,385	383	1,660	2,657	4,385	1,284	
1960	24,183	743	740	8,418	1,426	380	1,652	2,737	4,490	1,287	1,766
1961	24,457	712	707	8,535	1,482	389	1,678	2,767	4,629	1,310	1,760
1962	24,632	687	685	8,456	1,517	396	1,689	2,830	4,830	1,338	1,748
1963	24,661	691	657	8,322	1,545	406	1,670	2,863	4,947	1,385	1,735
1964	24,950	657	630	8,450	1,583	412	1,656	2,884	5,166	1,355	1,720
1965	25,204	605	597	8,561	1,621	419	1,648	2,909	5,327	1,374	1,696
1966	25,355	582	550	8,584	1,645	432	1,623	2,921	5,477	1,422	1,681
1967	24,992	542	526	8,319	1,556	434	1,617	2,795	5,530	1,471	1,762
1968	24,841	519	463	8,240	1,520	422	1,597	2,770	5,618	1,484	1,786
1969	24,857	492	421	8,353	1,459	406	1,561	2,711	5,736	1,465	1,853
1970	24,753	466	410	8,342	1,339	391	1,572	2,675	5,802	1,481	1,902
1971	24,511	432	396	8,058	1,262	377	1,568	2,610	5,910	1,509	2,021
1972	24,489	427	379	7,779	1,300	356	1,543	2,640	6,144	1,553	1,997
1973	25,057	432	363	7,830	1,380	344	1,524	2,744	6,461	1,585	2,032
1974	25,130	414	349	7,873	1,329	347	1,506	2,761	6,614	1,596	1,996
1975	25,040	397	352	7,490	1,314	353	1,518	2,763	6,861	1,657	1,994
1976	24,828	393	348	7,246	1,309	353	1,475	2,723	7,057	1,631	1,949
1977	24,850	388	350	7,292	1,270	347	1,468	2,753	7,134	1,614	1,904
1978	24,999	382	353	7,257	1,264	340	1,483	2,780	7,314	1,605	1,904
1979	25,375	367	349	7,193	1,289	348	1,497	2,869	7,572	1,617	1,903
1980	25,306	360	349	6,840	1,278	351	1,504	2,877	7,708	1,592	2,011
1981	24,323	351	338	6,087	1,143	347	1,443	2,767	7,652	1,573	2,118
1982	23,987	354	326	5,764	1,049	340	1,383	2,706	7,643	1,549	2,190
1982		...	...	5,912	1,059	686	1,332	2,956	9,134	1,593	
1983	23,792	349	...	5,641	1,016	662	1,452	2,987	9,222	1,600	2,260

25

	Output per person employed		Ave. weekly hrs of manual workers	Ave. weekly earnings of manual workers	Unemployment		Vacancies unfilled	Industrial stoppages	
	Whole economy	Mfg						Working days lost	Workers involved
	Index nos., 1980 = 100			£	'000	%	'000	'000	'000
1900	38·1	...	(54)	1·40	450	2·5	...	3,088	185
1901	38·5	...	...	...	600	3·3	...	4,130	179
1902	39·1	...	...	...	730	4·0	...	3,438	255
1903	38·5	...	...	...	870	4·7	...	2,320	116
1904	39·4	...	...	...	1,130	6·0	...	1,464	87
1905	40·2	...	...	...	950	5·0	...	2,368	92
1906	40·2	...	...	...	690	3·6	...	3,019	218
1907	40·9	...	...	...	710	3·7	...	2,148	146
1908	41·0	...	...	...	1,520	7·8	...	10,785	293
1909	41·3	...	...	...	1,510	7·7	...	2,687	297
1910	40·3	...	(54)	...	930	4·7	...	9,867	514
1911	40·8	...	...	...	600	3·0	...	10,155	952
1912	41·7	...	...	...	670	3·3	...	40,890	1,462
1913	42·3	...	...	1·60	430	2·1	...	9,804	664
1914	...	...	...	...	660	3·3	...	9,878	447
1915	...	...	...	...	200	1·1	...	2,953	448
1916	...	...	...	...	70	0·4	...	2,446	276
1917	...	...	...	...	100	0·6	...	5,647	872
1918	...	...	...	...	140	0·8	...	5,875	1,116
1919	...	...	...	...	660	3·4	...	34,969	2,591
1920	39·8	26·2	...	...	391	2·0	...	26,568	1,932
1921	39·5	25·8	...	...	2,212	11·3	...	85,872	1,801
1922	42·6	28·7	...	...	1,909	9·8	...	19,850	552
1923	43·4	30·1	...	...	1,567	8·1	...	10,672	405
1924	45·0	32·5	46	3·00	1,404	7·2	...	8,424	613
1925	45·7	33·3	...	...	1,559	7·9	...	7,952	441
1926	44·8	33·2	...	...	1,759	8·8	...	162,233	2,734
1927	47·2	34·5	...	...	1,373	6·8	...	1,174	108
1928	47·0	34·5	...	...	1,536	7·5	...	1,388	124
1929	47·5	35·4	...	...	1,503	7·3	...	8,287	533
1930	47·7	36·4	...	...	2,379	11·2	...	4,399	307
1931	47·2	36·3	...	2·95	3,252	15·1	...	6,983	490
1932	47·1	36·1	...	...	3,400	15·6	...	6,488	379
1933	48·0	37·3	...	...	3,087	14·1	...	1,072	136
1934	49·2	38·9	...	...	2,609	11·9	...	959	134
1935	50·5	41·4	...	...	2,437	11·0	...	1,955	271
1936	51·6	42·9	...	...	2,100	9·4	...	1,829	316
1937	51·9	43·3	...	3·00	1,776	7·8	...	3,413	597
1938	51·0	42·6	46·3 / 47·7	3·45	2,164	9·3	...	1,334	274
1939	...	...	...	...	1,340	5·8	...	1,356	337
1940	...	...	...	4·45	710	3·3	...	940	299
1941	...	...	...	4·97	250	1·2	...	1,079	360
1942	...	...	...	5·57	110	0·5	...	1,527	456
1943	...	...	52·9	6·06	80	0·4	...	1,808	557
1944	...	...	51·2	6·22	70	0·4	...	3,714	821
1945	...	...	49·7	6·07	100	0·5	...	2,835	531
1946	49·9	...	47·6	6·04	400	1·9	629	2,158	526
1947	50·3	...	46·6	6·40	300	1·4	571	2,433	620
1948	52·6	46·2	46·7	6·90	298[a]	1·5[a]	467	1,944	424
1949	54·4	48·5	46·8	7·13	328	1·6	383	1,807	433
1950	56·0	50·9	47·6	7·52	332	1·6	364	1,389	302
1951	56·2	51·2	47·8	8·30	264	1·3	410	1,694	379
1952	55·9	49·4	47·7	8·92	368	2·2	275	1,792	415
1953	57·8	52·2	47·9	9·46	356	1·8	275 / 192	2,184	1,370
1954	59·5	53·6	48·5	10·22	303	1·5	228	2,457	448
1955	60·8	55·6	48·9	11·15	244	1·2	281	3,781	659
1956	60·9	55·5	48·5	11·90	258	1·3	241	2,083	507
1957	61·8	56·7	48·2	12·58	327	1·6	186	8,412	1,356
1958	62·4	57·1	47·7	12·83	451	2·2	137	3,462	523
1959	66·8	60·2	48·5	13·54	480	2·3	158	5,270	645
1960	69·0	62·5	48·0	14·53	377	1·7	213	3,024	814[b]
1961	69·5	62·1	47·4	15·34	347	1·6	214	3,046	771
1962	70·0	62·8	47·0	15·86	467	2·1	150	5,798	4,420
1963	72·2	65·7	47·6	16·75	558	2·6	145	1,755	590
1964	75·8	70·8	47·7	18·11	404	1·7	222	2,277	872[b]
1965	77·1	71·8	47·0	19·59	347	1·5	267	2,925	868
1966	77·9	73·1	46·0	20·30	361	1·6	257	2,398	530[b]
1967	80·5	75·7	46·2	21·38	559	2·5	175	2,787	732
1968	84·4	81·6	46·4	23·00	586	2·5	190	4,690	2,256
1969	86·0	83·6	46·5	24·82	581	2·4	202	6,846	1,656
1970	87·9	84·1	45·7	28·05	612	2·6	188	10,980	1,793
1971	90·0	86·0	44·7	30·93	792 / 751	3·5 / 3·3	131	13,551	1,175
1972	93·0	91·0	45·0	35·82	837	3·7	147	23,909	1,726
1973	96·2	98·9	45·6	40·92	596	2·6	307	7,197	1,513
1974	94·5	97·4	45·1	48·63	600	2·6	298	14,750	1,622
1975	92·9	94·8	43·6	59·58	941	4·0	154	6,012	789
1976	95·7	99·8	44·0	66·97	1,302	5·5	122	3,284	670
1977	98·3	101·4	44·2	72·89	1,403	5·8	155	10,142	1,155
1978	101·1	102·3	44·2	83·50	1,383	5·7	210	9,405	1,003
1979	102·7	103·9	44·0	96·94	1,296	5·3	241	29,474	4,583
1980	100·0	100·0	43·0	113·06	1,665	6·8	143	11,964	842
1981	102·3	103·1	43·0	125·58	2,520	10·5	97	4,266	1,499
1982	105·8	108·8	42·9	137·06	2,916	12·1	111	5,313	2,103
1983	109·8	116·1	43·3	149·13	3,105	12·9	145	3,754	571

a July figure.   b Excludes workers becoming involved after end of year in which stoppage began.

	Total imports	Food, beverages & tobacco	Basic materials	Fuels	Semi-manufact.	Finished manufact.	of which: Machinery & transport equipment
				£ mn			
1900	523	220	166	7	127		4
1901	522	224	162	6	127		4
1902	528	224	164	6	132		5
1903	543	231	168	6	136		5
1904	551	231	176	7	136		4
1905	565	231	182	7	142		6
1906	608	238	205	7	155		6
1907	646	247	235	7	154		7
1908	593	244	197	8	142		6
1909	625	254	214	7	147		6
1910	678	258	255	7	156		12
1911	680	264	248	7	160		13
1912	745	281	276	9	178		16
1913	769	290	272	12	142	49	17
1914	697	297	223	13	123	37	15
1915	852	381	273	13	143	39	19
1916	949	419	321	20	152	37	16
1917	1,064	455	354	34	136	83	18
1918	1,316	570	398	64	151	129	24
1919	1,626	706	616	40	186	74	28
1920	1,933	760	715	72	281	102	49
1921	1,086	563	260	69	139	52	30
1922	1,003	469	298	40	138	55	16
1923	1,096	506	322	37	165	61	19
1924	1,277	567	395	43	195	83	23
1925	1,321	566	418	42	206	70	28
1926	1,241	526	343	94	203	81	24
1927	1,218	535	337	52	207	83	30
1928	1,196	528	331	41	201	90	31
1929	1,221	532	337	45	206	82	37
1930	1,044	472	248	48	183	74	32
1931	861	414	172	30	161	74	26
1932	702	371	162	33	90	40	16
1933	675	338	178	31	87	37	14
1934	731	345	204	33	101	44	31
1935	756	353	208	35	109	47	21
1936	848	379	243	39	123	58	26
1937	1,028	429	308	50	164	71	34
1938	920	428	240	48	131	65	30
1939	886	397	234	48	140	60	34
1940	1,082	418	329	76	190	63	…
1941	986	420	220	97	170	71	…
1942	997	434	229	103	163	54	…
1943	1,234	512	254	156	213	84	…
1944	1,309	518	272	224	174	91	…
1945	1,104	489	284	148	105	59	42
1946	1,301	636	375	89	140	33	21
1947	1,798	798	540	105	261	68	37
1948	2,064	865	643	159	287	81	55
1949	2,268	958	730	149	309	101	77
1950	2,598	1,017	914	197	350	103	71
1951	3,892	1,282	1,520	316	636	140	82
1952	3,465	1,196	1,143	339	581	187	133
1953	3,328	1,304	1,055	313	445	196	160
1954	3,359	1,314	1,026	329	512	169	119
1955	3,860	1,424	1,121	408	689	206	147
1956	3,862	1,434	1,099	414	670	234	163
1957	4,139	1,478	1,165	466	744	268	189
1958	3,834	1,489	906	439	674	303	210
1959	4,087	1,519	946	467	750	377	253
1960	4,655	1,540	1,080	480	1,005	517	347
1961	4,546	1,484	1,009	482	975	556	366
1962	4,627	1,569	924	533	955	602	395
1963	4,989	1,676	989	560	1,050	651	407
1964	5,702	1,771	1,118	585	1,323	834	545
1965	5,760	1,708	1,110	611	1,369	882	606
1966	5,951	1,712	1,061	628	1,476	990	681
1967	6,440	1,762	1,011	732	1,597	1,244	868
1968	7,900	1,900	1,206	907	2,116	1,652	1,189
1969	8,317	1,930	1,251	911	2,300	1,834	1,320
1970	9,113	2,047	1,415	950	2,478	2,091	1,515
1971	9,799	2,176	1,316	1,253	2,449	2,452	1,755
1972	11,073	2,356	1,364	1,247	2,806	3,155	2,287
1973	15,724	3,094	2,024	1,733	3,999	4,665	3,374
1974	23,129	3,762	2,630	4,644	6,051	5,602	3,993
1975	24,046	4,335	2,285	4,316	5,798	6,769	4,905
1976	31,084	4,983	3,446	5,669	7,568	8,957	6,486
1977	36,219	5,937	3,886	5,255	9,156	11,480	8,466
1978	39,533	6,141	3,691	4,805	10,313	14,012	10,199
1979	46,925	6,517	4,180	5,782	12,694	16,995	12,226
1980	49,773	6,153	4,049	6,875	13,481	17,696	12,566
1981	51,169	6,537	4,000	7,166	12,533	19,460	13,399
1982	56,978	7,251	3,930	7,409	14,032	23,083	16,464
1983	65,993	7,853	4,723	7,067	16,960	27,945	20,231

Table UK.12 Value of exports by commodity group, 1900–83

	Total exports	Non-manufact.	Fuels	Manufact.	of which: Chemicals	Textiles	Metals & metal manufact.	Machinery & transport equipment
				£ mn				
1900	354	66	39	247	16	111	47	31
1901	348	71	30	242	15	112	40	29
1902	349	73	28	245	17	112	43	30
1903	361	73	27	254	18	117	45	29
1904	371	76	27	263	18	129	43	41
1905	408	85	26	291	20	141	49	34
1906	461	91	32	331	21	153	61	44
1907	518	101	42	368	23	170	70	50
1908	457	90	42	320	22	143	55	60
1909	469	103	37	322	23	146	56	42
1910	534	117	38	370	25	167	65	48
1911	557	119	38	390	26	181	68	48
1912	599	132	43	414	28	185	74	54
1913	635	130	54	441	29	190	81	64
1914	526	113	42	363	25	157	63	53
1915	484	116	39	315	29	138	59	31
1916	604	113	51	420	38	192	79	32
1917	597	84	51	442	33	222	63	28
1918	532	40	52	419	31	246	51	25
1919	964	198	92	662	48	372	89	70
1920	1,558	287	124	1,133	60	557	167	71
1921	810	142	48	611	20	244	83	76
1922	824	148	80	584	22	257	78	63
1923	886	177	114	584	25	251	96	44
1924	941	205	83	637	24	280	97	45
1925	927	218	60	635	22	269	92	63
1926	779	182	26	557	23	215	86	62
1927	832	186	54	577	25	215	95	59
1928	844	184	47	593	28	212	89	65
1929	839	172	57	592	30	198	94	69
1930	658	134	53	453	30	151	68	111
1931	455	97	39	301	24	99	41	71
1932	416	86	36	280	24	103	38	57
1933	417	85	36	283	24	101	45	56
1934	447	93	37	306	25	107	51	66
1935	481	92	40	337	28	108	57	79
1936	502	100	38	352	27	113	57	84
1937	596	113	49	422	32	127	82	103
1938	532	97	47	376	29	94	66	117
1939	486	88	46	341	31	94	51	99
1940	419	65	29	318	40	100	50	72
1941	337	41	10	281	35	96	34	54
1942	276	26	7	237	26	91	23	53
1943	240	26	8	204	30	72	17	49
1944	282	39	6	232	32	74	19	68
1945	450	105	8	316	49	90	45	83
1946	965	134	15	792	81	157	132	268
1947	1,201	110	11	1,007	84	195	145	400
1948	1,628	191	53	1,325	104	294	183	574
1949	1,832	196	70	1,495	110	331	212	676
1950	2,245	295	78	1,807	136	382	260	807
1951	2,693	297	72	2,210	194	513	259	892
1952	2,711	329	134	2,161	178	365	315	967
1953	2,661	292	153	2,091	173	364	312	943
1954	2,748	299	157	2,160	202	362	304	984
1955	2,993	336	146	2,372	235	344	365	1,082
1956	3,286	367	167	2,623	245	331	448	1,235
1957	3,497	374	157	2,850	268	345	473	1,317
1958	3,391	360	136	2,796	264	293	427	1,372
1959	3,553	372	123	2,951	295	282	453	1,446
1960	3,789	393	130	3,137	319	298	466	1,541
1961	3,955	414	128	3,289	328	286	482	1,635
1962	4,062	427	151	3,362	344	280	487	1,674
1963	4,378	456	170	3,607	369	298	476	1,820
1964	4,600	476	144	3,807	414	319	511	1,844
1965	4,932	496	137	4,120	448	309	581	2,005
1966	5,275	533	139	4,413	475	296	588	2,205
1967	5,244	526	136	4,403	496	279	610	2,142
1968	6,442	639	173	5,432	603	330	746	2,623
1969	7,352	677	177	6,278	690	383	847	2,987
1970	8,096	779	210	6,827	775	418	962	3,337
1971	9,070	865	239	7,703	873	444	1,008	3,932
1972	9,602	978	242	8,097	951	468	1,017	4,090
1973	12,087	1,297	374	10,042	1,257	629	1,313	4,853
1974	16,309	1,645	782	13,277	2,113	774	1,717	6,149
1975	19,607	1,987	827	16,033	2,145	729	1,849	8,298
1976	25,277	2,501	1,265	20,657	3,007	972	2,362	10,179
1977	31,990	3,177	2,092	25,765	3,817	1,193	2,877	12,456
1978	35,380	3,948	2,375	27,989	4,199	1,238	3,113	13,408
1979	40,637	4,221	4,324	30,870	4,911	1,339	3,610	14,235
1980	47,364	4,706	6,429	34,818	5,286	1,363	4,062	16,273
1981	50,698	4,926	9,616	34,639	5,500	1,186	3,724	16,705
1982	55,558	5,300	11,237	37,313	6,119	1,192	3,933	18,101
1983	60,534	5,821	13,127	39,919	6,929	1,285	4,270	18,314

Table UK.13 Value of exports and imports by area, 1900–83

	European Community		Rest of Europe		North America		Rest of world		of which: Japan	
	Exports to	Imports from	Exports to	Imports from	Exports to	Imports from	Exports to	Imports from	Exports to	Imports from
					£ mn					
1900	109	159	31	41	48	163	165	158	10	2
1901	98	160	30	40	48	164	171	157	8	2
1902	95	166	28	41	56	153	169	167	5	2
1903	99	168	28	42	55	151	177	180	5	2
1904	99	151	29	56	53	145	189	196	5	2
1905	109	155	31	57	64	144	203	202	10	2
1906	128	162	35	62	70	164	227	218	13	3
1907	147	164	40	62	79	164	251	259	12	3
1908	131	157	38	57	58	153	228	224	10	2
1909	131	163	36	57	79	147	222	253	9	4
1910	146	172	41	60	86	149	259	293	10	4
1911	152	176	44	62	80	152	279	289	12	3
1912	160	193	47	61	93	165	297	322	13	4
1913	167	208	50	63	88	175	328	328	15	4
1914	130	162	42	56	85	173	267	288	9	4
1915	144	95	39	72	73	282	226	391	5	9
1916	180	89	46	82	87	356	289	433	8	13
1917	193	73	36	68	78	465	288	427	6	15
1918	198	69	34	96	42	647	256	542	7	24
1919	414	184	127	54	84	663	335	721	15	24
1920	451	246	179	176	181	666	742	840	28	30
1921	200	200	66	91	86	340	454	450	22	9
1922	230	189	68	91	105	280	416	439	25	8
1923	271	257	66	95	116	269	429	472	27	7
1924	296	306	72	99	109	312	460	557	27	8
1925	278	311	66	98	114	321	465	588	17	7
1926	204	335	49	89	104	296	418	518	14	7
1927	240	328	57	98	98	260	432	529	15	8
1928	242	328	57	90	106	250	434	524	15	9
1929	246	333	60	97	100	246	428	541	14	9
1930	207	307	58	87	71	196	317	451	8	8
1931	157	274	40	73	48	140	206	370	6	7
1932	134	168	36	57	38	129	203	344	6	7
1933	126	145	37	59	45	125	204	342	4	6
1934	126	146	43	65	44	136	228	380	4	8
1935	130	151	42	67	54	146	246	388	4	8
1936	128	160	39	75	62	172	267	437	4	10
1937	149	184	48	91	72	208	320	540	5	12
1938	132	172	45	77	53	200	296	466	2	9
1939	118	166	44	75	61	200	257	440	1	9
1940	72	80	33	56	72	364	239	579	—	6
1941	25	35	19	30	72	446	221	475	—	1
1942	21	35	18	39	50	505	187	418	—	—
1943	14	29	31	31	45	739	150	435	—	—
1944	28	34	18	49	43	745	193	481	—	—
1945	131	52	33	67	46	527	242	455	—	—
1946	241	125	106	83	74	431	534	655	—	—
1947	231	206	144	122	107	536	705	924	—	5
1948	308	280	207	175	144	408	969	1,201	—	5
1949	338	393	198	204	145	447	1,151	1,224	1	11
1950	450	497	253	217	257	392	1,285	1,492	3	8
1951	487	699	328	420	294	641	1,584	2,132	9	17
1952	502	633	328	345	314	638	1,567	1,849	9	29
1953	569	583	374	311	334	559	1,460	1,875	18	9
1954	597	625	312	323	297	556	1,542	1,855	12	16
1955	504	710	344	388	344	764	1,801	1,998	14	24
1956	696	709	369	397	442	756	1,779	2,000	24	24
1957	724	739	370	434	483	809	1,920	2,157	29	24
1958	683	773	349	392	515	665	1,844	2,004	20	35
1959	734	816	374	418	631	689	1,814	2,164	33	43
1960	800	951	430	518	596	950	1,963	2,236	29	42
1961	970	993	506	520	570	846	1,909	2,187	44	40
1962	1,103	1,033	538	512	580	838	1,841	2,245	46	54
1963	1,237	1,126	603	540	583	883	1,955	2,440	53	54
1964	1,292	1,317	686	669	622	1,109	2,001	2,608	61	75
1965	1,327	1,370	737	692	728	1,131	2,141	2,566	53	78
1966	1,419	1,508	816	740	877	1,149	2,163	2,551	69	77
1967	1,428	1,720	818	840	862	1,263	2,137	2,617	88	91
1968	1,777	2,073	925	1,074	1,182	1,574	2,557	3,178	99	115
1969	2,126	2,168	1,114	1,154	1,223	1,636	2,888	3,359	129	105
1970	2,420	2,462	1,311	1,390	1,233	1,878	3,095	3,364	149	135
1971	2,591	2,840	1,441	1,518	1,445	1,758	3,559	3,663	158	202
1972	2,935	3,525	1,566	1,794	1,600	1,805	3,472	3,930	172	315
1973	3,927	5,262	1,946	2,596	1,938	2,395	4,234	5,611	274	446
1974	5,467	7,800	2,624	3,331	2,291	3,273	5,867	8,710	320	572
1975	6,391	8,872	3,003	3,408	2,369	3,248	7,786	8,479	311	674
1976	9,101	11,504	3,773	4,346	3,105	4,276	9,241	10,924	362	798
1977	11,848	14,160	4,734	5,083	3,791	4,984	11,521	11,936	471	1,061
1978	13,621	16,547	4,425	5,998	4,249	5,314	12,985	11,611	542	1,283
1979	17,479	20,888	5,559	7,192	4,792	6,197	12,663	12,556	606	1,488
1980	20,543	20,574	6,750	7,265	5,329	7,464	14,595	14,370	597	1,707
1981	20,940	21,718	6,293	7,799	7,121	7,588	16,344	14,064	613	2,206
1982	23,124	25,269	6,681	8,390	8,353	8,095	17,400	15,224	681	2,659
1983	26,516	30,098	7,516	10,444	9,342	9,027	17,160	16,424	798	3,355

Table UK.14 Balance of payments, 1900–83

	Imports (fob)	Exports (fob)	Services Debits	Services Credits	Interest, profits & dividends Debits	Interest, profits & dividends Credits	Current balance	Official reserves (end year)
				£ mn				
1900	485	356	50	111	8	112	34	...
1901	485	349	55	109	9	115	19	...
1902	491	350	46	110	10	119	24	...
1903	505	361	38	118	10	122	43	...
1904	512	372	39	120	11	124	52	...
1905	527	409	40	126	12	135	88	...
1906	568	462	43	139	14	148	121	...
1907	603	519	46	152	16	160	162	...
1908	550	457	46	140	17	168	150	...
1909	581	470	47	145	17	175	142	...
1910	632	536	51	155	19	189	174	...
1911	634	559	51	156	20	197	204	...
1912	694	600	54	168	22	209	203	...
1913	719	637	58	179	24	224	235	35
1914	660	540	80	145	25	215	134	...
1915	840	500	130	250	25	190	−55	...
1916	980	630	160	370	30	230	90	...
1917	1,040	620	220	465	40	235	50	...
1918	1,170	540	230	400	65	240	−275	...
1919	1,460	990	220	480	65	230	−45	88
1920	1,761 / 1,812	1,585 / 1,664	224	464	46	292	317 / 337	128
1921	1,022	874	172	292	44	222	193	128
1922	951	888	150	225	60	237	201	127
1923	1,011	914	146	247	64	240	183	128
1924	1,172	958	152	242	65	261	78	129
1925	1,208	943	149	215	63	295	52	147
1926	1,140	794	152	223	63	300	−18	151
1927	1,115	845	142	245	63	302	98	152
1928	1,095	858	140	234	64	304	124	153
1929	1,117	854	152	242	64	307	96	146
1930	953	670	147	214	62	277	36	148
1931	786	464	140	168	48	211	−103	121
1932	641	425	123	153	48	175	−51	206
1933	619	427	120	146	29	183	−8	372
1934	683	463	116	145	28	195	−22	415
1935	724	541	124	149	31	212	23	493
1936	784	523	135	174	34	229	−27	703
1937	950	614	144	229	37	242	−47	825
1938	849	564	152	193	37	229	−55	615
1939	800	500	200	300	90	250	−250	545
1940	1,000	400	550	200	100	260	−800	108
1941	1,100	400	450	200	130	270	−820	141
1942	800	300	550	300	170	270	−660	254
1943	800	240	700	500	190	280	−680	467
1944	900	270	800	700	210	290	−680	601
1945	700	450	1,000	350	230	310	−870	610
1946	1,063	960	762	470	113	198	−230	664
1947	1,541	1,180	687	472	111	261	−381	512
1948	1,790	1,639	644	557	125	360	26	457
1949	2,000	1,863	697	632	132	351	−1	603
1950	2,312	2,261	764	734	162	558	307	1,178
1951	3,424	2,735	907	913	211	553	−369	834
1952	3,048	2,769	885	991	248	500	163	659
1953	2,927	2,683	908	1,004	266	495	145	899
1954	2,989	2,785	972	1,052	290	540	117	986
1955	3,386	3,073	1,095	1,104	343	517	−155	757
1956	3,324	3,377	1,230	1,221	342	571	208	799
1957	3,538	3,509	1,240	1,327	334	583	233	812
1958	3,377	3,406	1,206	1,304	389	682	360	1,096
1959	3,642	3,527	1,243	1,329	396	658	172	977
1960	4,138	3,737	1,411	1,419	438	671	228	1,154
1961	4,043	3,903	1,467	1,488	422	676	47	1,185
1962	4,103	4,003	1,505	1,523	420	754	155	1,002
1963	4,450	4,331	1,577	1,546	444	842	125	949
1964	5,111	4,568	1,708	1,658	495	889	−358	827
1965	5,173	4,913	1,798	1,762	557	992	−30	1,073
1966	5,384	5,276	1,876	1,907	576	964	130	1,107
1967	5,840	5,241	2,015	2,183	601	979	−269	1,123
1968	7,145	6,433	2,235	2,592	776	1,110	−244	1,009
1969	7,478	7,269	2,452	2,874	844	1,342	505	1,053
1970	8,184	8,150	2,963	3,444	898	1,452	823	1,178
1971	8,853	9,043	3,340	3,965	984	1,486	1,124	2,526
1972	10,185	9,437	3,587	4,288	1,210	1,748	223	2,405
1973	14,523	11,937	4,510	5,296	1,566	2,823	−979	2,795
1974	21,745	16.394	5,653	6,728	1,871	3,286	−3,278	2,955
1975	22,663	19,330	6,342	7,857	2,068	2,831	−1,523	2,700
1976	29,120	25,191	7,775	10,278	2,606	3,961	−846	2,485
1977	34,012	31,728	8,565	11,921	3,916	4,013	53	10,975
1978	36,605	35,063	8,906	12,764	4,534	5,157	1,162	10,380
1979	44,136	40,687	10,406	14,561	6,915	7,949	−525	13,170
1980	45,909	47,422	11,520	15,876	8,441	8,280	3,629	13,275
1981	47,325	50,977	12,607	17,065	8,922	9,978	7,221	11,960
1982	53,181	55,565	13,838	17,544	9,411	10,576	5,206	12,939
1983	61,341	60,625	15,241	19,143	10,525	12,473	2,916	12,805

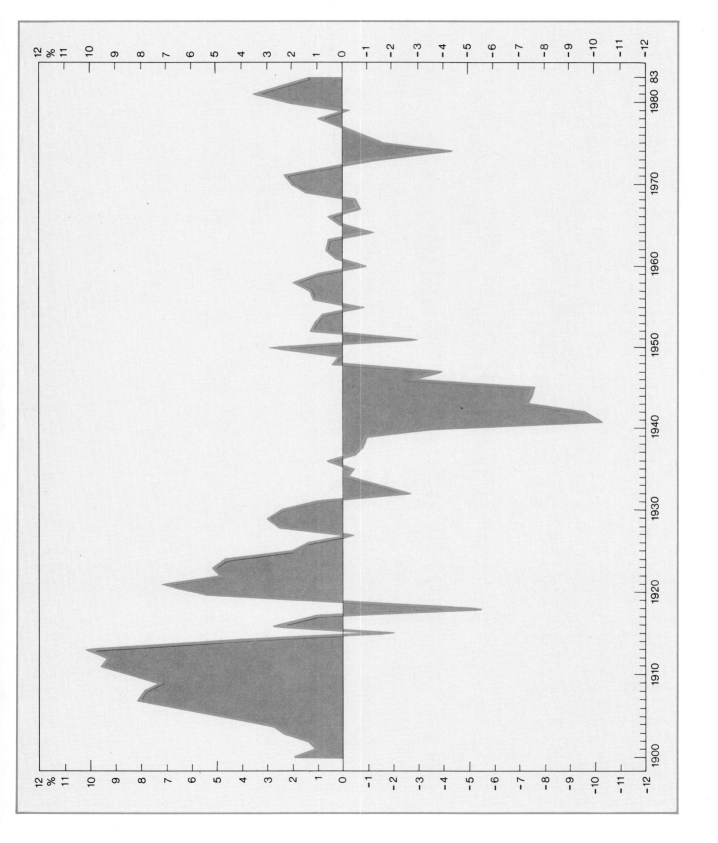

Chart UK. 14 Balance of payments, current balance as percent of gross domestic product, 1900–83

31

Table UK.15 Finance, 1900–83

		Interest rates				Total	Foreign exchange rates				
	Industrial ordinary share price index	Treasury bills, ave. 3 months tender rate	Gilt edged yields		Money stock (MI) (end of period)	consumer credit outstanding		French	German	Italian	Japanese
			Short-dated	2½% Consols			US $	Fr	mark	L	Y
	1980 = 100	%	%	%	£ mn	£ mn	Annual average, rates to £				
1900	4·5	3·996	...	2·51	...	...	4·872	25·38	20·72	...	9·91
1901	4·5	2·475	...	2·65	...	...	4·879	25·35	20·62	...	9·88
1902	4·1	2·963	3·12	2·65	...	...	4·876	25·33	20·61	...	9·81
1903	4·1	3·446	3·40	2·75	...	...	4·868	25·36	20·63	...	9·81
1904	4·1	2·904	3·40	2·83	...	...	4·872	25·33	20·61	...	9·92
1905	4·1	2·200	2·95	2·78	...	...	4·866	25·31	20·62	...	9·82
1906	4·1	3·000	3·17	2·83	...	...	4·857	25·37	20·71	...	9·85
1907	4·1	3·763	3·28	2·97	...	...	4·867	25·43	20·78	...	9·83
1908	3·7	2·246	2·91	2·90	...	...	4·868	25·32	20·66	...	9·83
1909	3·7	2·137	2·74	2·98	...	...	4·876	25·36	20·66	...	9·81
1910	4·1	3·058	2·91	3·08	...	...	4·868	25·45	20·71	...	9·86
1911	4·5	2·825	2·99	3·15	...	...	4·866	25·49	20·71	...	9·83
1912	4·5	2·004	3·04	3·28	...	...	4·870	25·50	20·75	...	9·81
1913	4·5	3·048	3·09	3·39	...	...	4·868	25·56	20·78	...	9·85
1914	...	...	...	...	...	...	4·884				9·90
1919	7·4	3·481	5·24	4·62	(1,501)	...	4·429	31·75	226·98	...	8·89
1920	7·4	6·212	6·23	5·32	(1,519)	...	3·661	52·47	404·59	104·6	7·62
1921	5·2	4·575	5·70	5·21	1,494	...	3·846	51·89	8,155·85	89·5	8·03
1922	6·0	2·571	4·78	4·42	1,424	...	4·427	54·60	...	93·2	9·32
1923	7·1	2·621	4·39	4·31	1,396	...	4·574	75·64	18·90	99·4	9·39
1924	7·1	3·392	4·36	4·39	1,393	...	4·417	85·24	20·28	101·3	10·52
1925	7·8	4·092	4·51	4·44	1,363	...	4·829	102·54	20·41	121·4	11·85
1926	8·2	4·512	4·35	4·55	1,365	...	4·858	152·38	20·46	125·8	10·36
1927	8·6	4·254	3·98	4·56	1,382	...	4·861	123·85	20·39	95·1	10·25
1928	10·1	4·146	4·73	4·47	1,424	...	4·866	124·10	20·39	92·6	10·49
1929	9·7	5·264	5·08	4·60	1,345	...	4·857	124·02	20·40	92·7	10·55
1930	7·8	2·484	4·31	4·48	1,388 1,303	...	4·862	123·88	20·38	92·8	9·86
1931	6·3	3·593	4·54	4·39	1,189	...	4·859 3·694	124·06 94·02	20·52 15·73	87·0	9·25
1932	6·0	1·486	3·64	3·74	1,317	...	3·504	89·19	14·74	68·4	12·60
1933	7·1	0·591	2·09	3·39	1,346	...	4·218	84·59	13·98	63·7	16·46
1934	8·9	0·727	1·78	3·10	1,377	...	5·041	76·94	12·80	58·8	16·78
1935	9·7	0·546	2·46	2·89	1,494	...	4·903	74·27	12·18	59·3	17·07
1936	11·2	0·583	2·45	2·93	1,670	...	4·971	82·97	12·33	70·4	17·12
1937	10·4	0·563	2·90	3·28	1,698	...	4·944	124·61	12·29	94·0	17·16
1938	8·6	0·611	2·72	3·38	1,663	...	4·890	170·65	12·17	92·9	17·15
1939	8·2	1·315	3·30	3·72	1,810	...	4·460	176·65	...	85·3	17·07
1940	6·7	1·028	2·78	3·40	2,235	...	4·03	176·62	...	72·3	16·84
1941	7·1	1·006	2·47	3·13	2,719	...	4·03	...	...	...	...
1942	7·8	1·004	2·32	3·03	3,133	...	4·03	...	...	...	...
1943	9·3	1·004	2·45	3·10	3,562	...	4·03	...	...	...	...
1944	10·4	1·004	2·37	3·14	4,069	...	4·03	...	...	...	...
1945	10·8	0·896	2·45	2·92	4,415	...	4·03	203·80	...	...	60·45
1946	11·9	0·504	2·08	2·60	4,956	...	4·03	480·00	...	...	...
1947	12·3	0·508	2·18	2·76	5,035	68	4·03	480·00	...	...	201·50
1948	11·9	0·509	2·02	3·21	5,126	105	4·03	879·73	...	...	1,088·1
1949	11·2	0·521	1·94	3·30	5,191	128	3·68	1,053·06	...	2,104	1,157·2
1950	11·5	0·516	2·03	3·54	5,283	167	2·80	980·00	...	1,749	1,010·2
1951	13·4	0·562	1·85	3·78	5,355	208	2·80	979·74	...	1,750	1,010·2
1952	11·2	2·196	2·98	4·23	4,950	241	2·79	981·48	...	1,750	1,010·2
1953	11·9	2·304	3·03	4·08	5,119	276	2·81	982·76	11·70	1,750	1,010·2
1954	15·6	1·794	2·61	3·75	5,358	384	2·81	981·64	11·73	1,750	1,006·6
1955	18·2	3·753	3·81	4·17	5,280	461	2·792	978·10	11·74	1,751	1,011·4
1956	17·1	4·945	4·67	4·73	5,300	376	2·796	982·74	11·71	1,751	1,005·1
1957	18·2	4·814	5·15	4·98	5,209	448	2·794	1,059·63	11·73	1,752	1,012·5
1958	18·6	4·563	4·75	4·98	5,191	556	2·810	1,177·51	11·72	1,745	1,010·5
1959	26·8	3·375	4·16	4·82	5,825	849	2·809	13·77	11·74	1,744	1,007·3
1960	33·9	4·887	5·60	5·42	5,707	935	2·808	13·77	11·71	1,743	1,008·2
1961	35·0	5·141	5·98	6·20	5,749	934	2·802	13·74	11·26	1,740	1,016·0
1962	32·8	4·171	5·31	5·98	5,890	887	2·808	13·76	11·224	1,743	1,007·8
1963	37·2	3·667	4·83	5·58	6,380 7,210	959	2·800	13·72	11·161	1,740	1,013·5
1964	39·8	4·594	5·54	6·03	7,450	1,115	2·793	13·68	11·099	1,743	1,001·1
1965	37·2	5·909	6·57	6·42	7,610	1,196	2·796	13·70	11·165	1,747	1,013·0
1966	37·6	6·122	6·77	6·80	7,600	1,104	2·793	13·72	11·168	1,744	1,012·5
1967	40·2	5·810	6·66	6·69	8,250 8,180	1,058	2·828	13·52	10·955	1,715	1,023·5
1968	56·8	7·031	7·59	7·39	8,640	1,089	2·394	11·86	9·555	1,492	856·3
1969	56·2	7·627	8·81	8·88	8,660	1,063	2·390	12·43	9·379	1,499	855·1
1970	49·8	6·999	7·89	9·16	9,420	1,127	2·396	13·24	8·736	1,502	857·8
1971	58·8	5·554	6·68	9·05	10,310 10,710	1,668	2·444	13·46	8·530	1,511	844·6
1972	74·9	5·541	7·68	9·11	12,370	2,106	2·502	12·62	7·975	1,460	752·3
1973	64·8	9·306	10·45	10·85	13,020	2,550	2·453	10·90	6·540	1,426	664·6
1974	38·1	11·357	12·51	14·95	14,460	2,386	2·340	11·25	6·049	1,522	682·7
1975	47·6	10·187	11·48	14·66	17,150	2,373	2·220	9·50	5·447	1,447	658·1
1976	57·0	11·157	12·06	14·25	19,000 3,860	2,716	1·805	8·61	4·552	1,497	535·4
1977	73·1	7·630	10·08	12·31	23,170	4,750	1·746	8·57	4·050	1,540	467·7
1978	82·3	8·535	11·32	11·92	27,364	6,234	1·920	8·64	3·850	1,628	402·7
1979	93·5	12·988	12·64	11·38	29,856	7,989	2·122	9·03	3·887	1,762	465·6
1980	100·0	15·127	13·84	11·86	31,044 34,452	9,126	2·328	9·82	4·227	1,992	525·6
1981	112·8	13·040	14·65	12·99	36,533	9,769	2·025	10·94	4·556	2,287	444·6
1982	130·7	11·424	12·79	11·91	40,664 9,693	11,356	1·749	11·48	4·243	2,364	435·2

Chart UK. 15   Share prices and interest rates, 1900–83

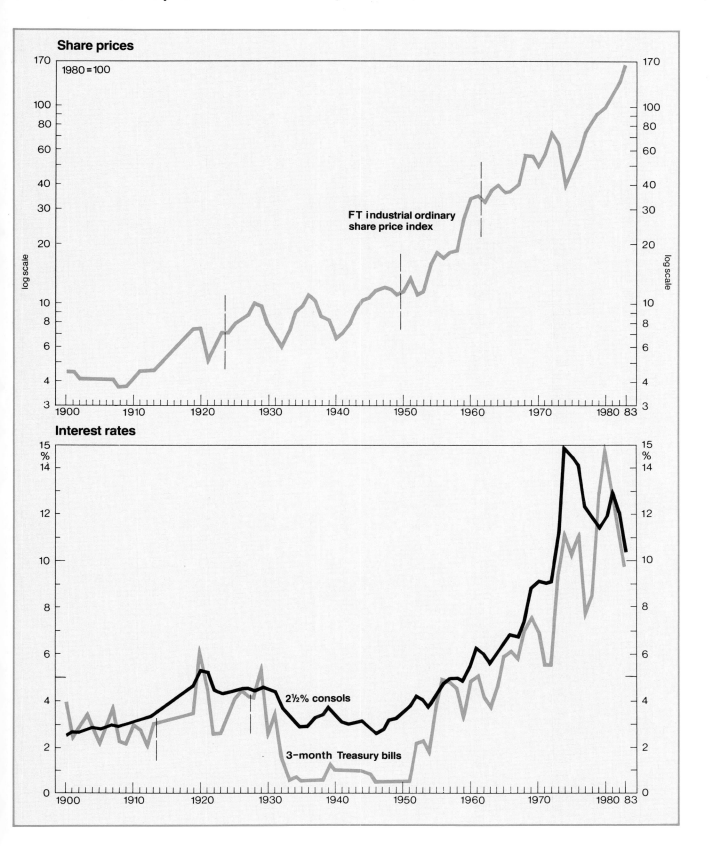

Share prices

1980 = 100

log scale

FT industrial ordinary
share price index

Interest rates

15
%

2½% consols

3-month Treasury bills

Table UK.16 Transport and energy, 1900–83

	Motor vehicle licences current		Railways		Airways	Energy consumption (primary fuel input basis)		
	Goods	Private	bn passenger km	bn freight net ton km	bn passenger km	Coal	Petroleum	Natural gas
	'000					mn tons coal or coal equiv.		
1900	...	...	...	...	...	165·9	1·5	...
1901	...	...	...	...	...	162·3	...	...
1902	...	...	...	...	...	167·7	...	...
1903	...	...	...	...	...	167·5	...	...
1904	4	8	...	...	...	167·4	...	...
1905	9	16	...	...	...	170·0	...	...
1906	12	23	...	...	...	175·5	...	...
1907	14	32	...	...	...	184·1	...	...
1908	18	41	...	...	...	177·7	...	...
1909	22	48	...	...	...	179·2	...	...
1910	30	53	...	...	...	181·4	2·0	...
1911	40	72	...	...	...	186·2	...	...
1912	53	88	...	...	...	180·9	...	...
1913	64	106	...	...	...	193·8	...	...
1914	82	132	...	...	...	188·3	...	...
1915	85	139	...	...	...	196·9	...	...
1916	82	142	...	...	...	205·5	...	...
1917	64	110	...	...	...	203·7	...	...
1918	41	78	...	...	...	187·8	...	...
1919	62	110	...	...	...	182·2	...	...
1920	101	187	30·9	31·4	...	186·4	...	...
1921	128	243	26·9	21·7	...	130·9	3·6	...
1922	151	315	28·5	27·5	...	166·1	4·1	...
1923	173	384	28·6	31·0	...	177·5	5·2	...
1924	203	474	29·9	31·2	...	184·5	6·0	...
1925	224	580	30·4	30·0	0·004	175·9	6·0	...
1926	257	684	27·0	23·0	0·006	123·0	7·6	...
1927	283	787	29·4	30·9	0·007	183·2	8·0	...
1928	306	885	29·9	29·0	0·010	170·4	8·1	...
1929	330	981	30·4	30·8	0·011	180·2	8·1	...
1930	348	1,056	29·4	29·1	0·010	171·1	9·1	...
1931	361	1,083	27·8	26·7	0·011	158·8	9·0	...
1932	370	1,128	26·7	24·4	0·026	156·1	9·1	...
1933	387	1,203	28·2	24·6	0·035	155·9	9·8	...
1934	413	1,308	29·8	26·5	0·047	167·5	10·4	...
1935	444	1,505	30·9	26·8	0·068	172·4	10·6	...
1936	471	1,675	32·0	28·5	0·066	182·4	11·0	...
1937	490	1,834	33·3	30·1	0·080	189·0	11·5	...
1938	506	1,984	30·6	26·6	0·086	178·5	12·6	...
1939	501	2,077	...	...	0·091	186·4	13·3	...
1940	455	1,454	...	...	0·068	197·5	11·7	...
1941	466	1,539	...	...	0·092	198·5	13·3	...
1942	466	883	...	39·0	0·164	199·7	13·1	...
1943	463	736	...	39·8	0·201	192·3	14·3	...
1944	463	773	...	40·0	0·288	189·9	20·9	...
1945	488	1,521	...	36·0	0·486	181·8	16·5	...
1946	475	1,807	47·0	33·7	0·584	189·1	13·9	...
1947	687	1,983	37·0	33·0	0·710	187·5	18·3	...
1948	788	2,003	34·2	35·4	0·892	195·3	19·0	...
1949	866	2,179	34·0	36·0	0·989	196·8	20·2	...
1950	920	2,308	32·5	36·2	1·278	204·3	22·9	...
1951	959	2,433	33·5	37·4	1·714	209·5	25·8	...
1952	990	2,565	32·9	36·6	1·999	207·4	26·9	...
1953	1,023	2,825	33·1	37·2	2·308	208·9	29·2	...
1954	1,061	3,173	33·3	36·1	2·438	215·8	32·4	...
1955	1,139	3,610	32·7	34·9	2·898	216·9	36·0	...
1956	1,206	3,981	34·0	35·1	3·383	217·4	39·1	...
1957	1,250	4,283	36·4	34·1	3·897	210·9	38·2	...
1958	1,304	4,651	35·6	30·1	4·137	201·8	49·1	0·1
1959	1,365	5,087	35·8	29·0	4·973	189·6	58·3	0·1
1960	1,439	5,657	34·7	30·5	6·371	198·6	68·1	0·1
1961	1,496	6,118	33·9	28·8	7·290	193·0	73·4	0·1
1962	1,563	6,710	31·7	26·3	7·836	194·0	80·8	0·1
1963	1,625	7,552	30·9	25·2	8·765	196·9	87·9	0·2
1964	1,677	8,441	32·0	26·2	10·339	189·6	96·1	0·4
1965	1,705	9,136	30·1	25·2	11·937	187·5	106·2	1·3
1966	1,682	9,758	29·7	23·6	13·360	176·8	114·8	1·2
1967	1,736	10,563	29·1	21·4	14·069	165·8	122·6	2·1
1968	1,682	11,087	28·7	22·7	14·095	167·3	129·4	4·8
1969	1,681	11,514	29·6	23·2	16·261	164·1	139·6	9·4
1970	1,672	11,828	30·4	24·5	17·432	156·9	150·0	17·9
1971	1,674	12,384	30·1	24·3	18·664	139·3	151·2	28·8
1972	1,701	13,044	29·1	21·0	22·169	122·4	162·2	40·9
1973	1,736[a]	13,521[a]	29·8	22·7	26·187	133·0	164·2	44·2
1974	1,817	13,977	30·9	21·6	25·397	117·9	152·5	52·9
1975	1,829	14,095	30·3	20·8	27·544	120·0	136·5	55·4
1976	1,813	14,401	28·4	20·4	31·078	122·0	134·2	58·8
1977	...	...	29·2	20·1	31·871	122·7	136·6	62·8
1978	1,766	14,518	30·7	19·9	40·442	119·9	139·3	65·1
1979	1,846	15,039	32·0	19·9	47·085	129·6	139·0	71·1
1980	1,827	15,560	31·7	17·6	50·164	120·8	121·4	71·1
1981	1,797	15,757	30·7	17·5	52·210	118·2	110·9	72·1
1982	1,762 / 583	16,210 / 17,204	27·4	15·9	46·404	110·7	111·1	71·7
1983	594	17,570	30·1	17·1	43·887	111·5	106·1	74·8

a See notes on p. 40.

Sources

(For sources used in specific tables, see Notes.)

1 *Annual Abstract of Statistics.* Central Statistical Office, London.

2 *Annual Statement of Trade* (now *Overseas Trade Statistics*). Department of Trade and Industry, London.

3 *Bankers' Almanac.* West Sussex, annual.

4 *Bank of England Quarterly Bulletin.* June 1970.

5 Bank of Japan, *100 Year Statistics of the Japanese Economy.* Tokyo, 1966.

6 Bowley, A L, *Wages and Income in the UK since 1860.* Cambridge University Press, 1937.

7 *British Business.* Department of Trade and Industry, London, 15 April 1983.

8 *The British Economy, Key Statistics 1900–1970.* London and Cambridge Economic Service, 1972.

9 *British Labour Statistics Historical Abstract 1886–1968.* Department of Employment, HMSO, London 1971.

10 *British Labour Statistics Year Book.* Department of Employment, London, 1972–76.

11 *Economic Trends Annual Supplement.* Central Statistical Office, London, 1984.

12 *Economic Trends.* Central Statistical Office, London, September 1983.

13 *Economic Trends.* Central Statistical Office, London, September 1984.

14 *Employment Gazette.* Department of Employment, London, monthly.

15 *Feinstein, C H, National Income, Expenditure and Output of the United Kingdom 1855–1965.* Cambridge University Press, 1972.

16 *Financial Statistics.* Central Statistical Office, London, monthly.

17 *Financial Statistics Explanatory Handbook.* Central Statistical Office, London, 1984.

18 Ghandi, J K S, PhD thesis, Cambridge University. Unpublished.

19 *International Financial Statistics Year Book.* United Nations, New York, 1978.

20 Johnson, H G, 'British Monetary Statistics'. *Economica.* New series. Vol XXVI, No. 101, London School of Economics, 1959.

21 Kendall, M G, (ed.), *Sources and Nature of the Statistics of the United Kingdom,* Vol. II. Royal Statistical Society, London, 1957.

22 Macmillan Report on *Finance and Industry.* (Cmd 3897), HMSO, London, 1930/31.

23 *Monthly Digest of Statistics.* Central Statistical Office, London.

24 *Monthly Digest of Statistics Supplement. Definitions and Explanatory Notes.* Central Statistical Office, London, 1984.

25 *National Accounts Statistics, Sources and Methods.* Central Statistical Office, HMSO, London, 1968.

26 *National Income and Expenditure.* Central Statistical Office, London, 1983 and earlier years.

27 *Overseas Trade Statistics Annual Supplement.* Department of Trade and Industry, London, 1984.

28 Prest, A R, *Consumers' Expenditure in the United Kingdom 1900–1919.* Cambridge University Press, 1954.

29 *Registrar General's Statistical Review of England and Wales,* Part II, *Population.* Annual.

30 *Reserves and Liabilities.* (Cmd 8354), HMSO, London, 1951.

31 Shinjo, H, *History of the Yen: 100 Years of Japanese Money Economy.* Kobe Institute, 1962.

32 Society of Motor Manufacturers and Traders, *The Motor Industry of Great Britain.* SMMT, London, 1926, 1947.

33 *Standard Industrial Classification Revised 1980.* HMSO, London, 1979.

34 Stone, Richard and Rowe, D A, *The Measurement of Consumers' Expenditure and Behaviour in the United Kingdom 1920–1938,* Vols I and II. Cambridge University Press, 1953 and 1966.

35 *Trade and Industry.* Department of Trade and Industry, London, February 1978.

36 *Transport Statistics, Great Britain 1971–1981.* Department of Transport, London, 1983.

37 *United Kingdom Balance of Payments* (the CSO 'Pink Book'). Central Statistical Office, London, 1984.

38 *United Kingdom National Accounts* (the CSO 'Blue Book'; formerly *National Income and Expenditure*). Central Statistical Office, London, 1984.

39 *United Nations Statistical Year Book.* New York, 1965.

NOTES

Table UK.1

Sources: **15, 38**

The official Central Statistical Office (CSO) estimates have been used from 1948. For 1900–47 estimates given in **15** have been linked to the official estimates and roughly converted to 1980 prices. Each category of expenditure has been re-referenced to 1980 independently, however, and this means that the total for gross domestic product may not equal the sum of the component categories. This applies for 1900–77. For further details see **38**.

There was a change in coverage of gross domestic fixed capital formation in 1948 and a consequent change in consumers' expenditure. For details see notes to Table UK.4 and **38**.

The value of physical increase in stocks between 1900 and 1920 and between 1939 and 1945 are orders of magnitude and are not based on direct measurement. For further details see **15**, Chapter 9.3.

Southern Ireland is included in the estimates up to 1920; two figures are given for that year, the first line including and the second excluding Southern Ireland.

This table measures the national output from the expenditure side. For details of coverage of individual column headings and methodology, see **25, 26** and **38**.

Table UK.2

Sources: **15, 26, 38**

The CSO estimates have been used from 1948. For 1900–47 estimates from **15** have been linked to the official series.

From 1978, the indices have been weighted on the basis of net output in 1980. For earlier years (1948–77) successive weights based on 1948, 1954, 1958, 1963 and 1970 have been used. See **26**, 1983. The current series are classified on the basis of the Standard Industrial Classification (SIC), Revised 1980, described in **33**. The main difference between the previous classification (1968) and the 1980 classification is that some industries formerly classified under 'Mining and quarrying' and under 'Manufacturing' are now grouped into one category under the title 'Energy and water supply'. For further details see **26**, 1983.

For the period 1913–47 the data are based on 1948 classification and weights. For the period 1900–13 the classification is broadly comparable with later years. For further details see **15**, Chapter 10. Two figures are given for 1920, the first line including and the second excluding Southern Ireland.

For details of coverage of individual column headings and methodology, see **25, 26** and **38** and Studies in Official Statistics No. 25, *The Measurement of Changes in Production*, HMSO, London, 1976.

Table UK.3

Sources: **1, 8, 11, 13, 32**

For all series, annual figures from 1946 relate to 52 week periods.

Coal: production of deep mined and open cast coal. Includes coal consumed by the colliery and supplied to ancillary works, free coal and concessionary coal; excludes screening and washing losses. Up to 1937, includes coal produced at quarries other than open cast workings; in 1938 this output amounted to 23,352 tons.

Crude steel: steel ingots and steel for castings. From January 1974, the European Community definition of usable steel has been used; the difference in definition is minor.

Cars and commercial vehicles: chassis delivered as such are included; armoured fighting vehicles, battery driven electric vehicles and three wheeled vehicles are excluded. Up to 1939, estimates by the Society of Motor Manufacturers and Traders, **32**. For 1927–34 the figures are for years ended 30 September.

Chemicals and allied industries: index for the output of chemical and allied industries (SIC division 2, group 25) in the index of production and construction industries. The index was rebased in 1983; for details of minor changes made to the classification see **33**.

Cotton cloth: cloth made for sale including industrial use; represents the cloth in the loom state before undergoing finishing processes. Up to 1937, estimates from Census of Production data.

Manmade fibres and mixtures: cloth made wholly from continuous filament and spun rayon, nylon and other manmade fibres and mixture cloth. Up to 1937, estimates from Census of Production data.

Woollen and worsted woven fabrics: total deliveries of all fabrics woven in the wool textile industry except blankets. Includes mixtures and manmade fibres classified as wool or worsted. Up to 1937, estimated from Census of Production data, and figures are for production not deliveries.

Electricity generated: total generated for public supply excluding railway and transport authorities. Up to 1948, covers authorised undertakings excluding railway and transport undertakings. Northern Ireland and Scotland partly estimated by London and Cambridge Economic Service – see **8**.

Table UK.4

Sources: **15, 26, 38** and unpublished figures from the CSO.

From 1965, industries are classified as far as possible according to the SIC Revised 1980. For the years before 1978, totals differ from the sum of their components for the same reasons, as explained in notes to Table UK.1.

Agriculture, forestry and fishing: from 1965, changes in the value of breeding livestock are included in capital formation figures.

Distribution and business services: Expenditure on assets for leasing other than ships is included in this category. An analysis by user industry in current prices is given from 1975 in **26**, 1983 and **38**; see tabular summary.

Percentage of total capital expenditure on assets for leasing by user industry

	Agriculture, forestry & fishing	Mfg	Energy & construction	Transport	Other industries & services	Gen. govt
1975	2·8	54·3	4·3	14·3	11·4	12·9
1979	3·7	34·0	11·7	21·3	24·5	4·8
1983	6·6	37·8	5·5	10·2	32·9	7·0

Other services: Classes 91–99 of the SIC, Revised 1980, covering public administration and defence, education, health and other public services. Previously classified as 'Social and public services' but some changes in coverage have been made in recent years; some expenditure previously included in current expenditure is now treated as capital expenditure. For further details see **38**.

Dwellings: from 1948, all expenditure on improvements, including central heating, is included; this was previously included in 'Consumers' expenditure'.

Other new buildings and works: includes the transfer costs of land and buildings and purchases less sales of land and existing buildings. Expenditure on new buildings and works for civil accommodation overseas is now included, together with expenditure on minor road improvements (both previously treated as 'Current expenditure').

Vehicles: includes railway rolling stock, buses and coaches, motor vehicles and aircraft.

Plant and machinery: includes changes in the value of breeding livestock.

For further details of each category see **38**.

Up to 1965, industry and asset data are based on Feinstein, **15**. There have been some revisions to the total for gross fixed capital formation since Feinstein's estimates were published, but revisions have not been made to the industry and asset data by the CSO before 1965. The differences in the totals are relatively minor. Feinstein's estimates by type of asset have been roughly adjusted to the revised totals but the industry estimates are unadjusted.

Highways and street lighting have been deducted from Feinstein's estimates of total expenditure on 'Transport and communication' and added to 'Other services' to accord with current definitions.

Table UK.5

Sources: **11, 15, 26, 38**

Wages and salaries: include pay in cash and kind of H M Forces. From 1900–20 (first line) Southern Ireland is included.

Other income: includes income from self employment (before providing for depreciation and stock appreciation), rent, dividends and net interest including imputed rent of owner occupied dwellings; employers' contributions to national insurance and other pension funds, current transfers to charities from companies, national insurance benefits and other current grants from general government.

Taxes, etc.: includes taxes on income, national insurance contributions from individuals and net transfers abroad.

Personal disposable income: before providing for depreciation and stock appreciation.

Savings ratio: savings as a percentage of personal disposable income.

Gross trading profits of companies: before providing for depreciation and stock appreciation. Estimates of gross trading profits from 1969 onwards have been made by using Inland Revenue corporation tax data. For further details see **26**, 1983 p. 104.

Gross trading surpluses of public corporations and government enterprises: for details of public corporations currently included see **38**, p. 120.

For the period 1900–45 see estimates from **15**.

Table UK.6

Sources: **15, 26, 38**

The classification of consumers' expenditure was changed in 1983, and most of the data have been revised by the CSO back to 1948. The figures given in this table are classified by type of commodity and include expenditure of resident and non-resident households and individuals in the UK. 'Other services' includes adjustment for international travel and for final expenditure by private non-profit-making bodies. For further details of commodity classification and treatment of private non-profit-making bodies see **38**, p. 117, and **12**.

For the period 1900–47, estimates from **15** have been linked to the official estimates and roughly converted to 1980 prices. The conversion to 1980 prices reflects, of course, current tax rates which probably have risen more on some commodities than on others (e g alcoholic drink and tobacco). Some differences in coverage in Feinstein's estimates should be noted.

(a) For 1900–47, 'Rent, rates and water charges' include occupiers' costs of maintenance, repairs and improvements.
(b) For 1900–19, household textiles and hardware are included in the figures for 'Durable goods' and not in 'Other goods'.

For full details see **15**.

For 1948–51, expenditure on foods includes catering expenditure; from 1952; it is included in 'Other services'.

From 1900 to the first-line figures for 1920, Southern Ireland is included.

Table UK.7

Sources: **7, 8, 11, 27**

Producer prices: the name of this index was changed from the former 'Wholesale price index' in 1983 and the series revised back to 1974. At the same time, it was rebased on 1980 and reclassified in accordance with the SIC 1980 Revised. The reclassification affected the two indices given in this table: mineral oil refining is no longer included with 'Materials and fuels purchased by manufacturing industry', and petroleum products (rather than crude oil) are now a component of the input index (i e, first column in table). The indices are based on average prices for the year excluding VAT. The weights given to each commodity are revised from time to time to take account of the changing pattern of industry's sales and purchases. For further details see **7**.

For 1948–54 the index had a less comprehensive coverage; in particular, the first column excludes purchases by the food and drink industries in this period.

For the period 1900–48, the Board of Trade index for all articles was used. The index covers goods at all stages of processing, but raw materials predominate.

Consumer prices: the 'All items' index measures changes in the average level of prices of commodities and services purchased by the majority of households in the UK. From February 1975, the weights used to combine the items in the index have been revised each year on the basis of the Family Expenditure Survey for the year ended the previous June. Weights for previous periods are as follows.

1963–74	Weights were derived from the Family Expenditure Survey for three years ended the previous June adjusted to correspond with levels of prices ruling in January of the current year.
1962–63	Weights were derived from the Family Expenditure Survey for the three years July 1958–June 1961, adjusted to correspond with the level of prices ruling in January 1962.
1956–62 (Jan.)	Weights were based on expenditure in 1953/54 adjusted to correspond with the level of prices in January 1962.

Coverage of the index in the period 1900–52 was less comprehensive than for the current index. For further details see **8**.

Food: the current index is compiled in the same way as the 'All items' index and has been linked to the series in **8**. For the period 1900–14 the index is weighted on the basis of London urban working class family budgets in 1904 and covers London prices only.

Durable goods; Clothing and footwear; Housing: consumers' average value indices and not the retail price index. These are obtained by dividing the estimates of expenditure on these commodity groups for the year in question at current prices by a corresponding total revalued at 1980 prices. The coverage of the indices is therefore affected by the coverage of the expenditure series; see notes to Table UK.6.

Exports and Imports average value indices: the ratio of trade at current values in the year in question to the trade of that year, revalued at 1980 prices. The revaluation is based on the published indices of trade volume.

Terms of trade: the export average value index as a percentage of the import average value index.

Table UK.8

Sources: **1, 15, 28, 29, 34, 38**

Total home population: persons usually resident in the UK including those temporarily absent; overseas visitors and those temporarily present excluded. The figures are on this basis from 1973; previously, overseas visitors were included and absent residents excluded.

Figures for 1900–47 from **15**.

Up to 1919 Southern Ireland is included. The 1920 figure for total population including Southern Ireland is 46·82 m; see **15**.

The figures for 1915–20 and 1940–50 include members of the armed forces serving overseas and merchant seamen and exclude foreign forces in the UK.

Births: for England and Wales, number of births occurring in year; for Scotland and Northern Ireland, births registered in year. Up to 1938, the figures are for births occurring in Scotland and Northern Ireland and for births registered in England and Wales. Includes Southern Ireland up to 1919; the 1920 figure for births including Southern Ireland is 1,194,000.

Age distribution: the figures for 1973–80 have not been adjusted to the current definition of the home population; they will not therefore add to the total.

Geographical distribution: the figures for 1973–80 have not been adjusted to the current definition of the population; they will not therefore add to the total. The figures from 1971 to 1980 have been adjusted to the 1971 Census results. The South East region currently includes the following:

> Bedfordshire, Berkshire, Buckinghamshire, Poole, Essex, Greater London, Hampshire, Hertfordshire, Kent, Oxfordshire, Surrey, East and West Sussex, Isle of Wight.

For 1950–64, London and the South Eastern region were combined with the South to give a close approximation to the current South East. London and the South East included:

> part of Essex, part of Hertfordshire, Kent, London, administrative county of Middlesex, Surrey, East and West Sussex.

and the South included:

> Berkshire, Buckinghamshire, Dorset, Oxfordshire, Isle of Wight, Southampton (renamed Hampshire in 1959).

Significant boundary changes also took place in 1931. For further details see **29** for that year. Figures for 1940–47 are for civilians only for the South East.

Table UK.9

Sources: **1, 9, 10, 14, 15**

Employed labour force: includes employees in employment, self employed and H M Forces. For 1948–59 (first line), based on counts of national insurance cards; current figures based on Census of Employment data.

Employment by sector: from 1948 (second line), figures are for employees in employment. Industries are classified according to the SIC 1968 from 1959 (second line), because, at the time of printing, estimates for the UK on the SIC 1980 classification had not been published. Only the figures for 1982 (second line) and 1983 are given on the SIC 1980 classification. The figure for gas, electricity and water includes mining and quarrying. For 1948–59 (first line), the figures are classified according to the SIC 1948. The series from 1959 are on a consistent basis; for details see **14**, March 1975. There have been some revisions to the figures in this table as a result of the 1983 labour force survey, but again the revisions have been published for Great Britain only at the time of printing and are not therefore included in this table. See **14**, July 1984, for further details.

'Employees in employment series' have been used for this table, although in some ways it would be more useful to know the total numbers employed in each industry (i e including the self employed). An industrial analysis of the self employed is published from time to time in **14**, but the 'Employees in employment series' is published annually in **1** and can be more easily kept up to date. Figures are at mid year; end May 1949–1959 (first line); end June 1948 and from 1959.

For 1920–48 the figures do include employers and self-employed as estimated in **15** and are based on the SIC 1948. For the period 1921–38, the temporarily stopped are excluded from the estimates. Two figures are given for the employed labour force in 1920: the first line includes and the second excludes Southern Ireland. Industrial analysis figures for 1901 and 1911 are based on Census data and cover the working population, ie including the unemployed. They also include Southern Ireland.

For further details of coverage and method of estimation for the period 1900–48 see **15**, Chapter 11.

Self employed: the figures for the self employed have been adjusted in the light of the 1971 and 1981 Censuses of Population from 1971; earlier figures have not been adjusted. An industrial analysis of the self employed in Great Britain only is given in **14**, July 1984 (classified according to the SIC 1980); for a summary, see the table.

	Mfg	Services	Agriculture
1971	129	1,200	282
1973	133	1,138	259
1975	140	1,183	247
1977	142	1,155	254
1979	140	1,102	257
1981	146	1,273	250
1983	154	1,386	246

Table UK.10

Sources: **1, 8, 9, 10, 11, 13, 14, 15, 24**

Output per person employed; whole economy: an index of gross domestic product at factor cost (Table UK.2) divided by the employed labour force (Table UK.9).

Output per person employed; manufacturing: an index of output in manufacturing (Table UK.2) divided by the numbers employed in manufacturing.

Average weekly hours worked: from 1980, the figures are for full time manual workers on adult rates in manufacturing and certain other industries (mining and quarrying, building, transport, public utilities, governmental industrial establishments, laundries and dry cleaning, and railways). Before 1980, railways were excluded and the series was for adult male (over 18 years) full time manual workers. The figure for 1979 on the new basis is 43·9. The series is the average of actual hours worked including overtime in October each year. For 1940–45 figures are for July. Figures are based on the SIC 1958 for 1959–69 and on the SIC 1968 from second figure in 1969.

Figures for 1900, 1910, 1924 and 1938 (first line) are based on an index of average weekly hours worked per operative in Great Britain. In 1938, the index is based on one week in October; in 1924, on the first month in each quarter. Figures for 1924 and 1938 include adult males in building, manufacturing, public utilities and transport (excluding railways). Figures for 1900 and 1910 are for manufacturing only.

Average weekly earnings: the current series covers average earnings including bonus and overtime payments before any deductions in one week in October. Industry coverage is the same as for hours worked. Before 1980, the series was for adult males; the comparable figure for 1979 for the current series is £95.69.

Figures up to 1937 are based on **6** and are taken from **8**. They include adult males in manufacturing, coal mining, agriculture, building, transport and public utilities.

Unemployment: the current series is based on records of claimants at unemployment benefit offices. It therefore excludes unemployed people not claiming benefit but includes the severely disabled unemployed not previously included. The figures have been revised back to 1971 on the new basis. From 1983 the figures take account of the fact that some men over 60 do not now have to register at the unemployment offices.

For earlier years, the figures refer to registered unemployed at local unemployment offices or careers offices on one day in each month, capable of and available for work. (The severely disabled and adult students registered for vacation employment were excluded.)

The figures are annual averages and include school leavers.

The percentage figure is the number of unemployed expressed as a percentage of the estimated total number of employees in employment plus the unemployed.

Figures up to 1947 from **15**. For full details of method of calculation and coverage see **15**, Chapter 11.

Vacancies unfilled: annual averages. Up to 1953 (first line), vacancies notified to unemployment offices and careers offices; from 1953 (second line), vacancies notified to unemployment offices only. It is estimated that these vacancies represent about one third of the total unfilled vacancies.

Industrial stoppages: working days lost and workers involved through stoppages in progress during the year.

Table UK.11

Sources: **2, 8, 27**

In 1978 the Standard Industrial Trade Classification was revised and figures are now classified according to SITC (R2). Official figures for most of the series shown were revised back to 1963 and the earlier figures have been adjusted as far as possible to conform with the revised classification. For details of the revisions see **35**.

Imports include goods subsequently exported and are valued c i f. Up to 1947 they include silver bullion and specie. Munitions are excluded in the period 1940–45. Southern Ireland is included as part of the UK up to 1923.

Table UK.12

Sources: **2, 8, 27**

Exports are valued f o b and include re-exports. Figures are classified in accordance with SITC (R2) (see above). Official statistics have been adjusted for most of the columns in the table back to 1963, and figures for earlier years have been adjusted as far as possible to conform with the revised classification.

The Channel Islands have been treated as part of the UK throughout. Southern Ireland is treated as part of the UK up to 1923.

Up to 1947, silver bullion and specie are included; munitions are excluded in the period 1940–45.

'Non-manufactures' include food, beverages and tobacco, crude materials, animal and vegetable oils and fats.

Table UK.13

Sources: **2, 8, 27**

Imports are classified according to country of consignment, which is not necessarily the country of shipment, origin or manufacture. Exports are classified according to country of destination. Trade with Southern Ireland is treated as part of the UK up to 1923.

European Community: comprises France, Belgium, Luxembourg, Netherlands, Germany, Italy, Irish Republic, Denmark and Greece.

Rest of Western Europe: comprises Iceland, Faroe Islands, Norway, Sweden, Finland, Switzerland, Austria, Portugal, Spain, Andorra, Gibraltar, Vatican City, Malta, Yugoslavia and Turkey.

North America: comprises Canada, USA, Greenland, Puerto Rico, St Pierre and Menelon.

Figures for all years have been adjusted as far as possible to accord with these areas. (The Faroe Islands, Iceland, Puerto Rico, etc., were not always separately distinguished in the early Annual Statements of Trade, but trade with these areas is relatively small and should not affect the figures in the table.)

Table UK.14

Sources: **15, 37**

Imports are adjusted to a f o b basis and adjustments are made to both imports and exports for coverage.

Services: includes receipts and payments for sea transport and civil aviation, financial services including insurance, banking and commodity trading, together with government payments and receipts for services and transfers.

Interest, profits and dividends: includes earnings on direct investment and on portfolio investment. For treatment of oil companies' earnings see **37**, p. 29.

Current balance: net surplus (+) or deficit (−) on both visible and invisible trade together with transfers. (Transfers are not shown separately in this table.)

Up to 1920 (first line), Southern Ireland is included in 'Imports', 'Exports' and 'Current balance'.

For the period 1900–45 estimates published in **15** have been used for all the above series.

Official reserves: comprises gold and convertible currencies and IMF drawing rights. Gold was converted into SDRs at the official price of 35 SDRs per fine ounce until end 1977; from 1977, it has been valued at the market price at the end of the year. Other currencies are converted into sterling at their end year middle market rates. For further details see **37**.

Changes in the gold valuation also took place in 1932, 1945 and 1949. For details see **8**.

From 1900 to 1945 figures from **8** and **30**. Bank of England holding included up to 1938.

Table UK.15

Sources: 3, 5, 8, 11, 13, 16, 18, 19, 20, 22, 31, 39

Industrial ordinary share prices index: from 1962, the index is the FT–Actuaries index, which is a weighted arithmetic average of the percentage price changes of the constituent shares since April 1962. The FT–Actuaries index covers 500 industrial shares excluding financial and property companies. For earlier years, the index has been linked to the series given in **8**.

Treasury bills: weighted averages of discount rates at the weekly allotments of 91 day bills. For the period 1900–27 the average is unweighted, and for the period 1900–13 the rate is for 6 month bills.

Gilt edged yields: short-dated: gross redemption yield on representative stock of about four years' life; average of working days. Up to 1934, the series was calculated by F W Paish from *Economist* data; average of mid month figures.

2½ per cent Consols: flat yield gross of income tax and without adjustment for accrued interest; average of working days. For the period up to 1934, the yield was on the average price for the year. In 1900 the rate of interest was 2¾ per cent but the yield has been calculated at 2½ per cent since conversion had already been announced.

Money stock: the definition used here is M1, which currently comprises notes and coins in circulation with the public plus sterling sight deposits held with UK banks by the private sector only. For further details see **17**.

From 1981, the figures have been calculated on the basis of the new monetary sector. Breaks in the series from 1963 show the effect of changes in contributors.

For the period 1952–63 (first line), the figures are end December figures estimates published in **4**. For 1930–51 estimates made by Johnson, **20**, have been used. Figures for 1919–30 (first line) are based on the Macmillan Report, **22**.

Total consumer credit outstanding: figures are for Great Britain only. The current series has been compiled from 1976. It covers credit extended by finance houses, other specialist consumer credit grantors, clothing retailers, household goods retailers, mixed retail businesses and general mail order houses. Charges for credit and amounts outstanding on running account credit agreements are included between 1976 and 1982 (first line). For further details see **17**. Before 1976, figures refer to hire purchase and other installment credit business. For the period 1947–55, unpublished estimates by Ghandhi, **18**, have been used.

Foreign exchange rates: the current figures are averages of daily mean Telegraphic Transfer rates in London. Figures for the French franc and the German mark for 1919–38 are averages of daily quotations from *The Times* or the *Financial Times* (May–December 1922) given in **8**. For the period 1900–13 rates were calculated from **3**, also given in **8**. The Italian lira figures were calculated from data in **19** for the period 1949–54 and from **3** for the period 1926–40. The figure for 1955 is from 22 August. The figures for 1939 and 1940 refer to a broken period. The Japanese yen rate for the period 1900–40 is an average of the highest and lowest during the year taken from **5**. For 1945–48 it is based on the military exchange rate in September 1945, March 1947 and July 1948 which are quoted in **31**.

Table UK.16

Sources: 1, 8, 11, 13, 23, 36

Motor vehicles licences current: The series for Great Britain was reclassified in October 1982. Some 970,000 vans and light goods vehicles previously licensed as 'Goods vehicles' were regrouped under a new heading 'Private and light goods vehicles'. Northern Ireland classification is unchanged. See **1**, 1985. Before 1982 goods vehicles include general haulage vehicles, agricultural vans and lorries and general haulage tractors. From 1978, figures are based on the count of the licensed vehicle stock at the Driver and Vehicle Licensing Centre on 31 December each year. Vehicles operating under the Crown Vehicles scheme and under Defence permits are excluded.

For 1974–78, the method used was changing and the figures for this period are not strictly comparable with either earlier or later periods. For 1945–74 the figures are based on a sample count taken during the third quarter. For the period 1939–45 the figures are for licences current on 31 August; for 1921–25 they are for the quarter with the greatest number of licences current; and up to 1920 they are licences current at 31 March.

No figures are available for 1977 for Great Britain or for 1973 for Northern Ireland; the figure for 1973 in the table is for Great Britain only.

Goods vehicles exclude tractors for general haulage up to 1934.

Railways: figures are for Great Britain only. From 1963, free hauled traffic on revenue earning and on departmental trains is excluded. From 1972, freight carried by coaching trains is excluded: the figure for 1972 including this freight is 23·4 m net ton km.

Airways: figures include scheduled services of British Airways and private companies on both domestic and international routes. Charter flights are included up to 1938.

Coal: consumption by primary and secondary fuel producers plus disposals to final users and net foreign trade and stock changes in solid fuels. For the period 1923–38 colliery stock changes only are taken into account, and up to 1922 the figures are not adjusted for stock changes.

Petroleum: refinery throughput of crude oil plus net imports and stock changes minus deliveries of non-energy products. For 1900–38, estimates by A L King given in **8**.

Natural gas: production of natural gas excluding amount flared or reinjected but including imports and colliery methane used at collieries or sold from collieries. Non-energy supplies are included.

UNITED STATES OF AMERICA

CONTENTS

***Table* US.1** Gross national product at constant prices, 1900–83

	Personal consumption expenditures	Govt purchases	Gross private domestic fixed investment	Change in business inventories	Exports of goods & services	Imports of goods & services	**Gross national product at market prices**
				$ bn, 1972 prices			
1900	74·4	12·5	23·8	2·0	2·8		**115·5**
1901	83·5	12·8	26·3	3·1	3·1		**128·8**
1902	84·2	13·3	29·6	1·7	1·2		**130·0**
1903	89·3	14·5	28·9	1·9	1·8		**136·4**
1904	90·4	14·5	27·3	0·9	1·8		**134·9**
1905	95·6	15·6	29·6	2·3	1·7		**144·8**
1906	106·2	15·9	33·8	3·5	2·1		**161·5**
1907	108·2	17·6	35·4	1·8	1·2		**164·2**
1908	101·4	19·8	29·9	− 1·1	0·6		**150·6**
1909	112·4	18·2	34·3	3·8	0·3		**169·0**
1910	114·5	18·9	35·0	2·4	0·1		**170·9**
1911	120·0	22·2	31·2	2·0	0·9		**176·3**
1912	123·2	22·2	35·3	3·2	0·9		**184·8**
1913	127·2	21·7	38·2	3·2	1·7		**192·0**
1914	125·7	23·4	27·5	0·1	0·5		**177·2**
1915	123·5	24·3	26·0	0·6	8·2		**182·6**
1916	134·6	22·9	31·8	4·6	14·5		**208·4**
1917	131·7	33·7	27·6	1·3	9·2		**203·5**
1918	131·1	79·8	21·6	1·5	− 12·0		**222·0**
1919	136·9	46·8	27·7	7·9	5·1		**224·4**
1920	143·6	26·9	29·7	11·9	9·6		**221·7**
1921	152·8	31·6	26·6	− 0·3	5·8		**216·5**
1922	158·4	30·7	36·5	0·7	2·9		**229·2**
1923	172·8	30·7	45·0	7·6	3·4		**259·5**
1924	185·6	33·4	46·9	− 2·7	4·1		**267·3**
1925	180·2	35·5	51·9	4·4	1·7		**273·7**
1926	194·9	35·6	55·9	3·2	1·9		**291·5**
1927	199·3	38·1	53·4	1·0	2·4		**294·2**
1928	203·8	39·6	52·4	− 1·2	3·3		**297·9**
1929	215·1	41·0	51·2	4·6	16·7	− 12·9	**315·7**
1930	199·5	44·8	39·0	− 0·5	14·2	− 11·4	**285·6**
1931	191·8	46·3	26·7	− 3·0	11·7	− 10·0	**263·5**
1932	173·9	44·3	15·0	− 7·2	9·3	− 8·3	**227·1**
1933	170·5	42·9	13·2	− 4·9	9·1	− 8·6	**222·1**
1934	176·9	48·4	16·4	− 3·3	9·7	− 8·9	**239·1**
1935	187·7	49·6	21·0	2·9	10·5	− 11·8	**260·0**
1936	206·2	57·9	28·4	3·8	11·2	− 11·9	**295·5**
1937	213·8	55·8	33·4	6·3	14·0	− 13·2	**310·2**
1938	208·8	60·7	26·6	− 2·6	13·5	− 10·3	**296·7**
1939	219·8	63·0	32·0	1·6	14·3	− 10·9	**319·8**
1940	229·9	65·3	38·3	6·2	15·5	− 11·1	**344·1**
1941	243·6	97·8	43·8	12·0	16·4	− 13·2	**400·4**
1942	241·1	191·6	24·3	5·2	11·4	− 12·0	**461·7**
1943	248·2	271·3	18·0	0·1	9·8	− 15·7	**531·6**
1944	255·2	300·4	22·0	− 2·3	10·5	− 16·8	**569·1**
1945	270·9	265·4	31·4	− 3·6	13·8	− 17·5	**560·4**
1946	301·0	93·1	58·7	12·2	27·3	− 14·0	**478·3**
1947	305·8	75·7	70·2	− 0·2	32·2	− 13·3	**470·3**
1948	312·2	84·7	76·6	5·5	26·3	− 15·5	**489·8**
1949	319·3	96·8	69·8	− 4·4	25·8	− 15·2	**492·2**
1950	337·3	98·1	83·0	10·6	23·6	− 17·7	**534·8**
1951	341·6	133·7	80·2	13·7	28·6	− 18·5	**579·4**
1952	350·1	159·8	78·7	4·3	27·9	− 20·0	**600·8**
1953	363·4	170·1	83·8	1·5	26·6	− 21·8	**623·6**
1954	370·0	156·0	85·3	− 2·2	27·8	− 20·9	**616·1**
1955	394·1	152·3	96·1	7·7	30·7	− 23·4	**657·5**
1956	405·4	153·5	96·8	5·8	35·3	− 25·2	**671·6**
1957	413·8	161·2	95·5	1·5	38·0	− 26·1	**683·8**
1958	418·0	169·8	89·3	− 1·8	33·2	− 27·6	**680·9**
1959	440·4	170·6	100·9	7·0	33·8	− 31·1	**721·7**
1960	452·0	172·8	101·2	3·5	38·4	− 30·7	**737·2**
1961	461·4	182·9	100·9	3·0	39·3	− 30·9	**756·6**
1962	482·0	193·2	109·7	7·8	41·8	− 34·3	**800·3**
1963	500·5	197·6	117·5	7·5	44·8	− 35·4	**832·5**
1964	528·0	202·6	125·9	7·1	50·3	− 37·5	**876·4**
1965	557·5	209·8	140·1	11·8	51·7	− 41·6	**929·3**
1966	585·7	229·7	146·2	16·8	54·4	− 47·9	**984·8**
1967	602·7	248·5	142·7	12·2	56·7	− 51·3	**1,011·4**
1968	634·4	260·2	152·6	9·0	61·2	− 59·3	**1,058·1**
1969	657·9	257·4	160·4	11·1	65·0	− 64·1	**1,087·6**
1970	672·1	251·1	154·8	3·8	70·5	− 66·6	**1,085·6**
1971	696·8	250·1	165·8	8·1	71·0	− 69·3	**1,122·4**
1972	737·1	253·1	184·8	10·2	77·5	− 76·7	**1,185·9**
1973	767·9	253·3	200·4	17·2	97·3	− 81·8	**1,254·3**
1974	762·8	260·3	183·9	11·6	108·5	− 80·7	**1,246·3**
1975	779·4	265·2	161·5	− 6·7	103·5	− 71·4	**1,231·6**
1976	823·1	265·2	176·7	7·8	110·1	− 84·7	**1,298·2**
1977	864·3	269·2	200·9	13·3	112·9	− 90·9	**1,369·7**
1978	903·2	274·6	220·7	16·0	126·7	− 102·7	**1,438·6**
1979	927·6	278·3	229·1	7·3	146·2	− 109·0	**1,479·4**
1980	931·8	284·3	212·9	− 4·4	159·1	− 108·8	**1,475·0**
1981	950·5	287·0	219·6	11·3	160·2	− 116·4	**1,512·2**
1982	963·3	292·7	204·7	− 10·4	147·6	− 118·0	**1,480·0**
1983	1,009·2	291·9	224·6	− 3·6	139·5	− 126·9	**1,534·7**

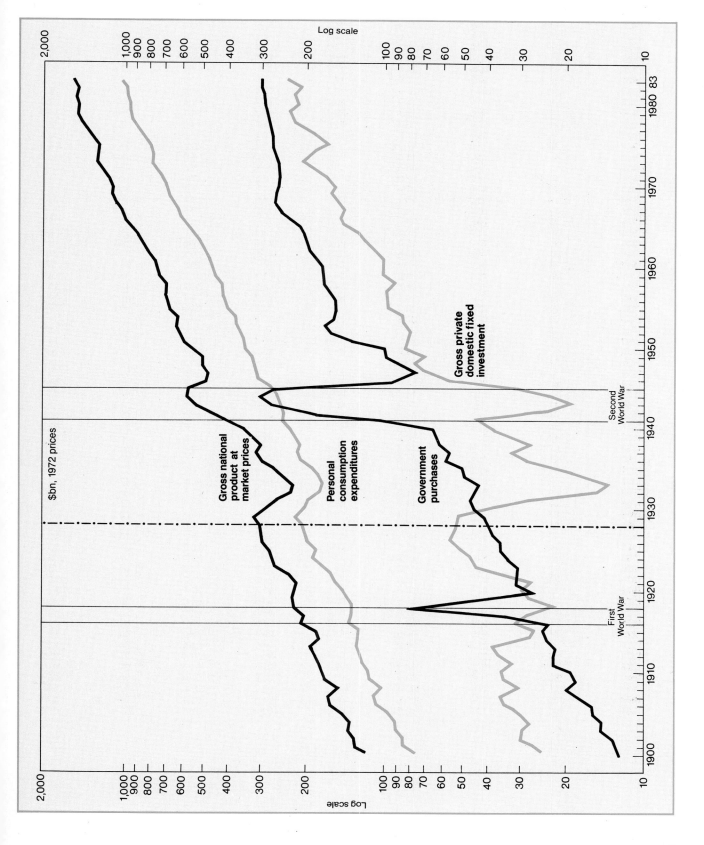

Chart US.1 Gross national product at constant prices, 1900–83

Log scale

$bn, 1972 prices

Gross national product at market prices

Personal consumption expenditures

Government purchases

Gross private domestic investment

First World War

Second World War

43

					Industrial production			
	Business	Farm	Govt	Gross domestic product	Total industrial output	Mfg	Mining	Public utilities
				Index nos., 1980 = 100				
1909	11·8	56·3	8·2	12·5	...	...	...	...
1910	12·1	57·7	8·7	12·8	...	...	...	...
1911	12·6	56·0	9·0	13·2	...	...	...	...
1912	13·1	62·9	9·3	13·9	...	...	...	...
1913	13·4	56·9	9·6	14·0	...	...	...	...
1914	12·6	62·6	10·1	13·5	...	...	...	...
1915	12·3	64·9	10·5	13·4	...	...	...	...
1916	13·5	61·7	10·8	14·4	...	...	...	...
1917	13·3	63·7	13·7	14·6	...	...	...	...
1918	14·4	62·3	26·9	16·9	...	...	...	...
1919	14·2	61·7	18·8	15·8	9·5	10·1	21·5	1·9
1920	13·6	61·7	14·1	14·8	10·0	10·4	25·0	2·1
1921	12·7	54·0	14·0	13·8	7·7	7·9	20·0	1·9
1922	14·9	60·0	13·7	15·8	9·8	10·4	21·4	2·1
1923	16·8	62·0	13·9	17·5	11·7	12·1	29·6	2·5
1924	16·9	60·6	14·5	17·7	11·0	11·4	27·0	2·6
1925	18·3	66·3	15·0	19·0	12·0	12·8	27·8	2·9
1926	19·5	63·4	15·4	20·1	12·8	13·4	30·2	3·4
1927	19·5	64·9	15·9	20·2	12·7	13·4	30·2	3·6
1928	19·8	62·9	16·3	20·4	13·3	14·1	29·9	4·0
1929	20·7	67·4	16·8	21·6	14·7	15·6	32·4	4·4
1930	18·7	65·1	17·7	19·5	12·2	12·8	28·1	4·5
1931	16·4	72·6	17·9	18·1	10·1	10·4	24·2	4·3
1932	13·6	71·7	17·5	15·6	8·0	8·0	20·2	4·0
1933	13·1	71·1	18·5	15·2	9·3	9·5	23·0	3·9
1934	14·5	59·7	21·0	16·4	10·2	10·4	24·1	4·2
1935	16·0	64·9	22·4	17·9	11·8	12·3	26·2	4·5
1936	18·2	60·0	26·1	20·3	13·9	14·7	30·1	5·1
1937	19·5	69·1	24·9	21·3	15·2	16·0	33·9	5·7
1938	18·0	70·9	26·7	20·4	10·2	12·3	29·3	5·7
1939	19·6	72·0	27·1	22·0	12·6	14·7	31·7	6·3
1940	21·5	70·0	28·3	23·6	17·0	17·3	35·2	6·9
1941	25·1	74·9	35·5	27·5	21·5	22·1	37·4	7·8
1942	28·0	81·7	52·6	31·8	24·7	25·8	38·6	8·8
1943	30·0	79·1	83·2	36·6	30·1	32·1	39·5	9·7
1944	30·6	77·4	95·8	39·2	32·2	34·7	42·3	10·3
1945	30·0	73·1	94·1	38·6	27·7	29·1	41·5	10·5
1946	29·7	73·7	48·8	32·9	23·8	24·1	40·8	10·9
1947	30·5	68·6	37·3	32·3	26·8	26·9	46·1	11·8
1948	32·3	73·7	37·3	33·6	28·0	27·9	48·5	13·2
1949	31·9	73·1	40·0	33·8	26·4	26·4	43·0	14·1
1950	34·8	77·1	41·6	36·7	30·5	30·7	48·0	16·0
1951	37·1	73·7	50·8	39·7	33·1	33·2	52·7	18·2
1952	38·4	75·4	55·0	41·2	34·4	34·5	52·2	19·8
1953	40·1	79·1	54·6	42·8	37·3	37·7	53·6	21·5
1954	39·5	81·1	54·1	42·2	35·3	35·1	52·6	23·1
1955	42·7	83·7	54·4	45·1	39·8	39·7	58·6	25·8
1956	44·0	82·6	55·7	46·0	41·6	41·3	61·7	28·4
1957	44·7	80·6	57·3	46·8	42·1	41·7	61·8	30·3
1958	44·2	83·7	58·0	46·7	39·4	38·9	56·7	31·7
1959	47·6	79·4	59·3	49·5	44·1	43·8	59·2	34·9
1960	48·6	83·4	61·2	50·5	45·0	44·6	60·4	37·3
1961	49·6	82·6	63·6	51·8	45·4	44·7	60·8	39·4
1962	52·5	82·3	65·9	54·8	49·1	48·8	62·5	42·4
1963	54·8	84·6	67·6	57·0	52·0	51·7	65·0	45·3
1964	58·1	82·3	69·9	59·9	55·6	55·3	67·6	49·2
1965	62·1	85·1	72·4	63·6	61·1	61·2	70·1	52·2
1966	65·7	80·6	77·6	67·4	66·5	66·8	73·9	56·2
1967	67·4	84·3	82·1	69·3	68·0	68·2	75·2	58·9
1968	70·9	82·9	85·1	72·4	72·3	72·6	78·4	63·8
1969	73·1	84·3	87·2	74·5	75·6	75·7	81·5	69·0
1970	72·5	88·9	87·5	74·4	73·3	72·6	84·4	73·3
1971	74·7	93·1	87·9	76·8	74·6	73·8	82·6	76·8
1972	79·7	91·1	88·6	81·1	81·4	81·1	85·1	82·1
1973	85·0	90·3	89·4	85·5	88·3	88·5	86·3	85·6
1974	83·8	90·9	91·5	84·9	88·0	88·3	86·8	84·6
1975	82·5	96·0	93·1	84·2	80·1	79·3	84·9	85·9
1976	87·5	91·7	94·0	88·5	88·8	88·9	85·9	89·3
1977	93·1	94·6	94·9	93·3	94·0	94·4	88·9	92·1
1978	98·4	93·1	97·2	97·9	99·4	100·1	93·3	95·0
1979	100·8	97·7	98·3	100·3	103·5	104·5	94·3	97·8
1980	100·0	100·0	100·0	100·0	100·0	100·0	100·0	100·0
1981	102·6	115·1	100·4	102·6	102·7	102·6	107·0	99·5
1982	100·3	111·1	100·6	100·5	94·3	93·9	94·9	99·3
1983	105·1	110·9	100·9	104·3	100·4	101·1	87·7	101·5

Table US.2 (Supplementary) Output by industry, index numbers, 1947–83

	Gross national product	Agriculture, forestry & fishing	Mining	Mfg	Construction	Transport & public utilities	Distributive trades	Services
	\multicolumn{8}{c}{Index nos., 1980 = 100}							
1947	31·9	65·9	50·0	32·7	43·9	30·3	30·9	26·0
1948	33·2	70·7	52·3	34·6	50·8	30·2	31·7	26·9
1949	33·4	70·2	45·8	32·8	50·8	28·1	32·5	27·6
1950	36·3	73·4	50·9	37·4	56·1	29·5	35·6	29·1
1951	39·3	71·2	56·0	41·6	62·3	32·6	35·9	30·0
1952	40·7	73·2	55·1	43·0	64·7	32·6	37·0	31·2
1953	42·3	76·4	56·5	45·9	66·7	33·4	38·2	32·2
1954	41·8	78·4	54·6	42·6	69·0	32·8	38·4	33·0
1955	44·6	80·5	61·1	47·2	73·2	35·6	41·9	35·2
1956	45·5	79·4	64·4	47·5	78·4	37·3	43·2	36·9
1957	46·4	77·9	63·9	47·8	78·4	38·1	43·9	38·6
1958	46·2	80·7	58·8	43·7	80·6	37·2	43·8	39·9
1959	48·9	76·7	61·6	48·8	87·2	39·7	46·9	42·2
1960	50·0	80·5	62·5	48·9	88·3	41·2	47·8	43·8
1961	51·3	79·7	63·0	49·0	89·5	42·0	48·3	45·7
1962	54·3	79·4	64·4	53·2	92·7	44·1	51·4	47·9
1963	56·4	81·5	67·1	57·6	95·6	46·6	53·3	49·6
1964	59·4	79·7	69·9	61·7	100·0	48·8	56·6	52·0
1965	63·0	82·2	72·7	67·4	104·2	52·6	60·3	54·5
1966	66·8	78·4	76·4	72·6	104·6	56·9	63·6	57·2
1967	68·6	81·7	78·7	72·5	102·3	58·5	65·1	59·9
1968	71·7	80·5	81·5	76·4	109·0	63·2	69·1	62·3
1969	73·7	81·9	84·3	79·0	106·9	66·3	70·6	65·2
1970	73·6	86·2	87·5	74·4	102·3	68·0	71·7	66·5
1971	76·1	90·0	85·2	76·0	110·9	70·0	75·4	68·5
1972	80·4	88·7	88·0	83·3	113·8	74·7	81·1	72·1
1973	85·1	88·5	88·9	92·7	115·1	79·2	85·8	75·8
1974	84·6	89·7	88·9	88·8	102·1	80·2	84·2	78·3
1975	83·6	93·0	87·5	82·5	92·5	81·3	85·3	79·2
1976	88·0	89·7	88·4	90·4	101·1	85·0	89·5	82·3
1977	92·9	92·5	90·3	96·6	105·4	89·6	93·9	87·5
1978	97·5	92·7	93·1	101·8	112·6	96·1	99·5	92·3
1979	100·3	97·5	96·3	104·6	111·5	100·3	101·9	97·1
1980	100·0	100·0	100·0	100·0	100·0	100·0	100·0	100·0
1981	102·5	113·5	104·2	102·5	96·0	102·3	102·8	103·9
1982	100·3	110·5	100·0	95·9	93·7	99·3	101·8	105·6
1983	104·0	98·0	97·2	100·9	96·2	102·1	108·5	108·4

	Coal	Raw steel	Passenger cars	Chemicals	Metals		
					Copper	Lead	Zinc
	mn tons		'000	Index nos., 1980 = 100	'000 tons		
1900	192·6	10·2	4	...	275·0	333·7	112·4
1901	204·8	13·4	7	...	273·1	336·6	127·7
1902	236·1	14·9	9	...	299·2	333·8	142·3
1903	256·5	14·4	11	...	316·6	334·7	144·4
1904	252·8	13·8	22	...	368·6	357·0	169·4
1905	285·9	19·9	24	...	403·2	352·3	184·9
1906	311·1	23·0	33	...	415·9	367·1	203·9
1907	358·1	23·0	43	...	384·3	330·9	229·5
1908	301·7	14·0	64	...	434·0	299·6	212·4
1909	344·5	23·8	124	...	511·0	349·4	274·3
1910	378·4	25·7	181	...	493·6	347·2	294·3
1911	368·2	23·5	199	...	505·7	387·0	300·7
1912	408·3	30·9	356	...	566·5	401·1	349·8
1913	434·0	30·9	462	...	560·5	438·3	375·4
1914	383·5	23·2	548	...	520·9	457·9	377·2
1915	401·5	29·2	896	...	674·9	491·8	533·5
1916	455·9	42·4	1,526	...	909·8	545·6	637·9
1917	500·6	45·2	1,746	...	859·7	570·2	647·4
1918	525·6	44·4	943	...	866·4	510·2	577·1
1919	422·6	34·6	1,652	...	549·9	389·7	497·9
1920	515·9	41·9	1,906	...	555·5	450·7	533·0
1921	377·3	20·9	1,468	...	211·5	375·6	232·8
1922	383·1	35·3	2,274	...	437·5	433·3	428·2
1923	512·2	44·4	3,625	...	670·3	496·4	554·0
1924	438·8	37·5	3,186	...	728·6	540·8	578·8
1925	471·8	45·1	3,735	...	761·2	620·9	644·8
1926	520·2	48·0	3,692	...	782·5	620·4	702·7
1927	469·7	44·7	2,937	...	748·4	603·7	651·8
1928	454·3	51·3	3,775	...	821·0	569·0	630·7
1929	485·3	56·0	4,455	...	905·0	587·9	657·3
1930	424·1	40·6	2,787	...	639·7	506·5	540·1
1931	346·6	25·8	1,948	...	479·8	367·0	372·2
1932	281·0	13·6	1,104	...	216·0	265·8	258·7
1933	302·7	23·3	1,561	...	172·9	247·4	348·6
1934	326·0	26·5	2,161	...	215·4	260·6	398·0
1935	337·8	34·6	3,274	...	350·6	300·4	469·8
1936	398·3	48·5	3,679	...	557·5	338·3	522·2
1937	404·2	51·3	3,929	...	763·9	421·8	568·3
1938	316·2	28·8	2,020	...	506·0	335·4	468·7
1939	358·2	47·9	2,889	...	660·7	375·6	529·6
1940	418·0	60·7	3,717	...	796·6	414·9	603·4
1941	466·4	75·1	3,780	...	869·2	418·6	679·6
1942	528·6	78·0	223	...	979·9	450·1	696·7
1943	535·4	80·5	—	...	989·6	411·2	675·1
1944	562·1	81·3	—	...	882·2	378·2	651·9
1945	524·0	72·3	70	...	701·2	354·5	557·4
1946	484·4	60·4	2,149	...	552·2	304·4	521·5
1947	572·1	77·0	3,558	9·5	768·9	348·5	578·4
1948	543·9	80·4	3,909	10·3	757·3	354·3	571·5
1949	397·2	70·7	5,119	10·1	682·9	371·9	538·1
1950	468·4	87·8	6,666	12·7	824·9	390·8	565·5
1951	484·1	95·4	5,338	14·3	842·1	352·2	618·0
1952	423·5	84·5	4,321	15·0	839·5	354·0	604·2
1953	414·8	101·2	6,117	16·2	840·4	310·8	496·6
1954	355·4	80·1	5,559	16·5	758·0	295·2	429·6
1955	421·5	106·1	7,920	19·2	905·9	306·6	466·9
1956	454·4	104·5	5,816	20·6	1,001·7	320·1	492·0
1957	447·0	102·2	6,113	21·8	986·0	306·8	482·4
1958	372·4	77·4	4,258	22·5	888·4	242·6	373·8
1959	373·8	84·7	5,591	26·2	748·3	231·9	385·8
1960	376·9	90·1	6,675	27·2	979·9	223·8	395·0
1961	365·6	88·9	5,543	28·6	1,057·1	237·6	421·3
1962	383·0	89·1	6,933	31·7	1,114·4	215·0	458·6
1963	416·3	99·1	7,638	34·7	1,100·6	229·9	480·2
1964	441·8	115·3	7,752	38·1	1,131·1	259·5	521·5
1965	464·6	119·3	9,306	42·4	1,226·2	273·2	554·5
1966	484·3	121·6	8,598	46·2	1,296·6	297·0	519·5
1967	501·3	115·4	7,437	48·3	865·5	287·5	498·4
1968	494·6	119·3	8,822	52·9	1,092·8	325·9	480·3
1969	508·5	128·2	8,224	57·2	1,401·2	461·8	501·8
1970	547·0	119·3	6,547	58·2	1,560·1	518·7	484·5
1971	500·8	109·2	8,585	60·8	1,380·7	525·3	456·3
1972	539·8	120·8	8,824	69·4	1,510·5	561·6	433·6
1973	537·1	136·8	9,658	74·6	1,558·6	547·0	434·5
1974	547·0	132·1	7,331	77·0	1,448·8	602·4	453·6
1975	587·9	105·8	6,713	71·1	1,281·9	563·4	425·5
1976	616·0	116·1	8,500	82·6	1,456·9	553·4	440·0
1977	626·9	113·6	9,201	89·7	1,364·4	537·1	408·2
1978	603·3	124·3	9,165	95·4	1,357·2	529·8	303·0
1979	704·0	123·6	8,419	101·6	1,443·3	525·3	267·6
1980	747·5	101·4	6,400	100·0	1,181·2	550·7	317·5
1981	742·4	109·6	6,255	104·2	1,538·2	445·4	312·4
1982	756·2	67·7	5,049	94·7	1,139·6	512·4	300·3
1983	708·3	75·6	6,739	103·9	1,038·1	449·0	273·7

Chart US.3 Industrial production, selected series, 1900–83

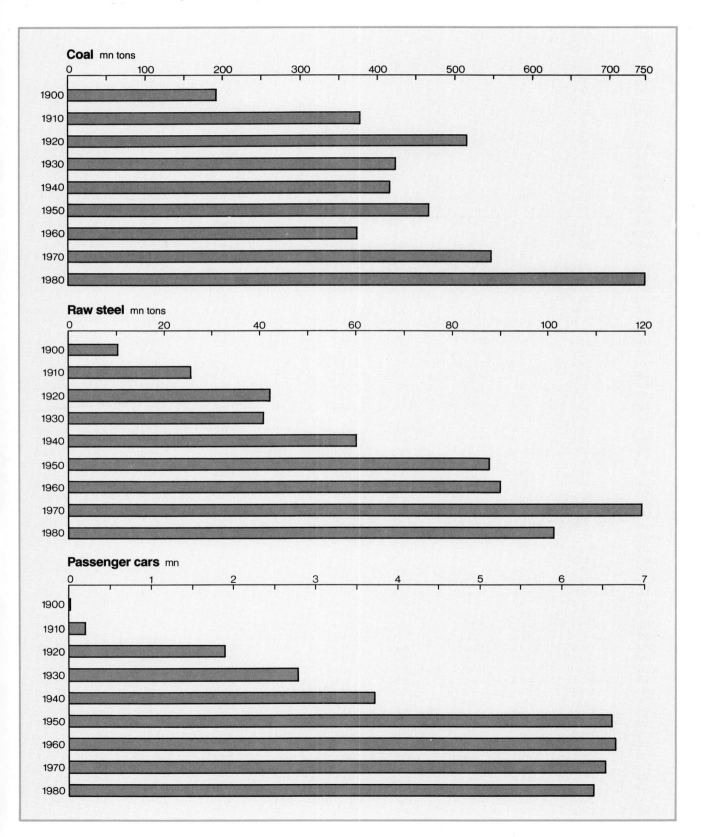

Table US.4 Gross domestic private investment by type of asset, 1900–83

	Total private investment	Type of asset				Investment in non-residential construction by sector				
		Non-residential construction	Plant & machinery	Transport equipment	Non-farm, residential construction	Industrial & commercial	Public utilities	Farm	Mining	Other
			\$ bn, 1972 prices							
1900	26·6	17·0	5·3		6·6	...	...	...	...	...
1901	28·6	18·4	6·0		6·5	...	...	...	...	...
1902	30·0	19·7	6·3		6·5	...	...	...	...	...
1903	31·4	19·3	6·7		7·8	...	...	...	...	...
1904	33·1	19·4	7·4		8·6	...	...	...	...	...
1905	34·5	19·5	8·0		9·1	...	...	...	...	...
1906	34·7	19·3	7·8		9·8	...	...	...	...	...
1907	36·2	20·0	8·1		10·5	...	...	...	...	...
1908	37·4	21·7	8·4		9·9	...	...	...	...	...
1909	36·7	21·8	8·1		9·4	...	...	...	...	...
1910	36·7	21·8	8·1		9·5	...	...	...	...	...
1911	38·6	23·0	8·8		9·5	...	...	...	...	...
1912	37·4	21·5	9·0		9·1	...	...	...	...	...
1913	35·5	19·2	8·8		9·4	...	...	...	...	...
1914	36·1	18·1	9·7		9·6	...	...	...	...	...
1915	35·4	16·4	10·7		8·8	...	...	...	...	...
1916	33·5	13·8	11·8		7·4	...	...	...	...	...
1917	34·4	13·5	13·0		6·8	...	...	...	...	...
1918	35·7	14·2	14·3		5·7	...	...	...	...	...
1919	34·4	13·8	13·8		5·4	...	...	...	...	...
1920	35·5	14·2	13·2		7·2	...	...	...	...	...
1921	39·2	15·4	13·1		10·2	...	...	...	...	...
1922	42·6	16·5	13·1		13·0	...	...	...	...	...
1923	47·2	17·7	13·5		16·6	...	...	...	...	...
1924	53·6	20·0	15·1		19·3	...	...	...	...	...
1925	57·4	21·7	16·2		20·5	...	...	...	...	...
1926	59·1	22·8	16·5		20·9	...	...	...	...	...
1927	60·4	23·9	17·6		19·6	...	...	...	...	...
1928	57·7	23·6	17·7		16·7	...	...	...	...	...
1929	51·2	21·1	9·4	7·1	13·6	9·2	6·2	0·6	1·3	3·8
1930	39·1	17·8	7·5	5·6	8·1	6·6	6·3	0·3	1·0	3·6
1931	26·7	11·2	5·2	3·4	6·8	3·5	4·2	0·2	0·6	2·7
1932	15·0	6·5	3·1	1·9	3·5	1·8	2·3	0·1	0·7	1·6
1933	13·2	5·0	2·9	2·7	2·7	2·0	1·3	0·1	0·6	1·0
1934	16·4	5·4	3·9	3·3	3·8	2·1	1·5	0·1	0·8	0·9
1935	21·0	6·0	5·5	4·2	5·4	2·1	1·7	0·3	1·0	0·9
1936	28·4	8·1	7·6	5·8	6·9	3·0	2·3	0·4	1·2	1·2
1937	33·4	10·5	8·8	6·6	7·5	4·2	2·9	0·5	1·5	1·4
1938	26·6	8·3	6·6	4·1	7·6	2·5	2·5	0·4	1·3	1·6
1939	32·0	8·7	7·1	5·1	11·0	2·6	2·9	0·5	1·3	1·4
1940	38·3	10·0	9·2	6·7	12·4	3·7	3·2	0·4	1·4	1·3
1941	43·8	12·0	10·9	7·8	13·1	5·1	3·4	0·5	1·5	1·5
1942	24·3	6·8	8·0	3·0	6·6	1·8	2·8	0·4	1·0	0·8
1943	18·0	4·2	7·0	2·8	4·0	0·6	1·9	0·5	0·9	0·3
1944	22·0	5·5	10·2	3·0	3·4	0·9	2·4	0·5	1·2	0·5
1945	31·4	8·3	14·4	4·9	3·7	2·8	2·7	0·5	1·4	0·9
1946	58·7	18·9	15·6	7·8	16·4	7·9	3·7	1·8	1·6	3·9
1947	70·2	17·4	21·1	10·7	21·0	6·0	5·3	1·7	1·8	2·6
1948	76·6	18·4	22·1	10·8	25·3	5·6	6·2	1·6	2·2	2·8
1949	69·8	17·9	17·6	10·8	23·5	4·5	6·5	1·5	2·2	3·2
1950	83·0	19·2	19·7	11·4	32·7	5·2	6·3	1·6	2·6	3·5
1951	80·2	20·7	21·2	11·3	27·0	6·7	6·3	1·5	2·7	3·5
1952	78·7	20·6	22·0	9·8	26·3	6·3	6·6	1·6	3·0	3·1
1953	83·8	22·6	23·0	11·0	27·2	7·2	7·1	1·4	3·3	3·6
1954	85·3	23·6	22·5	9·6	29·6	7·8	6·5	1·3	3·7	4·3
1955	96·1	25·4	24·2	12·1	34·4	9·6	6·1	1·3	3·9	4·5
1956	96·8	28·3	26·2	11·2	31·1	11·8	7·3	1·3	3·8	4·1
1957	95·5	28·4	26·3	11·9	28·8	11·4	7·5	1·2	3·6	4·7
1958	89·3	26·8	23·9	9·1	29·5	9·8	7·0	1·2	3·4	5·4
1959	100·9	27·4	25·0	11·8	36·8	10·1	6·5	1·6	3·5	5·7
1960	101·2	29·5	25·6	12·3	33·7	11·7	6·7	1·4	3·3	6·4
1961	100·9	30·2	25·2	11·8	33·8	12·4	6·2	1·5	3·3	6·8
1962	109·7	31·6	26·8	14·2	37·1	13·2	6·3	1·6	3·5	7·0
1963	117·5	31·9	29·5	14·2	41·9	12·9	6·8	1·6	3·3	7·3
1964	125·9	34·4	32·8	16·2	42·4	14·4	7·3	1·5	3·5	7·7
1965	140·1	40·6	37·7	19·8	42·0	18·9	8·2	1·6	3·5	8·4
1966	146·2	43·4	43·3	22·0	37·4	20·5	9·2	1·7	3·3	8·7
1967	142·7	42·0	43·3	21·1	36·3	18·8	9·9	1·9	3·1	8·3
1968	152·6	42·8	42·9	24·8	42·2	18·7	11·2	1·7	3·2	8·0
1969	160·4	45·0	46·7	26·2	42·5	20·1	11·3	1·8	3·3	8·5
1970	154·8	43·9	48·3	22·7	39·9	18·5	12·0	2·0	3·1	8·3
1971	165·8	42·8	45·7	24·9	52·4	18·0	11·9	2·0	2·9	8·0
1972	184·8	44·1	49·7	28·7	62·3	18·2	12·5	1·7	3·1	8·6
1973	200·4	47·4	58·0	34·4	60·6	20·2	13·5	2·3	3·1	8·3
1974	183·9	43·6	61·1	32·7	46·5	18·8	12·5	2·4	3·4	6·5
1975	161·5	38·3	53·9	28·8	40·6	14·9	11·2	2·7	4·0	5·5
1976	176·7	39·5	55·7	32·1	47·8	14·4	12·3	2·8	4·2	5·8
1977	200·9	40·4	64·1	37·7	58·8	15·3	11·6	3·0	4·8	5·7
1978	220·7	44·6	69·3	41·4	60·5	18·2	12·5	3·2	5·1	5·6
1979	229·1	49·1	79·2	43·7	57·1	21·4	13·5	3·0	5·3	5·9
1980	212·9	48·8	81·2	37·8	45·1	21·0	12·6	2·5	6·6	6·1
1981	219·6	53·2	86·0	37·8	42·5	23·3	12·7	2·3	8·3	6·6
1982	204·7	53·3	80·5	35·0	35·9	24·1	12·6	1·7	7·9	7·0
1983	224·6	49·2	85·2	38·7	51·6	21·0	11·8	1·6	6·9	7·9

Chart US.4   Gross domestic private investment by type of asset, 1900–83

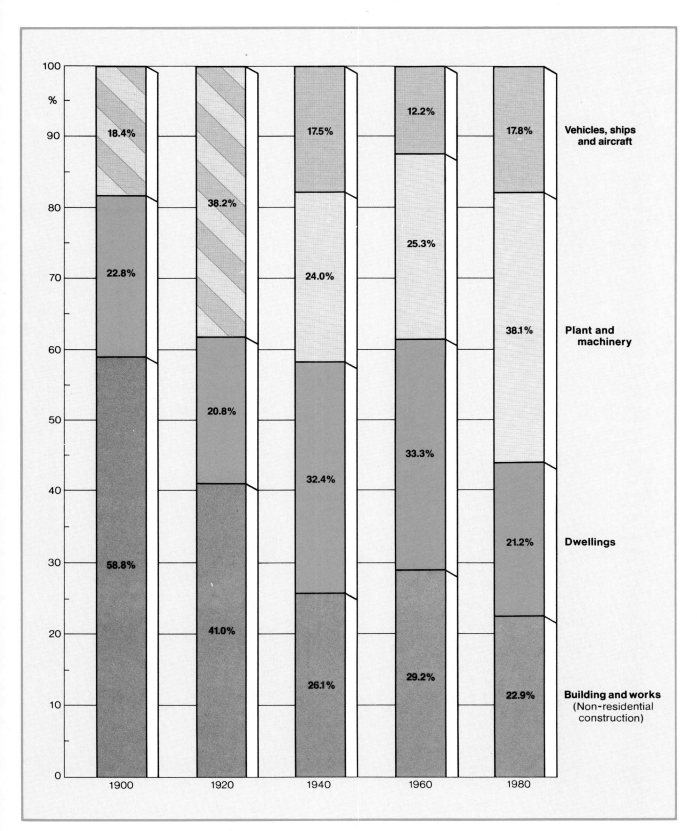

	Wages & salaries	Other income	Taxes etc	Personal disposable income	Personal outlays	Personal savings	Savings ratio	Gross trading profits
				$ bn				
1900	9·4	6·9	...	...	...	...	...	...
1901	10·1	7·2	...	...	...	...	...	...
1902	10·9	7·7	...	...	...	...	...	...
1903	11·7	8·0	...	...	...	...	...	...
1904	11·9	8·3	...	...	...	...	...	...
1905	13·1	8·5	...	...	...	...	...	...
1906	14·1	9·2	...	...	...	...	...	...
1907	14·7	9·8	...	...	...	...	...	...
1908	13·5	9·5	...	...	...	...	...	...
1909	15·5	11·1	...	...	...	...	...	...
1910	16·5	11·8	...	...	...	...	...	...
1911	16·7	11·5	...	...	...	...	...	...
1912	17·5	12·1	...	...	...	...	...	...
1913	19·0	12·6	...	...	...	...	...	...
1914	18·7	12·6	...	...	...	...	...	...
1915	19·5	13·2	...	...	...	...	...	...
1916	22·8	16·1	...	...	...	...	...	...
1917	27·2	19·3	...	...	...	...	...	...
1918	35·3	21·8	...	...	...	...	...	...
1919	39·6	23·4	...	...	...	...	...	...
1920	46·0	22·5	...	...	...	...	...	...
1921	37·0	19·8	...	...	...	...	...	...
1922	38·1	19·2	...	...	...	...	...	...
1923	44·6	21·1	...	...	...	...	...	...
1924	44·4	22·7	...	...	...	...	...	...
1925	46·0	24·1	...	...	...	...	...	...
1926	49·0	24·6	...	...	...	...	...	...
1927	48·9	25·1	...	...	...	...	...	...
1928	49·7	26·3	...	...	...	...	...	...
1929	52·1	27·5						
1930	50·5	34·6	2·7	82·4	79·1	3·3	4·0	9·9
	46·2	30·1	2·6	73·8	71·1	2·7	3·6	3·7
1931	39·2	26·5	2·0	63·7	61·4	2·2	3·5	−0·4
1932	30·5	19·8	1·6	48·7	49·3	−0·6	—	−2·3
1933	29·0	18·0	1·6	45·6	46·5	−0·9	—	−1·0
1934	33·7	20·2	1·7	52·2	52·0	0·2	0·4	2·3
1935	36·7	23·8	2·0	58·5	56·4	2·1	3·6	3·6
1936	42·0	26·7	2·4	66·3	62·8	3·5	5·3	6·3
1937	46·1	28·2	3·5	70·9	67·5	3·4	4·8	6·9
1938	43·0	25·5	3·4	65·2	64·9	0·4	0·6	4·0
1939	46·0	27·2	3·0	70·0	67·8	2·2	3·1	7·2
1940	49·9	28·7	3·2	75·3	72·0	3·4	4·5	10·0
1941	62·1	34·1	4·1	92·2	81·8	10·3	11·2	17·9
1942	82·1	41·7	7·1	116·6	89·4	27·2	23·3	21·7
1943	105·8	47·1	19·6	133·0	100·1	32·9	24·7	25·3
1944	116·7	49·8	21·1	145·6	109·0	36·6	25·1	24·2
1945	117·5	54·9	23·1	149·1	120·4	28·7	19·2	19·8
1946	112·0	67·7	20·7	158·9	145·2	13·7	8·6	24·8
1947	123·1	69·2	26·5	168·7	163·5	5·2	3·1	31·8
1948	135·5	75·7	23·2	188·0	176·9	11·1	5·9	35·6
1949	134·7	73·8	20·7	187·9	180·4	7·5	4·0	29·2
1950	147·0	83·2	23·6	206·6	194·7	11·9	5·8	42·9
1951	171·3	87·2	32·3	226·0	210·0	16·1	7·1	44·5
1952	185·3	90·1	37·8	237·7	220·4	17·4	7·3	39·6
1953	198·5	93·0	39·5	252·2	233·7	18·5	7·3	41·2
1954	196·8	97·3	37·1	257·1	240·1	17·0	6·6	38·7
1955	211·7	103·9	40·6	275·0	258·5	16·4	6·0	49·2
1956	228·3	110·0	45·5	292·9	271·6	21·3	7·3	49·6
1957	239·3	118·4	49·1	308·6	286·4	22·3	7·2	48·1
1958	240·5	132·5	49·0	319·0	295·4	23·6	7·4	41·9
1959	258·9	133·5	53·9	338·4	317·3	21·1	6·2	52·6
1960	271·9	139·7	59·6	352·0	332·3	19·7	5·6	49·8
1961	279·5	147·9	61·7	365·8	342·7	23·0	6·3	49·7
1962	298·0	155·9	67·1	386·8	363·5	23·3	6·0	55·0
1963	313·4	164·5	72·1	405·9	384·0	21·9	5·4	59·6
1964	336·1	175·6	71·2	440·6	411·0	29·6	6·7	66·5
1965	362·0	191·9	78·2	475·8	442·1	33·7	7·1	77·2
1966	398·4	207·6	92·3	513·7	477·7	36·0	7·0	83·0
1967	427·0	223·7	102·7	547·9	503·6	44·3	8·1	79·7
1968	469·6	243·8	120·1	593·4	551·5	41·9	7·1	88·5
1969	515·7	265·4	142·0	638·9	598·3	40·6	6·4	86·7
1970	548·7	290·1	143·7	695·3	639·5	55·8	8·0	75·4
1971	581·5	318·1	147·4	751·8	691·1	60·7	8·1	86·6
1972	635·2	350·5	175·5	810·4	757·7	52·6	6·5	100·6
1973	702·6	405·1	193·3	914·5	835·5	79·0	8·6	125·6
1974	765·2	450·7	218·2	998·3	913·2	85·1	8·5	136·7
1975	806·4	508·9	219·3	1,096·1	1,001·8	94·3	8·6	132·1
1976	889·9	556·8	252·3	1,194·4	1,111·9	82·5	6·9	166·3
1977	983·2	618·4	287·6	1,314·0	1,236·0	78·0	5·9	194·7
1978	1,106·5	696·1	328·5	1,474·0	1,384·6	89·4	6·1	229·1
1979	1,237·4	794·7	382·1	1,650·2	1,553·5	96·7	5·9	252·7
1980	1,356·6	897·3	425·1	1,828·9	1,718·7	110·2	6·0	234·6
1981	1,493·2	1,040·8	492·2	2,041·7	1,904·3	137·4	6·7	221·2
1982	1,568·7	1,127·2	515·4	2,180·5	2,044·5	136·0	6·2	165·5
1983	1,658·8	1,204·7	523·8	2,340·1	2,222·0	118·1	5·0	203·2

Table US.6 Consumers' expenditure at constant prices, selected commodities, 1900–83

	Food	Fuel	Clothing & footwear	Consumer durables (excl. cars)	Motor vehicles & parts	Housing	Household operation	Other services
	\$ bn, 1972 prices							
1900	26·9		10·9	7·0			32·0	
1901	28·2		11·5	7·3			34·3	
1902	29·4		12·0	7·4			36·4	
1903	30·5		12·6	7·8			38·5	
1904	31·6		13·1	8·3			40·9	
1905	33·4		13·5	8·7			43·7	
1906	33·8		13·8	8·7			45·4	
1907	35·0		14·4	9·2			47·8	
1908	36·1		14·7	9·5			49·9	
1909	37·0		15·1	9·5			51·7	
1910	37·6		15·8	9·8			53·0	
1911	39·4		16·5	10·4			55·1	
1912	40·6		16·8	10·4			56·2	
1913	41·0		17·2	10·5			57·2	
1914	41·5		17·6	11·0			58·9	
1915	41·7		17·5	11·5			61·0	
1916	42·1		17·2	11·4			62·8	
1917	42·3		17·2	12·2			65·5	
1918	43·7		16·9	12·8			69·3	
1919	44·8		16·8	12·4			73·2	
1920	45·0		17·5	12·5			76·6	
1921	48·0		18·6	14·1			80·8	
1922	50·4		19·4	15·1			86·3	
1923	52·2		20·9	16·7			88·4	
1924	54·0		21·9	19·2			91·2	
1925	56·0		23·0	21·0			95·0	
1926	57·4		23·7	21·9			99·2	
1927	58·5		25·0	22·8			102·3	
1928	59·2		25·3	22·4			107·5	
1929	52·5	7·1	25·6	11·8	9·1	20·4	13·1	62·6
1930	51·6	7·0	23·0	10·0	6·6	20·2	12·7	56·6
1931	51·9	6·8	22·7	9·3	5·0	20·0	11·8	52·6
1932	48·8	6·4	20·3	7·7	3·2	19·5	10·5	47·1
1933	47·8	6·6	18·2	6·9	3·8	19·2	10·0	47·7
1934	51·1	6·9	19·3	7·4	4·7	20·1	11·0	45·2
1935	53·4	7·2	20·7	8·4	6·6	20·3	11·5	47·7
1936	60·4	7·8	22·6	10·3	8·3	20·6	12·2	51·1
1937	63·5	8·1	22·5	10·9	8·6	20·9	12·9	52·8
1938	64·9	7·9	22·7	10·0	5·7	21·3	12·3	50·1
1939	67·2	8·5	24·4	11·1	7·5	21·7	13·0	51·4
1940	70·1	9·0	25·2	12·1	9·1	22·4	13·7	52·7
1941	73·7	9·8	26·9	14·1	10·1	23·6	13·5	54·7
1942	75·2	8·6	27·7	12·4	3·3	24·6	14·1	56·8
1943	77·3	7·2	29·7	11·0	3·0	25·6	13·2	61·4
1944	82·7	7·2	28·8	10·2	2·8	26·5	13·3	63·0
1945	89·3	8·3	29·9	11·4	3·0	27·1	13·7	65·5
1946	93·9	11·6	30·9	17·8	7·6	29·3	14·9	72·5
1947	90·3	12·3	29·4	20·0	11·1	31·9	15·8	73·3
1948	89·0	12·7	29·7	19·8	12·7	33·6	16·4	74·7
1949	89·9	12·6	29·8	19·3	16·2	35·7	16·8	74·0
1950	91·4	13·6	30·7	21·9	20·7	38·1	18·2	76·6
1951	93·4	14·0	30·3	21·2	17·9	40·8	19·0	77·4
1952	96·1	14·5	31·8	21·5	16·5	43·4	19·3	78·2
1953	99·1	15·0	32·1	22·3	19·8	45·7	19·9	80·0
1954	100·4	15·3	32·0	22·7	19·8	47·9	20·4	82·2
1955	104·6	16·6	33·6	25·3	25·8	50·3	22·5	84·8
1956	108·1	17·3	34·5	26·5	22·3	52·8	24·0	88·2
1957	110·1	17·6	34·2	25·9	22·7	55·4	24·7	90·2
1958	110·2	18·4	34·6	25·7	19·6	57·9	25·4	92·6
1959	114·4	18·9	36·3	27·4	23·3	60·9	26·4	97·5
1960	115·6	19·2	36·6	27·0	24·4	64·0	27·6	100·8
1961	117·4	19·0	37·3	27·2	22·1	67·0	28·4	104·8
1962	119·2	19·6	38·9	29·0	25·7	70·7	29·8	108·3
1963	120·7	20·2	39·6	31·0	28·7	74·0	30·9	112·9
1964	125·4	21·2	42·6	34·6	30·2	77·4	32·4	120·0
1965	130·9	22·3	44·2	37·8	34·8	81·6	33·9	125·4
1966	134·6	23·4	46·9	43·0	35·4	85·3	35·7	130·8
1967	136·7	24·0	46·9	44·8	34·7	89·1	37·5	137·1
1968	142·4	25·2	49·0	48·0	40·3	93·5	39·0	143·1
1969	145·6	26·4	50·0	49·9	41·9	98·4	41·0	149·4
1970	150·0	27·6	49·4	50·9	38·2	102·0	42·3	155·0
1971	151·2	28·8	51·8	52·7	45·5	106·4	43·1	160·4
1972	154·9	30·4	55·4	58·7	52·4	112·5	45·2	167·6
1973	153·6	31·6	59·3	64·8	56·5	118·2	47·4	173·6
1974	152·7	29·0	58·7	65·3	47·0	124·2	47·6	176·2
1975	156·9	29·8	60·9	65·2	47·5	128·3	49·9	181·1
1976	164·1	31·4	63·8	69·3	57·3	134·9	52·0	187·8
1977	170·6	32·1	67·5	74·5	63·5	141·3	55·1	196·6
1978	171·8	33·0	73·6	79·9	66·9	148·5	57·8	205·7
1979	176·1	32·1	76·7	84·6	62·6	154·8	60·1	212·4
1980	181·0	29·0	77·9	83·0	54·4	159·8	62·3	216·7
1981	180·9	28·7	82·6	84·6	56·3	164·8	62·7	221·3
1982	182·3	28·9	84·2	83·5	57·0	167·5	63·5	228·8
1983	188·9	30·1	88·5	90·9	66·6	171·3	64·1	240·0

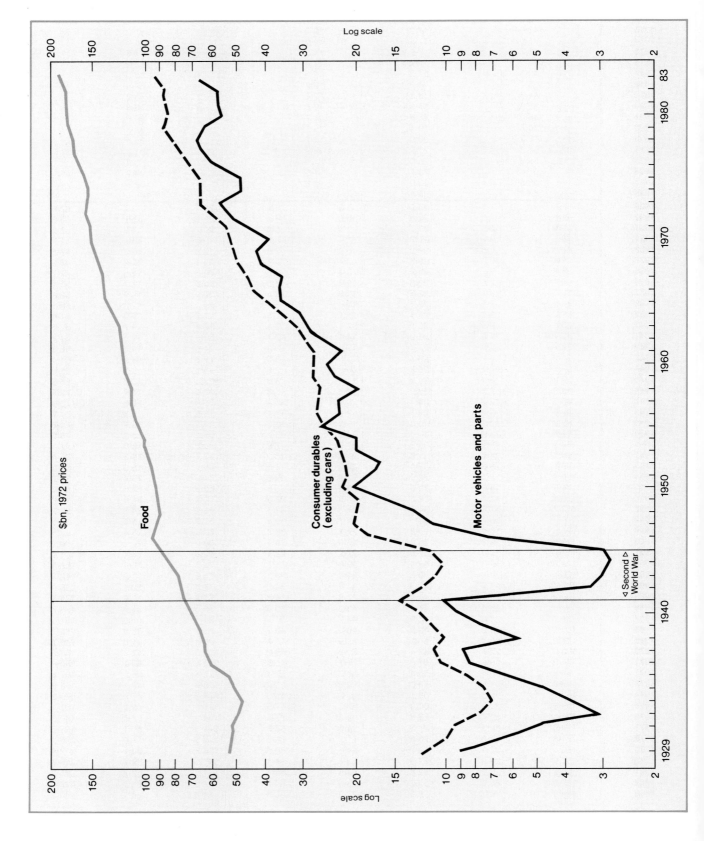

Chart US.6 Consumers' expenditure at constant prices, selected commodities, 1929–83

Log scale

$bn, 1972 prices

Food

Consumer durables (excluding cars)

Motor vehicles and parts

◁ Second ▷ World War

Log scale

52

Table US.7 Prices, 1900–83

	Producer prices		Consumer prices				Unit value exports	Unit value imports
	All commodities	Industrial commodities	All items	Food	Apparel & upkeep	Rent		
			Index nos., 1980 = 100					
1900	10·8	...	10·1	...	...	...	11·2	8·7
1901	10·6	...	10·1	...	...	...	11·0	8·3
1902	11·3	...	10·5	...	...	...	11·3	8·1
1903	11·4	...	10·9	...	...	...	12·0	8·4
1904	11·5	...	10·9	...	...	...	12·0	8·6
1905	11·5	...	10·9	...	...	...	11·6	9·1
1906	11·9	...	10·9	...	...	...	12·5	9·5
1907	12·5	...	11·3	...	...	...	13·3	10·0
1908	12·1	...	10·9	...	...	...	12·5	8·8
1909	13·0	...	10·9	...	...	...	13·1	8·8
1910	13·6	...	11·3	...	...	...	14·1	9·5
1911	12·5	...	11·3	...	...	...	13·0	9·6
1912	13·3	...	11·7	...	...	...	13·3	10·1
1913	13·4	13·5	12·0	11·7	16·5	25·9	13·9	10·0
1914	13·1	12·8	12·2	12·0	16·6	25·9	...	...
1915	13·3	13·1	12·3	11·8	17·0	26·0	...	...
1916	16·4	17·0	13·2	13·3	18·6	26·4	...	...
1917	22·6	22·2	15·5	17·1	22·3	26·1	...	...
1918	25·2	24·0	18·3	19·7	30·2	26·6	...	...
1919	26·6	25·0	21·0	22·0	40·1	28·8	30·5	17·8
1920	29·6	31·2	24·3	24·7	47·7	33·9	33·0	22·2
1921	18·7	20·3	21·7	18·8	36·8	38·9	21·5	12·5
1922	18·6	19·8	20·3	17·6	29·9	40·0	20·0	12·0
1923	19·3	20·2	20·7	18·1	29·9	41·0	22·8	14·1
1924	18·8	19·3	20·7	18·0	30·2	42·5	21·0	13·8
1925	19·8	19·9	21·3	19·5	29·1	42·7	21·3	15·0
1926	19·2	19·4	21·5	20·1	28·6	42·3	19·5	14·6
1927	18·4	18·2	21·1	19·4	28·0	41·6	18·3	13·6
1928	18·6	17·9	20·8	19·2	27·6	40·6	18·6	13·2
1929	18·3	17·7	20·8	19·4	27·3	39·7	18·5	12·4
1930	16·6	16·4	20·2	18·5	26·8	38·6	16·5	10·1
1931	14·0	14·5	18·5	15·2	24·4	36·5	12·7	7·9
1932	12·5	13·6	16·6	12·7	21·5	32·8	11·0	6·2
1933	12·7	13·8	15·7	12·3	20·8	28·2	11·4	6·2
1934	14·4	15·1	16·2	13·7	22·8	26·5	13·5	7·1
1935	15·4	15·1	16·6	14·7	23·0	26·4	13·7	7·2
1936	15·5	15·3	16·8	14·8	23·2	27·1	14·0	7·7
1937	16·6	16·4	17·4	15·4	24·4	28·3	14·9	8·6
1938	15·1	15·8	17·0	14·3	24·2	29·2	13·8	7·7
1939	14·8	15·8	16·8	13·9	23·9	29·2	13·5	7·8
1940	15·1	16·0	17·0	14·2	24·1	29·3	14·5	8·4
1941	16·8	17·2	17·9	15·4	25·3	29·9	15·6	9·0
1942	19·0	18·4	19·8	18·1	29·5	30·5	18·9	10·4
1943	19·8	18·7	21·0	20·2	30·8	30·5	20·8	11·3
1944	20·0	19·0	21·3	19·9	33·0	30·6	23·8	12·1
1945	20·3	19·3	21·8	20·4	34·7	30·7	23·7	12·4
1946	23·2	21·1	23·7	23·4	38·0	30·9	22·5	13·8
1947	28·5	25·8	27·1	28·4	44·1	31·9	26·9	17·0
1948	30·8	28·0	29·2	30·8	47·0	34·0	28·5	18·8
1949	29·3	27·4	28·9	29·6	45·2	35·5	26·5	17·9
1950	30·4	28·4	29·2	30·0	44·5	36·7	25·8	19·4
1951	33·9	31·3	31·2	33·3	48·5	38·2	29·6	24·4
1952	33·0	30·6	32·2	33·9	48·1	39·8	29·5	23·1
1953	32·5	30·9	32·4	33·4	47·7	41·9	29·2	22·2
1954	32·6	30·9	32·6	33·3	47·6	43·4	28·8	22·6
1955	32·7	31·6	32·5	32·8	47·4	44·0	29·1	22·6
1956	33·8	33·0	33·0	33·1	48·4	44·8	30·2	22·8
1957	34·7	34·0	34·1	34·1	49·2	45·7	31·1	23·2
1958	35·2	34·1	35·1	35·6	49·3	46·5	30·8	22·1
1959	35·3	34·7	35·3	35·0	49·7	47·2	30·9	21·7
1960	35·3	34·7	35·9	35·4	50·5	47·9	31·1	22·0
1961	35·2	34·5	36·3	35·8	51·0	48·5	31·7	21·7
1962	35·3	34·5	36·7	36·1	51·2	49·1	31·5	21·2
1963	35·2	34·5	37·1	36·7	51·8	49·6	31·4	21·4
1964	35·3	34·6	37·6	37·2	52·3	50·1	31·8	21·9
1965	36·0	35·1	38·3	38·0	52·8	50·6	32·8	22·2
1966	37·2	35·8	39·4	39·8	54·2	51·3	33·8	22·8
1967	37·2	36·4	40·5	40·2	56·4	52·2	34·5	23·0
1968	38·2	37·3	42·2	41·7	59·4	53·4	34·9	23·2
1969	39·6	38·6	44·5	43·8	62·9	55·2	36·1	23·9
1970	41·1	40·0	47·1	46·2	65·4	57·5	38·2	25·6
1971	42·4	41·5	49·1	47·6	67·5	60·1	39·4	26·9
1972	44·3	42·9	50·7	49·7	68·9	62·2	40·5	28·9
1973	50·1	45·8	53·9	56·9	71·5	64·9	47·4	34·1
1974	59·6	56·0	59·8	65·0	76·8	68·2	60·1	51·3
1975	65·1	62·4	65·3	70·5	80·2	71·7	67·2	55·4
1976	68·1	66·4	69·0	72·7	83·2	75·5	69·6	57·1
1977	72·3	71·0	73·5	77·3	86·9	80·1	72·4	62·0
1978	77·9	76·2	79·2	83·0	89·5	85·6	77·4	66·9
1979	87·7	86·1	88·1	92·1	93·4	91·9	88·0	79·7
1980	100·0	100·0	100·0	100·0	100·0	100·0	100·0	100·0
1981	109·2	110·7	110·4	107·9	104·8	108·7	109·2	105·5
1982	111·4	113·6	117·1	112·2	107·5	116·9	110·4	103·8
1983	112·8	114·9	120·9	114·6	110·1	123·6	111·6	99·5

	Total population	Births	Age distribution				Geographical distribution			
			0–14	15–34	35–64	65 & over	North-East	North Central	South	West
	mn	'000	mn				mn			
1900	76·1	...	26·1	27·1	19·7	3·1				
1901	77·6	...	26·5	27·7	20·2	3·2	...	...	...	...
1902	79·2	...	26·9	28·3	20·8	3·3	...	...	...	...
1903	80·6	...	27·2	28·9	21·3	3·3	...	...	...	...
1904	82·2	...	27·5	29·5	21·8	3·4	...	...	...	...
1905	83·8	...	27·8	30·2	22·3	3·5	...	...	...	...
1906	85·4	...	28·2	30·8	22·9	3·6	...	...	...	...
1907	87·0	...	28·5	31·4	23·4	3·7	...	...	...	...
1908	88·7	...	28·8	32·1	24·0	3·8	...	...	...	...
1909	90·5	2,718	29·2	32·8	24·6	3·9	...	...	...	...
1910	92·4	2,777	29·6	33·5	25·3	4·0	25·87	29·89	29·39	7·08
1911	93·9	2,809	30·0	33·9	25·9	4·1	...	...	...	...
1912	95·3	2,840	30·4	34·2	26·5	4·2	...	...	...	...
1913	97·2	2,869	31·0	34·7	27·2	4·3	...	...	...	...
1914	99·1	2,966	31·6	35·2	28·0	4·4	...	...	...	...
1915	100·5	2,965	32·0	35·4	28·6	4·5	...	...	...	...
1916	102·0	2,964	32·5	35·6	29·3	4·6	...	...	...	...
1917	103·3	2,944	32·9	35·7	29·9	4·7	...	...	...	...
1918	103·2	2,948	33·3	34·5	30·5	4·8	...	...	...	...
1919	104·5	2,740	33·4	35·4	30·9	4·9	...	...	...	...
1920	106·5	2,950	33·8	36·2	31·5	4·9	29·66	34·02	33·13	9·21
1921	108·5	3,055	34·4	36·9	32·2	5·1	...	...	...	...
1922	110·1	2,882	34·8	37·3	32·7	5·2	...	...	...	...
1923	112·0	2,910	35·2	38·0	33·3	5·4	...	...	...	...
1924	114·1	2,979	35·6	38·9	34·0	5·6	...	...	...	...
1925	115·8	2,909	35·9	39·4	34·7	5·8	...	...	...	...
1926	117·4	2,839	36·1	39·9	35·4	6·0	...	...	...	...
1927	119·0	2,802	36·3	40·4	36·3	6·1	...	...	...	...
1928	120·5	2,674	36·3	40·8	37·1	6·3	...	...	...	...
1929	121·8	2,582	36·2	41·1	38·0	6·5	...	...	...	...
1930	123·1	2,618	36·0	41·5	38·8	6·7	34·43	38·59	37·86	12·32
1931	124·1	2,506	35·8	41·9	39·4	6·9	...	...	...	...
1932	124·8	2,440	35·5	42·2	40·0	7·1	...	...	...	...
1933	125·6	2,307	35·1	42·6	40·5	7·4	...	...	...	...
1934	126·4	2,396	34·7	43·0	41·1	7·6	...	...	...	...
1935	127·3	2,377	34·4	43·4	41·7	7·8	...	...	...	...
1936	128·1	2,355	33·9	43·8	42·2	8·0	...	...	...	...
1937	128·8	2,413	33·6	44·2	42·8	8·3	...	...	...	...
1938	129·8	2,496	33·3	44·6	43·4	8·5	...	...	...	...
1939	130·9	2,466	33·1	45·0	44·0	8·8	...	...	...	...
1940	132·6	2,559	32·9	45·5	44·7	9·0	35·98	40·14	41·67	14·38
1941	133·9	2,703	32·9	45·8	45·4	9·3	...	...	...	...
1942	135·4	2,989	33·1	46·0	46·1	9·6	...	...	...	...
1943	137·3	3,104	33·7	46·3	46·9	9·9	...	...	...	...
1944	138·9	2,939	34·1	46·5	47·6	10·1	...	...	...	...
1945	140·5	2,858	34·6	46·4	48·4	10·5	...	...	...	...
1946	141·9	3,411	35·1	46·3	49·1	10·8	...	...	...	...
1947	144·7	3,817	36·7	46·4	49·9	11·2	...	...	...	...
1948	147·2	3,637	38·0	46·4	50·7	11·5	...	...	...	...
1949	149·8	3,649	39·4	46·3	51·6	11·9	...	...	...	...
1950	152·3	3,632	40·8	46·2	52·3	12·4	39·48	44·46	47·20	20·19
1951	154·9	3,823	42·3	46·1	53·1	12·8	...	...	...	...
1952	157·6	3,913	43·9	46·0	53·9	13·2	...	...	...	...
1953	160·2	3,965	45·4	45·9	54·7	13·6	...	...	...	...
1954	163·0	4,078	47·1	45·9	55·4	14·0	...	...	...	...
1955	165·9	4,097	48·7	45·8	56·2	14·5	...	...	...	...
1956	168·9	4,218	50·3	45·9	57·1	14·9	...	...	...	...
1957	172·0	4,308	51·9	46·0	58·0	15·4	...	...	...	...
1958	174·9	4,255	53·1	46·6	58·7	15·8	...	...	...	...
1959	177·1	4,245[a]	54·4	47·0	59·5	16·2	...	...	...	...
	177·8		54·7	47·2	59·7	16·2				
1960	180·7	4,258[b]	56·1	47·5	60·4	16·7	44·68	51·62	54·97	28·05
1961	183·7	4,268	57·6	47·9	61·1	17·1	...	...	...	...
1962	186·6	4,167	57·9	49·4	61·8	17·5	...	...	...	...
1963	189·2	4,098	58·5	50·6	62·4	17·8	...	...	...	...
1964	191·9	4,027	58·9	51·9	62·9	18·1	...	...	...	...
1965	194·3	3,760	59·3	53·2	63·4	18·5	...	...	...	...
1966	196·6	3,606	59·3	54·7	63·8	18·8	...	...	...	...
1967	198·7	3,521	59·1	56·4	64·2	19·1	...	...	...	...
1968	200·7	3,502	58·9	58·1	64·6	19·4	...	...	...	...
1969	202·7	3,600	58·3	59·9	64·8	19·7	...	...	...	...
1970	205·1	3,731	57·9	61·9	65·1	20·1	49·13	56·66	63·05	34·97
1971	207·7	3,556	57·7	63·9	65·5	20·6	49·49	57·03	64·11	35·57
1972	209·9	3,258	57·0	66·1	65·8	21·0	49·62	57·29	65·22	36·11
1973	211·9	3,137	56·2	68·2	66·0	21·5	49·48	57·44	66·23	36·70
1974	213·9	3,160	55·2	70·2	66·3	22·1	49·33	57·55	67·22	37·30
1975	216·0	3,144	54·4	72·3	66·6	22·7	49·33	57·65	68·12	37·95
1976	218·0	3,168	53·4	74·3	67·1	23·3	49·29	57·83	68·94	38·63
1977	220·2	3,327	53·0	76·0	67·7	23·9	49·19	58·05	69·79	39·37
1978	222·6	3,333	52·0	77·4	68·7	24·5	49·09	58·26	70·64	40·24
1979	225·1	3,494	51·4	78·9	69·6	25·1	49·00	58·41	71·55	41·14
1980	227·7	3,612	51·3	80·3	70·4	25·7	49·14	58·87	75·37	43·17
1981	229·8	3,646	51·2	81·4	71·0	26·3	49·34	58·96	76·86	44·20
1982	232·1	3,704	51·4	81·3	72·6	26·8	49·46	58·93	78·14	45·02

a Including Alaska.
b Including Alaska and Hawaii.

Table US.9 Labour market: employment, 1900–83

			Employment by sector						
	Number in civil work	Employed in agriculture	Mining	Mfg	Transport & public utilities	Distributive trades	Services	Govt	Self employed
	mn					'000			
1900	27·0	11·1	637	5,468	2,282	2,502	2,048	1,094	...
1901	27·9	10·9	703	5,817	2,404	2,765	2,202	1,129	...
1902	28·8	10·8	685	6,305	2,754	2,827	2,240	1,191	...
1903	29·5	10·9	834	6,527	2,666	2,979	2,333	1,229	...
1904	29·8	11·1	801	6,199	2,743	2,992	2,371	1,277	...
1905	30·9	11·2	889	6,739	2,905	3,170	2,461	1,335	...
1906	32·6	11·5	894	7,226	3,110	3,442	2,620	1,386	...
1907	33·2	11·5	1,051	7,322	3,114	3,486	2,666	1,448	...
1908	32·1	11·2	900	6,570	3,069	3,299	2,606	1,507	...
1909	33·9	11·2	998	7,661	3,229	3,585	2,790	1,564	...
1910	34·6	11·3	1,068	7,828	3,366	3,570	2,893	1,630	...
1911	35·0	11·1	1,052	7,870	3,426	3,813	3,011	1,672	...
1912	36·2	11·1	1,083	8,322	3,552	4,073	3,107	1,717	...
1913	37·0	11·0	1,182	8,751	3,570	4,232	3,239	1,757	...
1914	36·3	10·9	1,027	8,210	3,445	4,128	3,304	1,809	...
1915	36·2	11·0	1,022	8,210	3,439	4,091	3,331	1,861	...
1916	38·0	10·8	1,168	9,629	3,579	4,476	3,534	1,916	...
1917	38·2	10·8	1,267	9,872	3,722	4,320	3,554	2,000	...
1918	38·5	10·7	1,311	10,167	3,877	4,110	3,578	2,461	...
1919	39·2	10·5	1,133	10,659	3,711	4,514	3,349	2,676	...
1920	39·2	10·4	1,239	10,658	3,998	4,467	3,512	2,603	...
1921	37·1	10·4	962	8,527	3,459	3,960	4,053	2,528	...
1922	39·6	10·6	929	9,120	3,505	4,708	4,232	2,538	...
1923	42·4	10·6	1,212	10,300	3,882	5,194	4,422	2,607	...
1924	42·0	10·6	1,101	9,671	3,807	5,047	4,509	2,720	...
1925	43·7	10·7	1,089	9,939	3,826	5,576	4,075	2,800	...
1926	44·8	10·7	1,185	10,156	3,942	5,784	4,323	2,846	...
1927	44·9	10·5	1,114	10,001	3,895	5,908	4,506	2,915	...
1928	45·1	10·5	1,050	9,947	3,828	5,874	4,671	2,995	...
1929	47·6	10·5	1,087	10,702	3,916	6,123	4,919	3,065	10,320
1930	45·5	10·3	1,009	9,562	3,685	5,797	4,821	3,148	10,311
1931	42·4	10·3	873	8,170	3,254	5,284	4,561	3,264	10,352
1932	38·9	10·2	731	6,931	2,816	4,683	4,244	3,225	10,350
1933	38·8	10·1	744	7,397	2,672	4,755	4,141	3,166	10,371
1934	40·9	9·9	883	8,501	2,750	5,281	4,349	3,299	10,493
1935	42·3	10·1	897	9,069	2,786	5,431	4,448	3,481	10,645
1936	44·4	10·0	946	9,827	2,973	5,809	4,685	3,668	10,567
1937	46·3	9·3	1,015	10,794	3,134	6,265	4,920	3,756	10,495
1938	44·2	9·7	891	9,440	2,863	6,179	4,868	3,883	10,338
1939	45·8	9·6	854	10,278	2,936	6,426	4,949	3,995	10,266
1940	47·5	9·5	925	10,985	3,038	6,750	5,150	4,202	10,150
1941	50·4	9·1	957	13,192	3,274	7,210	5,430	4,660	10,090
1942	53·8	9·3	992	15,280	3,460	7,118	5,575	5,483	9,947
1943	54·5	9·1	925	17,602	3,647	6,982	5,611	6,080	9,431
1944	54·0	9·0	892	17,328	3,829	7,058	5,606	6,043	9,273
1945	52·8	8·6	836	15,524	3,906	7,314	5,703	5,944	9,349
1946	55·2	8·3	862	14,703	4,061	8,376	6,372	5,595	9,913
1947	57·8 / 57·0	8·3 / 7·9	955	15,545	4,166	8,955	6,753	5,474	10,199
1948	58·3	7·6	994	15,582	4,189	9,272	6,981	5,650	10,211
1949	57·6	7·7	930	14,441	4,001	9,264	7,068	5,856	10,064
1950	58·9	6·2	901	15,241	4,034	9,386	7,245	6,026	9,996
1951	60·0	6·7	929	16,393	4,226	9,742	7,503	6,389	9,699
1952	60·2	6·5	898	16,632	4,248	10,004	7,734	6,609	9,637
1953	61·2	6·3	866	17,549	4,290	10,247	7,946	6,645	9,475
1954	60·1	6·2	791	16,314	4,084	10,235	8,169	6,751	9,329
1955	62·2	6·4	792	16,882	4,141	10,535	8,538	6,914	9,149
1956	63·8	6·3	822	17,243	4,244	10,858	8,886	7,278	8,981
1957	64·1	5·9	828	17,174	4,241	10,886	9,146	7,616	8,821
1958	63·0	5·6	751	15,945	3,976	10,750	9,246	7,839	8,611
1959	64·6	5·6	732	16,675	4,011	11,127	9,636	8,083	8,428
1960	65·8	5·5	712	16,796	4,004	11,391	10,007	8,353	8,305
1961	65·7	5·2	672	16,326	3,903	11,337	10,308	8,594	8,177
1962	66·7	4·9	650	16,853	3,906	11,566	10,736	8,890	8,009
1963	67·7	4·7	635	16,995	3,903	11,778	11,107	9,225	7,722
1964	69·3	4·5	634	17,274	3,951	12,160	11,571	9,596	7,652
1965	71·1	4·4	632	18,062	4,036	12,716	12,013	10,074	7,526
1966	72·9	4·0	627	19,214	4,158	13,245	12,556	10,784	7,271
1967	74·4	3·8	613	19,447	4,268	13,606	13,230	11,391	7,188
1968	75·9	3·8	606	19,781	4,318	14,099	13,904	11,839	7,115
1969	77·9	3·6	619	20,167	4,442	14,705	14,681	12,195	7,199
1970	78·7	3·5	623	19,367	4,515	15,040	15,193	12,554	7,093
1971	79·4	3·4	609	18,623	4,476	15,352	15,569	12,881	7,117
1972	82·2	3·5	628	19,151	4,541	15,949	16,184	13,334	7,198
1973	85·1	3·5	642	20,154	4,656	16,607	16,903	13,732	7,264
1974	86·8	3·5	697	20,077	4,725	16,987	17,589	14,170	7,458
1975	85·8	3·4	752	18,323	4,542	17,060	18,057	14,686	7,420
1976	88·8	3·3	779	18,997	4,582	17,755	18,822	14,871	7,392
1977	92·0	3·3	813	19,682	4,713	18,516	19,770	15,127	7,639
1978	96·0	3·4	851	20,505	4,923	19,542	20,976	15,672	7,988
1979	98·8	3·3	958	21,040	5,136	20,192	22,087	15,947	8,272
1980	99·3	3·4	1,027	20,285	5,146	20,310	23,050	16,241	8,665
1981	100·4	3·4	1,139	20,170	5,165	20,547	23,893	16,031	8,759
1982	99·5	3·4	1,143	18,853	5,081	20,401	24,404	15,803	8,927
1983	100·8	3·4	1,021	18,678	4,943	20,508	25,141	15,747	9,219

55

	Productivity		Average weekly hrs of mfg production workers	Average weekly earnings of mfg production workers	Unemployment		Industrial disputes	
	Gross private domestic product per manhour	Output per manhour in mfg					Workers involved	Man days idle
	Index nos., 1980 = 100			$	'000	%	'000	mn
1900	17·4	13·7	...	...	1,420	5·0	568	...
1901	18·6	14·6	...	...	1,205	4·0	564	...
1902	17·9	15·3	...	...	1,097	3·7	692	...
1903	18·3	14·8	...	...	1,204	3·9	788	...
1904	18·3	15·5	...	...	1,691	5·4	574	...
1905	18·7	15·6	...	...	1,381	4·3	302	...
1906	20·1	15·8	...	...	574	1·7	...	...
1907	20·1	15·2	...	...	945	2·8	...	...
1908	19·1	14·2	...	...	2,780	8·0	...	...
1909	20·5	16·1	51·0	9·74	1,824	5·1	...	...
1910	20·1	15·9	...	...	2,150	5·9	...	...
1911	20·5	15·2	...	...	2,518	6·7	...	...
1912	20·9	17·5	...	...	1,759	4·6	...	...
1913	21·6	18·3	...	...	1,671	4·3	...	...
1914	20·2	18·4	49·4	10·92	3,120	7·9	...	...
1915	21·0	20·7	...	11·22	3,377	8·5	...	...
1916	22·6	20·4	...	12·63	2,043	5·1	...	...
1917	21·4	19·0	...	14·97	1,848	4·6	...	...
1918	23·2	18·9	...	19·12	536	1·4	...	...
1919	24·7	18·0	46·3	21·84	546	1·4	...	...
1920	24·5	19·1	47·4	26·02	2,132	5·2	1,420	...
1921	26·2	22·1	43·1	21·94	4,918	11·7	1,099	...
1922	25·9	25·0	44·2	21·28	2,859	6·7	1,613	...
1923	27·5	24·1	45·6	23·56	1,049	2·4	757	...
1924	28·7	25·6	43·7	23·67	2,190	5·0	655	...
1925	28·6	27·3	44·5	24·11	1,453	3·2	428	...
1926	29·4	27·8	45·0	24·38	801	1·8	330	...
1927	29·9	28·5	45·0	24·47	1,519	3·3	330	26·20
1928	29·9	29·7	44·4	24·70	1,982	4·2	314	12·60
1929	31·3	31·1	44·2	24·76	1,550	3·2	289	5·35
1930	30·1	31·3	42·1	23·00	4,340	8·7	183	3·32
1931	30·4	32·3	40·5	20·64	8,020	15·9	342	6·89
1932	29·2	30·2	38·3	16·89	12,060	23·6	324	10·50
1933	28·6	32·9	38·1	16·65	12,830	24·9	1,170	16·90
1934	31·5	34·4	34·6	18·20	11,340	21·7	1,470	19·60
1935	32·6	36·7	36·6	19·91	10,610	20·1	1,120	15·50
1936	34·2	36·9	39·2	21·56	9,030	16·9	789	13·90
1937	34·2	36·4	38·6	23·82	7,700	14·3	1,860	28·40
1938	35·2	35·9	35·6	22·07	10,390	19·0	688	9·15
1939	36·6	39·2	37·7	23·64	9,480	17·2	1,170	17·80
1940	37·6	41·1	38·1	24·96	8,120	14·6	577	6·70
1941	39·8	42·6	40·6	29·48	5,560	9·9	2,360	23·00
1942	39·9	43·4	43·1	36·68	2,660	4·7	840	4·18
1943	40·5	44·0	45·0	43·07	1,070	1·9	1,980	13·50
1944	43·2	43·4	45·2	45·70	670	1·2	2,120	8·72
1945	45·5	42·8	43·5	44·20	1,040	1·9	3,470	38·00
1946	44·2	39·4	40·3	43·32	2,270	3·9	4,600	116·00
1947	44·2	41·7	40·4	49·13	2,311	3·9	2,170	34·60
1948	46·5	44·3	40·0	53·08	2,276	3·8	1,960	34·10
1949	47·2	46·1	39·1	53·80	3,637	5·9	3,030	50·50
1950	50·9	48·6	40·5	58·28	3,288	5·3	2,410	38·80
1951	52·4	50·2	40·6	63·34	2,055	3·3	2,220	22·90
1952	54·1	51·1	40·7	66·75	1,883	3·0	3,540	59·10
1953	55·2	52·0	40·5	70·47	1,834	2·9	2,400	28·30
1954	56·1	52·8	39·6	70·49	3,532	5·5	1,530	22·60
1955	58·3	55·5	40·7	75·30	2,852	4·4	2,650	28·20
1956	58·9	55·1	40·4	78·78	2,750	4·1	1,900	33·10
1957	60·4	56·1	39·8	81·19	2,859	4·3	1,390	16·50
1958	62·3	55·9	39·2	82·32	4,602	6·8	2,060	23·90
1959	64·3	58·6	40·3	88·26	3,740	5·5	1,880	69·00
1960	65·2	59·0	39·7	89·72	3,852	5·5	1,320	19·10
1961	67·3	60·6	39·8	92·34	4,714	6·7	1,450	16·30
1962	69·9	63·2	40·4	96·56	3,911	5·5	1,230	18·60
1963	72·5	67·7	40·5	99·23	4,070	5·7	941	16·10
1964	75·6	71·1	40·7	102·97	3,786	5·2	1,640	22·90
1965	78·3	73·3	41·2	107·53	3,366	4·5	1,550	23·30
1966	80·7	74·0	41·4	112·19	2,875	3·8	1,960	25·40
1967	82·5	74·0	40·6	114·49	2,975	3·8	2,870	42·10
1968	85·3	76·7	40·7	122·51	2,817	3·6	2,649	49·02
1969	85·5	78·0	40·6	129·51	2,832	3·5	2,481	42·87
1970	86·2	77·8	39·8	133·33	4,093	4·9	3,305	66·41
1971	89·2	82·5	39·9	142·44	5,016	5·9	3,280	47·59
1972	92·4	86·7	40·5	154·71	4,882	5·6	1,714	27·07
1973	94·7	91·4	40·7	166·46	4,365	4·9	2,251	27·95
1974	93·5	89·3	40·0	176·80	5,156	5·6	2,778	47·99
1975	95·5	91·8	39·5	190·79	7,929	8·5	1,746	31·24
1976	98·7	95·9	40·1	209·32	7,406	7·7	2,420	37·86
1977	101·1	98·3	40·3	228·90	6,991	7·1	2,040	35·82
1978	101·7	99·1	40·4	249·27	6,202	6·1	1,623	36·92
1979	100·5	99·8	40·2	269·34	6,137	5·8	1,727	34·75
1980	100·0	100·0	39·7	288·62	7,637	7·1	1,366	33·29
1981	101·4	103·5	39·8	318·00	8,273	7·6	1,081	24·73
							729	16·91
1982	102·3	105·3	38·9	330·26	10,678	9·7	656	9·06
1983	104·9	109·7	40·1	354·08	10,717	9·6	909	17·46

Table US.11 Value of imports by commodity group, 1900–83

	Total imports	Food, feeds & beverages	Industrial supplies & materials	of which: Petroleum & products	Capital goods (excl. autos)	Consumer goods (non-food) (excl. autos)	Motor vehicles parts & engines
				$ mn			
1900	850	231	416	—		203	
1901	823	236	382	—		206	
1902	903	215	457	—		231	
1903	1,026	236	532	—		258	
1904	991	250	488	—		253	
1905	1,118	291	574	—		252	
1906	1,227	274	644	—		308	
1907	1,434	309	762	—		364	
1908	1,194	293	570	—		332	
1909	1,312	330	683	1		299	
1910	1,557	327	863	1		368	
1911	1,527	353	813	2		361	
1912	1,653	426	867	3		360	
1913	1,813	406	998	5		408	
1914	1,894	476	969	11		449	
1915	1,674	510	828	15		336	
1916	2,392	599	1,448	11		346	
1917	2,952	738	1,823	15		392	
1918	3,031	743	1,884	22		405	
1919	3,904	1,101	2,310	27		493	
1920	5,278	1,816	2,586	33		877	
1921	2,509	668	1,221	68		620	
1922	3,113	717	1,733	79		663	
1923	3,792	891	2,468	80	17	364	1
1924	3,610	942	2,245	103	14	369	1
1925	4,227	918	2,855	109	16	394	1
1926	4,431	953	2,979	126	23	433	2
1927	4,185	950	2,727	115	24	439	2
1928	4,091	951	2,618	134	27	446	3
1929	4,399	955	2,837	145	39	516	3
1930	3,061	684	1,943	146	29	347	2
1931	2,091	523	1,268	93	14	239	1
1932	1,333	404	742	61	8	142	—
1933	1,450	403	861	26	7	141	—
1934	1,655	514	933	37	11	155	—
1935	2,047	635	1,183	38	14	182	—
1936	2,423	728	1,443	41	17	215	1
1937	3,084	844	1,856	45	23	255	1
1938	1,960	566	1,150	39	16	186	2
1939	2,318	600	1,431	44	13	198	1
1940	2,625	556	1,778	70	9	166	1
1941	3,345	655	2,271	82	13	119	—
1942	2,756	575	1,868	37	27	116	—
1943	3,381	892	1,834	85	23	190	—
1944	3,929	1,178	1,961	113	21	240	—
1945	4,159	1,063	2,300	152	24	322	—
1946	5,003	1,328	3,065	159	32	492	5
1947	5,829	1,673	3,626	250	55	375	6
1948	7,207	1,986	4,508	416	103	434	35
1949	6,706	2,068	4,011	478	106	404	13
1950	8,954	2,642	5,493	592	111	540	23
1951	11,068	3,087	6,952	601	170	666	38
1952	10,817	3,156	6,537	692	227	663	56
1953	10,983	3,282	6,456	762	224	757	53
1954	10,369	3,317	5,764	829	220	787	53
1955	11,562	3,108	6,843	1,026	254	991	85
1956	12,902	3,190	7,674	1,286	364	1,133	145
1957	13,412	3,306	7,595	1,548	400	1,210	339
1958	13,419	3,472	6,944	1,625	460	1,195	555
1959	15,688	3,445	8,343	1,535	591	1,632	844
1960	15,072	3,286	7,887	1,544	562	1,901	633
1961	14,759	3,331	7,714	1,643	693	1,889	383
1962	16,453	3,573	8,573	1,765	758	2,276	521
1963	17,205	3,753	8,874	1,814	823	2,389	586
1964	18,749	3,915	9,563	1,907	1,039	2,694	767
1965	21,520	3,946	11,024	2,092	1,458	3,305	939
1966	25,618	4,499	12,162	2,127	2,136	3,912	1,910
1967	26,889	4,586	11,862	2,099	2,412	4,213	2,604
1968	33,226	5,271	14,159	2,359	2,819	5,375	4,256
1969	36,043	5,239	14,160	2,577	3,244	6,616	5,288
1970	40,356	6,152	15,415	2,960	3,985	7,404	5,925
1971	46,170	6,364	17,458	3,664	4,317	8,392	7,917
1972	56,364	7,264	20,689	4,699	5,836	11,111	9,634
1973	70,473	9,112	27,137	8,294	7,902	12,890	11,337
1974	102,576	10,568	53,049	26,463	9,734	14,380	12,358
1975	98,509	9,642	50,645	27,044	10,143	13,211	12,065
1976	123,478	11,546	62,925	34,598	12,279	17,165	16,768
1977	150,390	13,981	78,333	44,961	13,954	21,796	19,388
1978	174,757	15,397	82,380	42,197	19,643	28,943	25,095
1979	209,458	17,366	106,348	59,888	25,038	30,566	26,488
1980	244,871	18,127	129,211	78,795	30,463	34,445	27,978
1981	261,305	18,113	131,423	77,107	36,624	38,664	30,815
1982	243,941	17,118	108,202	60,835	38,153	39,658	34,304
1983	258,048	18,186	105,765	53,591	40,854	44,934	42,033

Table US.12   Value of exports by commodity group, 1900–83

	Total exports (incl. re-exports)	Food, feeds & beverages	Industrial supplies & materials	of which: Fuels & lubricants	Capital goods (excl. autos)	Consumer goods (excl. autos)	Motor vehicles & parts
				$ mn			
1900	1,394	546	493	105		332	
1901	1,488	583	559	102		318	
1902	1,382	514	520	103		322	
1903	1,420	508	557	100		327	
1904	1,461	445	642	118		349	
1905	1,519	401	689	119		402	
1906	1,744	524	733	124		460	
1907	1,881	513	860	132		481	
1908	1,861	521	824	155		489	
1909	1,663	439	760	152		440	
1910	1,745	369	842	151		499	
1911	2,049	385	1,030	153		598	
1912	2,204	419	1,079	179		672	
1913	2,466	503	1,149	218		776	
1914	2,365	430	1,174	225		725	
1915	2,769	962	947	206		807	
1916	5,483	1,069	1,728	294		2,625	
1917	6,234	1,316	2,148	394		2,706	
1918	6,149	1,953	2,025	491		2,069	
1919	7,920	2,641	2,545	503		2,564	
1920	8,228	2,035	2,841	953		3,205	
1921	4,485	1,358	1,394	572		1,627	
1922	3,832	1,047	1,426	442		1,292	
1923	4,167	840	1,772	533		1,478	
1924	4,591	966	1,944	560		1,588	
1925	4,910	890	2,854	581	415	287	324
1926	4,809	835	2,784	759	445	289	328
1927	4,865	883	2,685	597	478	287	397
1928	5,128	762	2,879	627	543	308	509
1929	5,240	753	2,827	668	657	343	547
1930	3,843	542	2,111	585	547	255	284
1931	2,424	374	1,321	336	326	176	152
1932	1,611	243	996	254	131	102	78
1933	1,674	204	1,105	241	134	96	92
1934	2,133	224	1,308	285	218	127	192
1935	2,283	216	1,372	303	265	145	232
1936	2,456	203	1,424	322	342	182	246
1937	3,249	283	1,899	445	509	217	354
1938	3,094	433	1,560	446	528	202	277
1939	3,177	321	1,670	452	583	219	260
1940	4,021	246	2,045	397	954	234	259
1941	5,020	...	...	...	...	...	...
1942	8,003	...	...	...	...	...	...
1943	12,842	...	...	...	...	...	...
1944	14,162	...	...	...	...	...	...
1945	9,585	...	...	...	...	...	...
1946	9,770	2,206	3,864	752	1,660	1,084	556
1947	15,359	3,178	5,997	1,275	3,199	1,333	1,153
1948	12,654	2,659	4,865	1,149	2,626	1,033	939
1949	12,053	2,335	4,877	870	2,562	923	772
1950	10,277	1,482	4,358	777	2,144	850	746
1951	15,038	2,433	6,190	1,392	2,526	1,111	1,218
1952	15,203	2,201	5,553	1,303	2,812	1,015	1,024
1953	15,775	1,838	4,826	1,041	2,929	1,086	998
1954	15,112	1,713	5,479	970	2,919	1,097	1,072
1955	15,553	2,119	6,065	1,141	3,071	1,134	1,276
1956	19,096	2,807	7,383	1,508	3,834	1,246	1,395
1957	20,859	2,781	8,669	1,839	4,487	1,336	1,349
1958	17,912	2,590	6,436	1,092	4,752	1,314	1,123
1959	17,642	2,871	6,146	868	4,617	1,371	1,187
1960	20,600	3,170	7,924	841	5,511	1,396	1,266
1961	21,037	3,418	7,705	772	5,910	1,441	1,188
1962	21,714	3,829	7,132	806	6,443	1,455	1,301
1963	23,387	4,282	7,822	953	6,604	1,558	1,468
1964	26,650	4,849	9,185	924	7,463	1,751	1,729
1965	27,521	4,928	8,917	895	8,039	1,799	1,929
1966	30,430	5,489	9,613	902	8,892	2,035	2,354
1967	31,622	4,998	9,971	1,150	9,913	2,111	2,784
1968	34,636	4,813	11,004	1,081	11,072	2,334	3,453
1969	38,006	4,688	11,776	1,220	12,346	2,576	3,888
1970	43,246	5,849	13,704	1,698	14,442	2,734	3,652
1971	44,181	6,110	12,703	1,702	15,372	2,913	4,698
1972	49,813	7,500	13,858	1,705	16,791	3,510	5,160
1973	71,453	15,089	19,630	1,961	21,663	4,714	6,416
1974	98,641	18,489	29,802	3,627	30,398	6,284	8,352
1975	108,112	19,086	29,651	4,753	36,269	6,476	10,240
1976	115,419	19,712	31,864	4,684	38,678	7,916	11,372
1977	121,293	19,591	34,169	4,763	39,312	8,817	12,286
1978	143,766	25,032	38,800	4,502	45,948	10,308	14,621
1979	182,024	29,617	57,046	6,676	57,510	12,485	16,698
1980	220,782	35,313	70,211	8,775	72,600	16,249	16,168
1981	233,739	37,888	67,300	10,725	80,173	15,868	18,362
1982	212,275	31,352	61,483	13,008	72,678	14,307	15,914
1983	200,538	30,940	56,461	9,857	67,248	13,444	17,044

Table US.13 Value of exports and imports by areas, 1900–83

	Europe		of which: UK		Germany		Rest of America		Asia		of which: Japan	
	Exports to	Imports from	Exports to	Imports from	Exports to	Imports from	Exports to	Imports from	Exports to	Imports from	Exports to	Imports from
							$ mn					
1900	1,040	441	534	160	187	97	227	224	68	146	29	33
1901	1,137	430	631	143	192	100	241	255	53	122	19	29
1902	1,008	475	549	166	173	102	242	271	69	136	21	38
1903	1,029	547	524	190	194	120	256	297	62	159	21	44
1904	1,058	499	537	166	215	109	286	319	65	156	25	47
1905	1,021	541	523	176	194	118	318	378	135	175	52	52
1906	1,200	633	583	210	235	135	383	375	111	192	38	53
1907	1,298	747	608	246	257	162	432	424	101	224	39	69
1908	1,284	608	581	190	277	143	409	364	113	191	41	68
1909	1,147	654	515	209	235	144	387	418	83	207	27	70
1910	1,136	806	506	271	250	169	479	503	78	210	22	66
1911	1,308	768	577	261	287	163	566	488	105	231	37	79
1912	1,342	820	564	273	307	171	648	549	141	249	53	81
1913	1,479	893	597	296	332	189	763	580	140	298	58	92
1914	1,486	896	594	294	345	190	654	650	141	305	51	107
1915	1,971	614	912	256	29	91	576	734	139	272	41	99
1916	3,813	633	1,887	305	2	6	1,145	1,086	388	551	109	182
1917	4,062	551	2,009	280	—	—	1,573	1,471	469	821	186	254
1918	3,859	318	2,061	149	—	—	1,628	1,585	498	939	274	302
1919	5,188	751	2,279	309	93	11	1,738	1,844	772	1,108	366	410
1920	4,466	1,228	1,825	514	311	89	2,553	2,424	872	1,397	378	415
1921	2,364	765	942	239	372	80	1,403	1,051	533	618	238	251
1922	2,083	991	856	357	316	117	1,142	1,181	449	827	222	354
1923	2,093	1,157	882	404	317	161	1,355	1,469	511	1,020	267	347
1924	2,445	1,096	983	366	440	139	1,404	1,461	515	931	253	340
1925	2,604	1,239	1,034	413	470	164	1,541	1,499	487	1,319	230	384
1926	2,310	1,278	973	383	364	198	1,620	1,580	565	1,409	261	401
1927	2,314	1,265	840	358	482	201	1,691	1,504	560	1,268	258	402
1928	2,375	1,249	847	349	467	222	1,802	1,530	655	1,169	288	384
1929	2,341	1,334	848	330	410	255	1,934	1,621	643	1,279	259	432
1930	1,838	911	678	210	278	177	1,357	1,195	448	854	165	279
1931	1,187	641	456	135	166	127	750	824	386	574	156	206
1932	784	390	288	75	134	74	462	539	292	362	135	134
1933	850	463	312	111	140	78	455	520	292	425	143	128
1934	950	490	383	115	109	69	648	628	401	489	210	119
1935	1,029	599	433	155	92	78	706	776	378	605	203	153
1936	1,043	718	440	200	102	80	821	910	399	708	204	172
1937	1,360	843	536	203	126	92	1,158	1,113	580	967	289	204
1938	1,326	567	521	118	107	65	1,040	753	517	570	240	127
1939	1,290	617	505	149	46	52	1,131	898	562	700	232	161
1940	1,645	390	1,011	155	—	5	1,501	1,089	619	981	227	158
1941	1,847	281	1,637	136	—	3	2,047	1,657	625	1,088	60	78
1942	4,009	220	2,529	134	—	—	2,205	1,762	688	340	—	—
1943	7,633	240	4,505	105	—	—	2,418	2,458	838	235	—	—
1944	9,364	289	5,243	84	—	—	2,627	2,965	996	322	—	—
1945	5,515	409	2,193	90	2	1	2,564	2,874	849	407	—	—
1946	4,122	804	855	158	83	3	3,684	2,762	1,327	887	102	81
1947	5,670	817	1,103	205	128	6	6,199	3,401	2,330	1,055	415[a]	35
1948	4,279	1,121	644	290	863	32	5,307	4,100	2,130	1,346	325[a]	63
1949	4,118	925	700	228	822	46	4,861	3,995	2,256	1,240	468	82
1950	3,306	1,449	548	335	440	104	4,902	5,064	1,540	1,638	418	182
1951	5,121	2,119	1,000	466	521	233	6,607	5,826	2,410	1,983	601	205
1952	5,089	2,029	787	485	450	212	6,682	6,025	2,541	1,813	633	229
1953	5,711	2,335	826	546	363	277	6,514	6,117	2,783	1,626	686	262
1954	5,118	2,083	808	501	505	278	6,521	5,896	2,577	1,467	693	279
1955	5,126	2,453	1,006	616	607	366	6,903	6,262	2,581	1,876	683	432
1956	6,437	2,963	985	726	943	494	8,243	6,856	3,418	1,996	998	558
1957	6,844	3,147	1,164	766	1,330	607	9,001	7,048	3,961	1,985	1,319	601
1958	5,570	3,341	905	864	888	629	7,999	6,703	3,411	1,984	987	667
1959	5,559	4,607	1,097	1,137	880	920	7,692	7,071	3,284	2,603	1,079	1,029
1960	7,406	4,268	1,487	993	1,275	897	7,684	6,864	4,186	2,722	1,447	1,149
1961	7,371	4,141	1,206	898	1,343	856	7,673	6,995	4,653	2,583	1,837	1,055
1962	7,758	4,621	1,128	1,005	1,581	962	7,724	7,591	4,676	2,960	1,574	1,358
1963	8,738	4,811	1,213	1,079	1,582	1,003	7,944	7,850	5,448	3,192	1,844	1,498
1964	9,436	5,307	1,532	1,143	1,606	1,171	9,207	8,390	5,802	3,620	2,009	1,768
1965	9,364	6,292	1,615	1,405	1,650	1,341	9,917	9,212	6,012	4,528	2,080	2,414
1966	10,003	7,857	1,737	1,786	1,674	1,796	11,429	10,829	6,733	5,276	2,364	2,963
1967	10,298	8,227	1,960	1,710	1,706	1,955	11,883	11,741	7,146	5,348	2,695	2,999
1968	11,347	10,337	2,289	2,058	1,709	2,721	13,411	14,148	7,582	6,911	2,954	4,054
1969	12,642	10,334	2,335	2,120	2,142	2,603	14,713	15,547	8,261	8,275	3,490	4,888
1970	14,817	11,395	2,536	2,194	2,741	3,127	15,612	16,928	10,023	9,621	4,652	5,875
1971	14,562	12,881	2,369	2,499	2,831	3,651	16,850	18,730	9,855	11,780	4,055	7,259
1972	16,181	15,744	2,658	2,987	2,808	4,250	19,690	21,930	11,297	15,117	4,963	9,064
1973	23,161	19,812	3,564	3,657	3,756	5,345	25,033	27,322	18,419	18,157	8,313	9,676
1974	30,070	24,625	4,574	4,061	4,985	6,324	35,745	40,325	25,785	27,345	10,679	12,338
1975	32,732	21,623	4,527	3,784	5,194	5,381	38,843	37,796	28,223	27,055	9,563	11,268
1976	35,901	23,640	4,801	4,254	5,731	5,592	41,074	43,356	29,729	39,367	10,145	15,504
1977	37,304	28,802	5,951	5,141	5,989	7,238	43,751	50,697	31,436	49,312	10,529	18,550
1978	43,608	36,483	7,116	6,514	6,957	9,962	50,394	56,473	39,630	58,264	12,885	24,458
1979	54,342	41,681	10,635	8,028	8,478	10,955	61,555	68,509	48,771	66,739	17,581	26,248
1980	67,512	46,602	12,694	9,842	10,960	11,693	74,114	78,687	60,168	80,299	20,790	30,714
1981	69,715	53,410	12,439	12,835	10,277	11,379	81,667	85,436	63,849	92,033	21,823	37,612
1982	63,664	53,413	10,645	13,095	9,291	11,975	67,312	84,467	64,822	85,170	20,966	37,744
1983	58,871	55,243	10,621	12,470	8,737	12,695	63,970	96,873	63,813	91,464	21,894	41,183

a Includes shipments under Army Civilian Program – $354 mn in 1947 and $246 mn in 1948.

Table US.14 Balance of payments, 1900–83

	Imports	Exports	Investment income		Net military transactions	Net travel & transport	Other services	Unilateral transfers	Current balance
			Receipts	Payments					
					$ mn				
1900	869	1,623	38	137	...	−148	...	−95	412
1901	912	1,585	47	135	...	−147	...	−104	334
1902	996	1,473	57	137	...	−139	...	−105	153
1903	1,019	1,575	67	139	...	−144	...	−115	225
1904	1,062	1,563	70	141	...	−151	...	−127	152
1905	1,215	1,751	76	145	...	−169	...	−133	165
1906	1,365	1,921	86	148	...	−198	...	−147	149
1907	1,469	2,051	87	153	...	−220	...	−177	119
1908	1,159	1,880	89	160	...	−223	...	−192	235
1909	1,522	1,857	100	164	...	−245	...	−187	−161
1910	1,609	1,995	108	172	...	−276	...	−204	−158
1911	1,576	2,228	114	190	...	−302	...	−224	50
1912	1,866	2,532	123	197	...	−335	...	−212	45
1913	1,829	2,600	137	210	...	−324	...	−207	167
1914	1,815	2,230	145	200	...	−304	...	−170	−114
1915	1,813	3,686	200	136	...	−189	...	−150	1,598
1916	2,423	5,560	250	118	...	−167	...	−150	2,952
1917	3,006	6,398	350	100	...	−167	...	−205	3,270
1918	3,103	6,432	450	100	−1,018	−203	...	−268	2,190
1919	3,995	8,891	719	130	−757	224	−84	−1,044	3,824
1920	5,384	8,481	596	120	−123	148	−75	−679	2,844
1921	2,572	4,586	445	105	−65	−64	−103	−509	1,613
1922	3,184	3,929	670	105	−42	−237	−34	−352	645
1923	3,866	4,266	840	130	−33	−219	−16	−365	477
1924	3,684	4,741	762	140	−36	−272	−20	−364	987
1925	4,291	5,011	912	170	−39	−337	1	−403	684
1926	4,500	4,922	953	200	−43	−307	1	−381	445
1927	4,240	4,982	981	240	−38	−343	−29	−357	716
1928	4,159	5,249	1,080	275	−44	−415	−59	−365	1,012
1929	4,463	5,347	1,139	330	−50	−463	−32	−377	771
1930	3,104	3,929	1,040	295	−49	−486	−3	−342	690
1931	2,120	2,494	766	220	−48	−366	10	−319	197
1932	1,343	1,667	527	135	−47	−278	16	−238	169
1933	1,510	1,736	437	115	−41	−179	30	−208	150
1934	1,763	2,238	437	135	−34	−200	58	−172	429
1935	2,462	2,404	521	155	−41	−211	72	−182	−54
1936	2,546	2,590	569	270	−38	−269	79	−208	−93
1937	3,181	3,451	577	295	−41	−343	129	−235	62
1938	2,173	3,243	585	200	−41	−209	86	−182	1,109
1939	2,409	3,347	541	230	−46	−219	82	−178	888
1940	2,698	4,124	564	−210	−61	−27	27	−210	1,509
1941	3,416	5,343	544	−187	−162	77	211	−1,136	1,274
1942	3,499	9,187	614	−158	−953	353	969	−6,336	177
1943	4,599	15,115	509	−155	−1,763	678	1,253	−12,907	−1,869
1944	5,043	16,969	573	−161	−1,982	799	1,297	−14,142	−1,690
1945	5,245	12,473	589	−231	−2,434	741	148	−7,113	−1,072
1946	5,067	11,764	772	−212	−493	733	310	−2,922	4,885
1947	5,973	16,097	1,102	−245	−455	946	145	−2,625	8,992
1948	7,557	13,265	1,921	−437	−799	374	175	−4,525	2,417
1949	6,874	12,213	1,831	−476	−621	230	208	−5,638	873
1950	9,081	10,203	2,068	−559	−576	−120	242	−4,017	−1,840
1951	11,176	14,243	2,633	−583	−1,270	298	254	−3,515	884
1952	10,838	13,449	2,751	−555	−2,054	83	309	−2,531	614
1953	10,975	12,412	2,736	−624	−2,423	−238	307	−2,481	−1,286
1954	10,353	12,929	2,929	−582	−2,460	−269	305	−2,280	219
1955	11,527	14,424	3,406	−676	−2,701	−297	299	−2,498	430
1956	12,803	17,556	3,837	−735	−2,788	−361	447	−2,423	2,730
1957	13,291	19,562	4,180	−796	−2,841	−189	482	−2,345	4,762
1958	12,952	16,414	3,790	−825	−3,135	−633	486	−2,361	784
1959	15,310	16,458	4,132	−1,061	−2,805	−821	573	−2,448	−1,282
1960	14,758	19,650	4,616	−1,237	−2,752	−964	579	−2,308	2,824
1961	14,357	20,108	4,999	−1,245	−2,596	−978	594	−2,524	3,822
1962	16,260	20,781	5,618	−1,324	−2,449	−1,152	809	−2,638	3,387
1963	17,048	22,272	6,157	−1,561	−2,304	−1,309	960	−2,754	4,414
1964	18,700	25,501	6,824	−1,784	−2,133	−1,146	1,041	−2,781	6,823
1965	21,510	26,461	7,437	−2,088	−2,122	−1,280	1,387	−2,854	5,432
1966	25,493	29,310	7,528	−2,481	−2,935	−1,331	1,365	−2,932	3,031
1967	26,866	30,666	8,020	−2,747	−3,266	−1,750	1,612	−3,125	2,583
1968	32,991	33,626	9,368	−3,378	−3,143	−1,548	1,630	−2,952	611
1969	35,807	36,414	10,912	−4,869	−3,328	−1,763	1,833	−2,994	399
1970	39,866	42,469	11,747	−5,516	−3,354	−2,038	2,180	−3,294	2,331
1971	45,579	43,319	12,707	−5,436	−2,893	−2,345	2,495	−3,701	−1,433
1972	55,797	49,381	14,764	−6,572	−3,420	−3,063	2,766	−3,854	−5,795
1973	70,499	71,410	21,808	−9,655	−2,070	−3,158	3,184	−3,881	7,140
1974	103,811	98,306	27,587	−12,084	−1,653	−3,184	3,986	−7,186	1,962
1975	98,185	107,088	25,351	−12,564	−746	−2,792	4,598	−4,613	18,116
1976	124,228	114,745	29,286	−13,311	559	−2,558	4,711	−4,998	4,207
1977	151,907	120,816	32,179	−14,217	1,528	−3,565	5,272	−4,617	−14,511
1978	176,020	142,054	42,245	−21,680	621	−3,573	6,013	−5,106	−15,446
1979	212,028	184,473	64,132	−32,914	−1,778	−2,935	5,735	−5,649	−964
1980	249,781	224,269	72,506	−42,063	−2,237	−997	7,277	−7,077	1,898
1981	265,086	237,085	86,411	−52,359	−1,115	144	8,048	−6,833	6,294
1982	247,667	211,198	83,862	−56,059	195	−1,008	8,339	−8,058	−9,199
1983	261,312	200,257	77,003	−53,495	515	−4,584	8,704	−8,651	−41,563

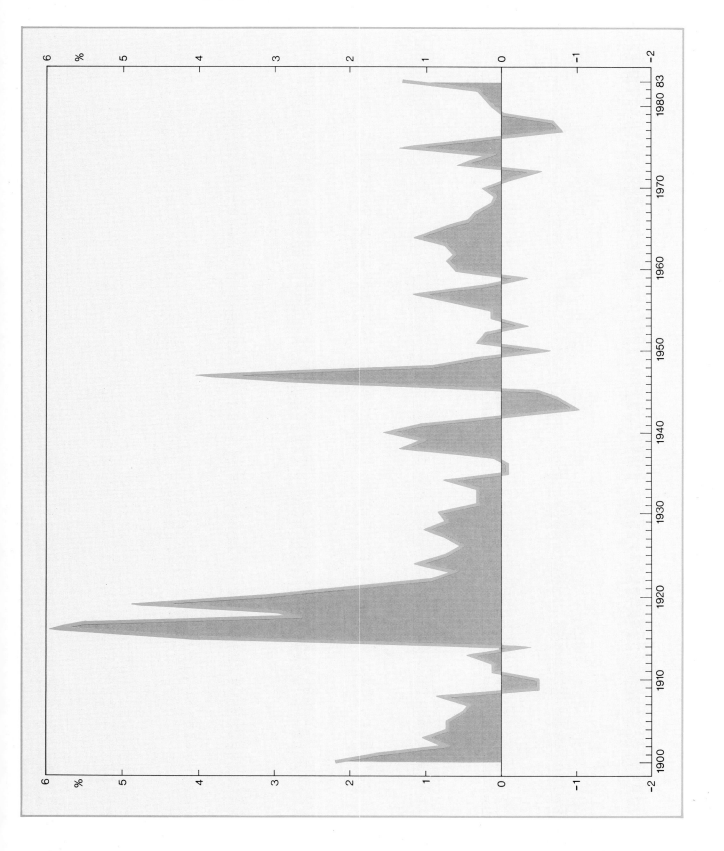

Chart US.14   Balance of payments, current balance as percent of gross national product, 1900–83

Table US.15 Finance, 1900–83

	Share prices		Interest rates				Money supply M1	Consumer credit outstanding	Ratio of consumer credit to PDY
	Standard & Poor's index	Dow Jones average	3 month Treasury bill yield	US govt bonds yield	Federal Reserve Bank High	Federal Reserve Bank Low			
	1980 = 100	$ per share	%	%	%		$ bn	$ mn	%
1900	5·2	...	...	...	3·94		6·50	...	...
1901	6·6	...	...	...	4·24		7·46	...	...
1902	7·1	...	...	...	5·05		8·14	...	...
1903	6·1	...	...	...	4·84		8·65	...	...
1904	5·9	...	...	...	3·10		9·12	...	...
1905	7·6	...	...	...	3·82		10·20	...	...
1906	8·1	...	...	...	5·71		10·99	...	...
1907	6·6	...	...	...	6·49		11·55	...	...
1908	6·6	...	...	...	3·24		11·48	...	...
1909	8·2	...	...	...	3·26		12·73	...	...
1910	7·9	...	...	...	4·03		13·36	...	...
1911	7·8	...	...	...	3·22		14·16	...	...
1912	8·0	...	...	...	4·16		15·17	...	...
1913	7·2	...	...	...	4·64		15·75	...	...
1914	6·8	...	...	...	6·00	5·00	16·41	...	...
1915	7·0	...	...	...	5·00	4·00	12·48	...	...
1916	8·0	...	...	...	4·00	3·00	14·70	...	...
1917	7·2	...	...	...	3·50	3·00	17·08	...	...
1918	6·4	...	...	...	4·00	3·50	18·96	...	...
1919	7·4	...	...	4·73	4·75	4·00	21·79	2,642	...
1920	6·7	...	...	5·32	7·00	4·75	23·73	2,964	...
1921	5·8	...	...	5·09	7·00	4·50	21·51	2,966	...
1922	7·1	...	...	4·30	4·50	4·00	21·67	3,166	...
1923	7·2	...	...	4·36	4·50	4·00	22·93	3,652	...
1924	7·6	...	...	4·06	4·50	3·00	23·67	4,025	...
1925	9·4	...	...	3·86	3·50	3·00	25·66	4,715	...
1926	10·6	...	...	3·68	4·00	3·50	26·18	5,227	...
1927	12·9	...	...	3·34	4·00	3·50	26·10	5,344	...
1928	16·8	...	...	3·33	5·00	3·50	26·38	6,258	...
1929	21·9	125·43	...	3·60	6·00	4·50	26·64	7,116	8·6
1930	17·7	95·64	...	3·29	4·50	2·00	25·76	6,351	8·7
1931	11·5	55·47	1·40	3·34	3·50	1·50	24·14	5,315	8·3
1932	5·8	26·82	0·88	3·68	3·50	2·50	21·11	4,026	8·2
1933	7·5	36·00	0·52	3·31	3·50	2·00	19·91	3,885	8·6
1934	8·3	39·16	0·26	3·12	2·00	1·50	21·86	4,218	8·0
1935	8·9	41·97	0·14	2·79	1·50	1·50	25·88	5,190	8·9
1936	13·0	58·98	0·14	2·69	1·50	1·50	29·55	6,375	9·7
1937	13·0	58·08	0·45	2·74	1·50	1·00	30·91	6,948	9·7
1938	9·7	43·10	0·05	2·61	1·00	1·00	30·52	6,370	9·8
1939	10·2	48·01	0·02	2·41	1·00	1·00	34·15	7,222	10·3
1940	9·3	45·28	0·01	2·26	1·00	1·00	39·65	8,338	11·0
1941	8·3	41·22	0·10	2·05	1·00	1·00	46·52	9,172	10·0
1942	7·3	36·04	0·33	2·46	1·00	0·50	55·36	5,983	5·1
1943	9·7	46·39	0·37	2·47	1·00	0·50	72·24	4,901	3·7
1944	10·5	51·39	0·38	2·48	1·00	0·50	85·34	5,111	3·5
1945	12·8	63·72	0·38	2·37	1·00	0·50	99·23	5,665	3·8
1946	14·4	71·01	0·38	2·19	1·00	0·50	106·46	8,384	5·3
1947	12·8	63·39	0·59	2·25	1·00	1·00	111·79	11,598	6·9
1948	13·1	66·32	1·04	2·44	1·50	1·00	112·31	14,447	7·7
1949	12·8	64·37	1·10	2·31	1·50	1·50	111·16	17,364	9·3
1950	15·5	77·69	1·22	2·32	1·75	1·50	114·14	21,471 / 24,956	10·4 / 12·1
1951	18·8	93·98	1·55	2·57	1·75	1·75	119·23	26,496	11·7
1952	20·6	103·71	1·77	2·68	1·75	1·75	125·22	31,727	13·3
1953	20·8	107·11	1·93	2·94	2·00	1·75	128·34	35,795	14·2
1954	25·0	124·24	0·95	2·55	2·00	1·50	130·27	37,133	14·4
1955	34·1	161·34	1·75	2·84	2·50	1·50	134·44	44,123	16·0
1956	39·3	174·54	2·66	3·08	3·00	2·50	136·02	47,984	16·4
1957	37·4	164·83	3·27	3·47	3·50	3·00	136·75	50,841	16·5
1958	38·9	169·27	1·84	3·43	3·00	1·75	138·35	51,284	16·1
1959	48·3	212·78	3·41	4·07	4·00	2·50	143·70	59,075	17·5
1960	47·1	204·57	2·93	4·01	4·00	3·00	143·5	63,525	18·0
1961	55·8	232·44	2·38	3·90	3·00	3·00	146·5	66,134	18·1
1962	52·5	221·07	2·78	3·95	3·00	3·00	149·2	72,351	18·7
1963	58·9	253·67	3·16	4·00	3·50	3·00	154·7	81,055	20·0
1964	68·5	294·23	3·55	4·15	4·00	3·50	160·2	90,713	20·6
1965	74·3	318·50	3·95	4·21	4·50	4·00	169·5	101,063	21·2
1966	71·8	308·70	4·88	4·66	4·50	4·50	173·7	107,413	20·9
1967	77·4	314·79	4·32	4·85	4·50	4·00	185·1	112,676	20·6
1968	83·1	322·19	5·34	5·25	5·50	4·50	199·4	123,790	20·9
1969	82·4	301·35	6·68	6·10	6·00	5·50	205·8	134,129	21·0
1970	70·1	243·92	6·46	6·58	6·00	5·50	216·5	139,355	20·0
1971	82·8	298·12	4·35	5·74	5·25	4·50	230·6	155,537	20·7
1972	92·0	319·36	4·07	5·63	4·50	4·50	251·9	175,286	21·6
1973	90·5	286·73	7·04	6·30	7·50	4·50	265·8	200,894	22·0
1974	69·8	237·33	7·89	6·98	8·00	7·50	277·4	210,634	21·1
1975	72·6	247·25	5·84	6·98	7·75	6·00	291·0	219,772	20·1
1976	85·9	303·91	4·99	6·78	6·00	5·25	310·4	244,932	20·5
1977	82·7	301·70	5·27	7·06	6·00	5·25	335·5	284,599	21·7
1978	80·9	283·63	7·22	7·89	9·50	6·00	363·2	332,849	22·6
1979	86·8	293·50	10·04	8·74	12·00	9·50	389·0	377,486	22·9
1980	100·0	328·20	11·51	10·81	13·00	10·00	414·9	381,689	20·9
1981	107·9	364·61	14·03	12·87	14·00	12·00	441·9	405,654	19·8
1982	100·8	345·40	10·61	12·23	12·00	8·50	480·5	423,852	19·5
1983	135·1	472·24	8·61	10·84	8·50	8·50	525·3	*473,507*	20·2

Chart US.15   Share prices and interest rates, 1900–83

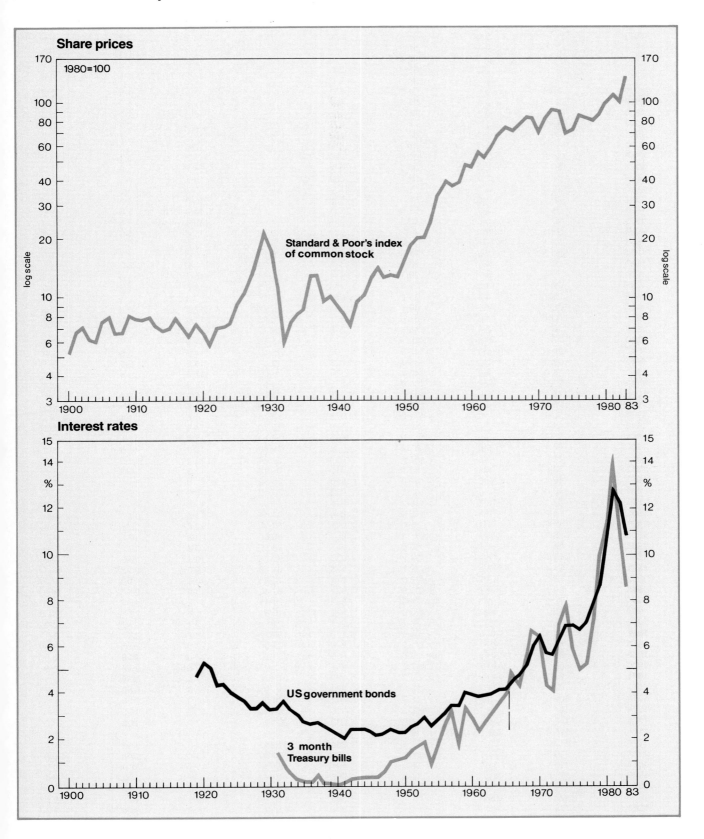

Share prices

1980=100

Standard & Poor's index
of common stock

log scale

Interest rates

US government bonds

3 month
Treasury bills

	Vehicle registrations		Railways		Airways	Energy consumption		
	Passenger cars	Goods vehicles	bn passenger km	bn freight ton km	bn passenger km	Coal	Crude petroleum	Natural gas
	mn					quadrillion Btu		
1900	0·008	—	25·7	232	—	6·8	0·2	0·3
1901	0·015	—	28·0	240	—	7·5	0·25	0·3
1902	0·023	—	31·7	257	—	7·8	0·4	0·3
1903	0·033	—	33·6	283	—	9·2	0·4	0·3
1904	0·055	—	35·2	286	—	9·0	0·5	0·3
1905	0·077	0·001	38·3	304	—	10·0	0·6	0·4
1906	0·106	0·002	40·5	353	—	10·5	0·6	0·4
1907	0·140	0·003	44·6	387	—	12·2	0·8	0·4
1908	0·194	0·004	46·8	356	—	10·5	0·8	0·4
1909	0·306	0·01	46·8	358	—	11·7	0·8	0·5
1910	0·458	0·01	52·0	417	—	12·7	1·0	0·5
1911	0·619	0·02	52·0	415	—	12·4	1·0	0·5
1912	0·902	0·04	53·3	432	—	13·4	1·1	0·6
1913	1·19	0·07	55·8	494	—	14·2	1·2	0·6
1914	1·66	0·10	57·0	473	—	12·9	1·3	0·6
1915	2·33	0·2	52·3	453	—	13·3	1·4	0·7
1916	3·37	0·3	55·2 / 56·6	561 / 598	—	14·7	1·5	0·8
1917	4·73	0·4	64·5	651	—	16·2	1·8	0·9
1918	5·56	0·6	69·5	669	—	17·0	1·9	0·8
1919	6·68	0·9	75·3	600	—	13·8	2·2	0·8
1920	8·13	1·1	76·3	677	—	15·5	2·7	0·8
1921	9·21	1·3	60·7	507	—	12·3	2·7	0·7
1922	10·70	1·6	57·6	559	—	12·6	3·1	0·8
1923	13·25	1·8	61·6	680	—	15·8	4·1	1·0
1924	15·44	2·2	58·3	641	—	14·7	3·9	1·2
1925	17·5	2·6	58·2	682	—	14·7	4·3	1·2
1926	19·3	2·9	57·4	731	—	15·9	4·5	1·3
1927	20·3	3·0	54·4	706	—	15·0	4·6	1·5
1928	21·4	3·3	51·0	713	—	14·9	5·0	1·6
1929	23·1	3·6	50·2	736	—	15·4	5·5	1·9
1930	23·0	3·7	43·3	631	0·16	13·6	5·9	2·0
1931	22·4	3·7	35·2	508	0·19	11·2	5·2	1·7
1932	20·9	3·5	27·4	384	0·24	9·3	4·7	1·6
1933	20·7	3·5	26·4	410	0·32	9·6	5·0	1·6
1934	21·5	3·7	29·1	441	0·37	10·4	5·0	1·8
1935	22·6	4·0	29·8	464	0·58	10·6	5·7	2·0
1936	24·2	4·3	36·2	558	0·77	12·0	6·3	2·2
1937	25·5	4·6	39·7	594	0·76	12·6	6·8	2·5
1938	25·3	4·6	34·9	477	0·85	10·0	6·7	2·3
1939	26·2	4·8	36·5	548	1·22	11·1	7·1	2·5
1940	27·5	5·0	38·3	613	1·85	12·5	7·7	2·7
1941	29·6	5·3	47·3	782	2·49	14·2	8·6	2·9
1942	28·0	5·0	86·4	1,048	2·67	15·6	8·0	3·1
1943	26·0	4·9	140·7	1,194	3·02	17·0	8·6	3·5
1944	25·6	4·9	154·0	1,212	4·01	17·0	9·7	3·8
1945	25·8	5·2	147·7	1,118	6·13	16·0	10·1	4·0
1946	28·2	6·2	104·3	973	11·29	14·5	10·5	4·1
1947	30·8	7·0	74·0	1,076	12·74	15·8	11·4	4·5
1948	33·4	7·7	66·3	1,048	12·70	14·9	12·6	5·0
1949	36·5	8·2	56·5	865	14·21	12·6	12·1	5·3
1950	40·4	8·8	51·2	968	16·48	12·9	13·5	6·2
1951	42·7	9·2	55·7	1,063	21·24	13·2	14·8	7·2
1952	43·8	9·4	54·7	1,010	25·13	11·9	15·3	7·8
1953	46·4	9·8	51·0	996	29·35	11·9	16·1	8·2
1954	48·5	10·0	47·1	903	33·16	10·2	16·1	8·5
1955	52·1	10·6	45·9	1,025	39·18	11·5	17·5	9·2
1956	54·2	10·9	45·4	1,064	44·44	11·8	18·6	9·8
1957	55·9	11·2	41·7	1,017	50·30	11·2	18·6	10·4
1958	56·9	11·4	37·5	907	50·68	9·8	19·2	11·0
1959	59·5	11·9	35·6	947	58·52	9·8	19·7	12·0
1960	61·7	12·2	34·3	935	62·53	10·1	19·9	12·6
1961	63·4	12·5	32·7	925	64·09	9·8	20·2	13·1
1962	66·1	13·1	32·0	974	70·41	10·1	21·0	13·9
1963	69·1	13·7	29·8	1,022	81·03	10·5	21·6	14·6
1964	72·0	14·3	29·4	1,082	94·11	11·2	22·2	15·5
1965	75·3	15·1	28·0	1,441	110·51	11·8	23·1	16·0
1966	78·1	15·8	27·7	1,221	128·54	12·7	25·7	17·3
1967	80·4	16·5	24·6	1,189	158·89	12·2	25·2	18·1
1968	83·6	17·3	21·2	1,226	183·36	12·6	26·8	19·4
1969	86·9	18·2	19·6	1,265	201·80	12·6	28·3	20·9
1970	89·2	19·2	17·4	1,251	211·92	12·6	29·4	21·9
1971	92·7	20·3	14·3	1,220	218·28	12·0	30·5	22·5
1972	97·1	21·7	13·8	1,280	245·23	12·4	32·9	22·7
1973	102·0	23·7	15·0	1,403	260·59	13·3	34·8	22·5
1974	104·8	25·1	16·5	1,393	262·14	12·9	32·8	21·8
1975	106·7	26·2	15·9	1,233	261·96	12·9	32·8	20·0
1976	110·4	28·2	16·6	1,306	287·99	13·7	35·2	20·3
1977	112·3	30·1	16·6	1,364	310·86	14·0	37·2	19·9
1978	116·6	31·8	16·4	1,403	364·89	13·8	38·0	20·0
1979	118·4	33·4	18·0	1,494	421·56	15·1	37·1	20·7
1980	121·6	34·1	17·7	1,503	410·62	15·4	34·2	20·4
1981	123·5	35·0	...	1,488	400·32	16·0	32·0	19·9
1982	123·7	35·8	...	1,305	417·76	15·3	30·2	18·5
1983	125·4a	36·6a	...	1,354	452·37	15·9	30·0	17·4

a Provisional.

SOURCES

(For sources used in specific tables, see Notes.)

1 *Business Statistics.* Department of Commerce, Bureau of Economic Analysis, Washington, DC, 1979, 1982.

2 *Current Population Reports*, Series P-25, Nos. 875 (1980), 911 and 917 (1982), 929 and 930 (1983). Bureau of the Census, Washington, DC.

3 *Economic Report of the President.* US Government Printing Office, Washington, DC, 1984.

4 *Employment and Earnings.* Bureau of Labor Statistics, Washington, DC, monthly.

5 *Employment and Earnings in the United States, 1909–78.* Bureau of Labor Statistics, Washington, DC, 1979.

6 *Federal Reserve Bulletin.* Board of Governors, Federal Reserve System, Washington, DC, monthly.

7 Friedman, M and Schwartz, A, *Monetary Statistics of the United States.* National Bureau of Economic Research, Columbia University Press, 1970.

8 *Handbook of Methods for Surveys and Studies.* Bulletin 1910, Bureau of Labor Statistics, Washington, DC, 1976.

9 *Historical Statistics of the United States Colonial Times to 1970*, Vols I and II. Department of Commerce, Bureau of the Census, Washington, DC, 1975.

10 Kendrick, J W, *Productivity Trends in the United States.* National Bureau of Economic Research, Princeton University Press, 1961.

11 Kuznets, S, *Capital in the American Economy. Its Formation and Financing.* National Bureau of Economic Research, Princeton University Press, 1961.

12 Lipsey, Robert E, *Price and Quantity Trends in the Foreign Trade of the United States.* National Bureau of Economic Research/Princeton University Press, 1963.

13 Martin, Robert F, *National Income in the United States, 1799–1938.* National Industrial Conference Board Studies No. 241, New York, 1939.

14 *National Income and Product Accounts of the United States, 1929–1976. Statistical Tables.* Department of Commerce, Bureau of Economic Analysis, Washington, DC, 1981.

15 *National Income and Product Accounts of the United States, 1976–79.* Department of Commerce, Bureau of Economic Analysis, Washington, DC, 1982.

16 *Statistical Abstract of the United States.* Department of Commerce, Bureau of the Census, Washington, DC, annual.

17 *Supplement* for *Producer Prices and Price Indexes.* Bureau of Labor Statistics, Washington, DC, annual.

18 *Survey of Current Business.* Department of Commerce, Bureau of Economic Analysis, Washington, DC, June 1982, 1983 and 1984.

19 *Survey of Current Business.* Department of Commerce, Bureau of Economic Analysis, Washington, DC, July 1982, 1983 and 1984.

NOTES

Table US.1

Sources: **10, 14, 15, 19**

The figures from 1929 are official Department of Commerce estimates. From 1960 data for Alaska and Hawaii are included.

Government expenditure includes gross fixed capital formation by government enterprises but excludes their current outlays.

The figures for 1900–28 are based on constant price estimates in **11** adjusted to Department of Commerce concepts by Kendrick, **10**. The figures are five year moving averages and have been linked to the official estimates to give a rough conversion to 1972 prices. Each category of expenditure has been re-referenced to 1972 prices independently. A net figure for imports and exports of goods and services has been obtained as a residual; this includes any statistical discrepancy caused by the independent re-referencing of the component categories.

For further details of coverage and methodology of current series see **14** and, for the earlier series, **10** and **11**.

Table US.2

Sources: **1, 6, 14, 15, 19**

The sectors distinguished in US data are 'non-farm', 'housing', 'households and institutions', 'farm', 'government' and 'the rest of the world'. In this table 'non-farm', 'housing' and 'households and institutions' have been brought together under 'Business'.

Government: includes all federal, state and local government agencies except government enterprises which are included under 'Business'. Transactions with the rest of the world have not been included. For further details see **14**.

Industrial production: the index measures changes in the volume of output in the manufacturing, mining, and gas and electricity industries. The current index is based on a 1976 revision which widened the coverage of the index. Compiled by the Federal Reserve Board. For further details of coverage and methodology see **1**.

Output by industry (supplementary table): the industrial classification in this table is on an establishment basis and is in accordance with the Standard Industrial Classification (SIC) 1972. The first column is for gross *national* product; in the main table gross *domestic* product has been given.

Table US.3

Sources: **1, 6, 9, 16**

The US unit of measurement is short tons; the published figures of coal, steel and other metals have been converted to metric tons by using the factor 0·90719.

Coal: bituminous coal. From 1951 auger production is included. Based on detailed annual reports from producers.

Passenger cars: figures refer to factory sales and are for passenger cars only. Production of passenger cars was discontinued in February 1942 but some vehicles remaining in factory stocks were sold in subsequent war years. Production was resumed in July 1945 but no new cars were actually produced until 1946.

Chemicals: part of the current index of industrial production. Coverage of the index has changed over the period. For further details see **1**.

Metals: figures for copper, lead and zinc refer to the recoverable metal content of domestic mine output. Figures for lead in 1928 and 1929 exclude the output of Virginia and for 1900–06, figures for lead and zinc are for primary production refined from domestic and foreign ores. Figures for copper for 1900–05 represent smelter production from domestic ores; difference in the series is slight.

Table US.4

Sources: **11, 14, 15, 19**

Official Department of Commerce estimates have been used from 1929. The series for producers' durable equipment has been roughly divided into plant and machinery and transport equipment.

Non-residential construction: includes industrial, commercial, religious and educational buildings, hospitals and institutions, public utilities, farm and mining exploration. Includes brokers' commissions.

Plant and machinery: includes residential purchases of fixed durable equipment as well as industrial and commercial.

Transport equipment: includes trucks, buses and truck trailers, automobiles, ships and boats, railroad equipment and instruments.

Non-farm residential construction: include new houses, farm and non-farm, together with improvements to existing houses and brokers' commissions.

For the period 1900–28, constant price estimates (five year moving averages) by Kuznets, **11**, have been used as the basis of the series. They have been linked to the official series and roughly converted to 1972 prices. Each series has been linked separately; components may not therefore add to the total. The figures for the total also differ from those given in Table US.1, which have been adjusted to Department of Commerce concepts (see notes to that table).

For further details of coverage and methodology see **11** and **14**.

Table US.5

Sources: **13, 14, 15, 19**

Official estimates have been used from 1929.

Wages and salaries: include pay in cash and in kind. Retroactive wages are counted when paid rather than when earned.

Other income: employers' contributions to private pension funds on behalf of employees, group health and life insurance, proprietors' income and rent (adjusted for depreciation and stock appreciation), dividends, interest and transfer payments.

For the period 1900–29 (first lines), estimates by Martin, **13**.

Taxes: include income tax payments and personal contributions for social insurance and also non-tax payments such as passport fees, fines and penalties, donations and fees paid to schools and hospitals operated by the government.

Personal disposable income: personal income less tax and non-tax payments.

Gross trading profits: represents the profits that accrue to industry. No adjustment is made for capital gains or losses, changes in inventory values because of price changes, or receipt of domestic and foreign dividends, except those received by mutual life assurance companies.

Table US.6

Sources: **11, 14, 15, 19**

Official Department of Commerce estimates have been used since 1929, classified by major commodity groups. The groups used in this table cover the following.

Food: all food and beverages including canteen purchases, military purchases and food produced and consumed on farms, and all meals purchased outside the home.

Fuel: includes gasoline and oil, fuel oil and coal but not electricity and gas.

Consumer durables: includes furniture and household equipment, ophthalmic products, durable toys, sports equipment and jewellery.

Housing: includes owner occupied housing and rented dwellings.

Household operation: includes electricity and gas, telephone, domestic services, water and other sanitary services.

Other services: transport, personal care, medical care, personal business, recreation, private education, religious and welfare activities, net foreign travel.

For the period 1900–28, estimates for broad categories of consumers' expenditure by Kuznets, **11**, in five year moving averages, have been roughly converted to 1972 dollars. The broad groups used by Kuznets do not fully accord with Department of Commerce concepts or with the current classification; they have been included in the table to give approximate magnitudes. Kuznets's groups have been used in the tables as follows.

Kuznets's group	Commodity group in Table US.6
Perishables	Food and fuel
Durables	Consumer durables including motor vehicles and parts
Semi durables	Clothing and footwear
Services	Housing, household operation and other services

Table US.7

Sources: **9, 16, 17, 19**

Producer prices: the indices measure average changes in prices received in primary markets by producers of commodities in all stages of processing. Previously called the 'Wholesale price index'. The sample includes 2,800 commodities produced in manufacturing, agriculture, forestry and fishing, mining, gas, electricity and public utilities.

The industrial commodities index includes crude materials for further processing such as hides and skins, chemicals and allied products, and fuels. For further details of coverage and methodology see **17**.

Consumer prices: from 1978, the index measures changes in the price of a 'fixed basket' of goods and services based on expenditure patterns of urban families in 1972–73 (covering approximately 80 per cent of the total non-institutional civilian population). Before 1978, the index used in the table was based on the expenditure patterns of wage earners' and clerical workers' families – CPI (W) – covering about half the population included in the current index. The CPI (W) was based first on expenditure patterns in 1917–19; revisions were made in 1940, 1953 and 1964. For further details see **16**, 1983.

Unit value exports and imports indices: from 1922, these indices have been compiled by the US Bureau of International Commerce. They are chain indices, chained annually.

For the period 1900–21, the indices are based on estimates made by Lipsey, **12**, also published in **9**.

Table US.8

Sources: **2, 9, 16**

Total population: mid year estimates (1 July). Includes armed forces stationed overseas. From 1959 (second line), the figures include Alaska and Hawaii.

Geographical distribution: excludes armed forces stationed abroad, and figures are as at 1 April each year. Current definition of areas is as follows, but there have been boundary changes from time to time; see **16**, 1983, Appendix.

North-East: Maine, New Hampshire, Vermont, Massachusetts, Rhode Island, Connecticut, New York, New Jersey, Pennsylvania.

North Central: Ohio, Indiana, Illinois, Michigan, Wisconsin, Minnesota, Iowa, Missouri, North Dakota, South Dakota, Nebraska, Kansas.

South: Delaware, Maryland, District of Columbia, Virginia, West Virginia, North Carolina, South Carolina, Georgia, Florida, Kentucky, Tennessee, Alabama, Mississippi, Arkansas, Louisiana, Oklahoma, Texas.

West: Montana, Idaho, Wyoming, Colorado, New Mexico, Arizona, Utah, Nevada, Washington, Oregon, California, Alaska, Hawaii.

Table US.9

Sources: **3, 4, 5, 16, 19**

Number in civil work: all those in civilian employment, including employees and self employed.

Employed in agriculture: includes employees and self employed.

Employment by sector: the estimates include all full and part time wage and salary earners who worked during or received pay for any part of the pay period which includes the twelfth of each month. Based on reports from establishments. Does not include self employed, proprietors or domestic workers. Those on the establishment pay roll at the time of the survey are included even though they may be on strike, on leave or sick. Employment in the government sector relates to civilian employment only. Data are classified in accordance with the SIC 1972.

The information provided by periodic censuses is used as a benchmark to establish the level of employment, and the sample data provide information measuring the changes between censuses. The current series is adjusted to March 1982. For further details see **5** and **4**, February 1967.

'Services' includes finance, insurance and real estate, plus other services such as laundry and dry cleaning.

From 1947, the figures refer to those aged 16 and over; previously they included those aged 14 and over. From 1960, Alaska and Hawaii are included in the data.

Self employed: active proprietors or partners who devote a majority of their working hours to their unincorporated businesses. The industry breakdown is summarised in the table.

	Agriculture, etc.	Manufacturing	Construction	Other
	'000			
1980	1,689	363	1,186	5,427
1981	1,684	366	1,166	5,543
1982	1,681	358	1,131	5,757
1983	1,603	375	1,171	6,070

Table US.10

Sources: **3, 4, 5, 9, 16, 19**

Average weekly hours and earnings: based on reports of establishments and covering those on the payroll at the time of the survey. 'Hours' include paid hours for full and part time production and related workers. 'Earnings' figures include pay for overtime, holidays and vacations, and sick leave but not fringe benefits, bonuses (unless earned and paid regularly) or payments in kind. For further details see **4**, February, 1967.

Productivity indices: obtained by dividing output indices by the corresponding index of manhours. From 1947, the series have been compiled by the Bureau of Labor Statistics. For full details see **8**, Chapters 30 and 31.

For 1900–46, the series are based on those published in **9**, which in turn are based on estimates by Kendrick, **10**.

Unemployment: includes those not working during the survey week but who are available and currently looking for work. The sample consists of about 60,000 households selected to represent the total population aged 16 years and over. Households are interviewed on a rotating basis so that three quarters of the sample is the same for any two consecutive periods. From January 1967, the lower age limit was raised from 14 to 16 years and the figures were revised back to 1947. The unemployment percentage is the number of unemployed expressed as a percentage of the civilian labour force (i e including the self employed and the unemployed). For further details see **5** and **4**, February 1967.

Industrial disputes: present series (from 1982) includes all known stoppages in effect during the year arising out of labour disputes involving 1,000 or more workers and continuing for at least one full day or shift. Figures cover all workers made idle for as long as one shift in establishments directly involved even though they may not be active participants. Indirect or secondary effects are not included. Up to 1981, the figures cover all work stoppages in effect during the year involving six or more workers.

Table US.11

Sources: **9, 18**

US import data are classified in two ways: by broad end-use and by economic class. The first classification is used in this table from 1923. For 1900–22 the figures are based on classification by economic class but have been broadly grouped according to end-use category given in the table. For details of the differences see **9**, p. 879. From 1946, imports include silver ore and bullion, and for 1946–59 US government imports of uranium ores and concentrates and oxides are included. For 1923–40 commodity categories (but not the total) are on an imports for consumption basis. For this reason, and because revisions to totals are not reflected in components, the columns will not always add to the total.

Table US.12

Sources: **9, 18**

The totals for exports include re-exports. Re-exports are included in the commodity detail only from 1925. The commodity classification is the same as for Table US.11, i e by broad end-use from 1925. Figures based on classification by economic class have been included under the appropriate headings in the table but coverage will differ. For details of differences see **9**, p. 879.

From 1946, exports include silver ore and bullion.

Table US.13

Sources: **9, 16, 18**

Europe: includes all East and West European countries together with Iceland and the Soviet Union.

Germany: from 1952, the data are for the Federal Republic of Germany.

Rest of America: includes Canada and all South American countries. US Virgin Island trade with foreign countries included from 1981.

Asia: includes Iran, Iraq, Jordan and Saudi Arabia together with East and South East Asia.

Revisions to the totals of imports and exports are not included in the geographical data.

Table US.14

Sources: **3, 9, 16, 18**

Imports and Exports: certain adjustments are made to the trade data for valuation, coverage and timing. Exports are on a f.a.s. transactions value basis in all years. Imports are on a customs valuation basis up to 1973 and f.a.s. transactions basis from 1974. For further description of adjustments, valuation and timing, see **1**.

Investment income: includes interest, dividends and earnings of unincorporated affiliates and reinvested earnings of incorporated affiliates on US direct investment abroad (net of foreign taxes); dividends and interest on foreign securities held by US residents; interest received on bank and commercial loans to foreigners; interest received by the US government on loans to foreign countries minus payments of income for investment in the USA in each of the above categories.

Other services: includes insurance, royalties and fees, miscellaneous government services.

Table US.15

Sources: **1, 7, 9, 16**

Standard and Poor's index of common stock: based on the aggregate value of the common stock of 500 companies. From July 1976, the index includes 400 industrial stocks, 20 transport, 40 public utilities and 40 finance. (Before 1976 the coverage was 425 industrial, 25 transport 50 public utilities.) The market value each year is expressed as a percentage of the average market value in the base period, 1941–43.

Dow Jones average: data published in the *Wall Street Journal*. Averages are compiled from daily closing prices of 65 representative stocks listed on the New York Stock Exchange. The composition of the stocks will change from time to time. For further details see **1**.

3 month Treasury bill yield: the rate is the open market rate in New York City.

US government bonds yield: the figures are unweighted averages of yields. For 1919–25, yields cover all outstanding, partially tax exempt, government bonds with a minimum repayment period of 8 years; for 1926–34, 12 year minimum repayment period; 1935–41, 15 year minimum repayment period. From 1942, the series is for fully taxable bonds; 1942–52, minimum repayment period 15 years; 1953–82, 10 years or more repayment period.

Money supply: defined as currency in circulation plus demand deposits at commercial banks and foreign demand balances at Federal Reserve banks. The figures are seasonally adjusted averages of daily figures in December from 1959. From 1908 to 1958 the figures are annual averages. For the period 1900–14, data in **7** have been used. The series for this period includes time deposits, and the figures for 1900–07 are for June.

Consumer credit outstanding: series compiled by the Board of Governors of the Federal Reserve system; figures are at end December each year. Figures prior to 1940 are based largely on Department of Commerce estimates. The series is updated periodically. Includes credit extended to individuals for the purchase of capital goods that may be used in part for business purposes. The series has been revised back to 1950; two figures are therefore given for 1950. The second line is the revised figure; the first one is consistent with the earlier years.

Table US.16

Sources: **9, 16**

Vehicle registrations: the series includes both private and publicly owned vehicles. 'Passenger cars' includes taxis, and 'Goods vehicles' covers both trucks (lorries) and buses. Based on information supplied to the US Federal Highway Administration by state vehicle registration departments. Data before 1921 are incomplete because not all states required vehicles to be registered. Figures for 1983 are provisional.

Railways: passenger km: series is for revenue passenger miles converted to km by using the factor 1·609. Covers all three classes of railway up to 1960 and then Class I only. (Railways are classified according to size of operating revenues; in 1969 Class I railways carried over 98 per cent of the traffic.) For years up to 1916, the figures are for year end 30 June; from 1916 (second line), figures refer to calendar years.

Railways: freight ton km: see note above for coverage and timing of data. Converted to freight ton km by using the factor 1·635.

Airways: passenger km: series covers both domestic and international flights on scheduled and chartered airlines. Converted to km by using the factor 1·609.

Energy consumption: series covers primary fuel input with the exception of hydroelectricity, expressed in Btu to give a common measurement. For details of conversion factors see **9**, pp. 567 and 568.

'Crude petroleum' includes domestically produced crude oil, natural gas liquids and lease condensate plus imported crude oil and products.

Part III

Statistical tables for France, Germany, Italy and Japan

FRANCE

CONTENTS

Table F.1   Gross domestic product at constant prices, 1930–83

	Consumers' expenditure	Govt current expenditure	Gross fixed capital formation	Value of physical change in stocks	Exports of goods & services	Imports of goods & services	Gross domestic product at market prices
				Fr bn, 1975 prices			
1930	...	...	...	...	...	...	**445·0**
1931	...	...	...	...	...	...	**426·1**
1932	...	...	...	...	...	...	**396·0**
1933	...	...	...	...	...	...	**396·0**
1934	...	...	...	...	...	...	**388·4**
1935	...	...	...	...	...	...	**373·3**
1936	...	...	...	...	...	...	**369·6**
1937	...	...	...	...	...	...	**381·0**
1938	258·6	99·2	42·8	3·8	26·8	−37·2	**377·1**
1946	...	...	...	...	...	...	**313·0**
1947	...	...	...	...	...	...	**339·4**
1948	...	...	...	...	...	...	**362·0**
1949	249·6	84·2	75·8	7·8	32·8	−38·8	**412·0**
1950	265·0	87·6	76·4	9·2	42·6	−40·1	**444·5**
1951	284·5	94·3	80·8	7·2	49·2	−45·4	**470·4**
1952	295·5	109·5	77·8	7·8	46·8	−48·5	**486·3**
1953	308·3	111·8	78·2	6·1	47·8	−48·0	**498·5**
1954	320·2	105·3	84·8	7·5	52·9	−49·9	**519·4**
1955	339·5	102·0	95·9	6·2	55·8	−53·3	**543·6**
1956	360·6	112·8	104·0	9·3	53·1	−63·9	**575·8**
1957	385·6	116·6	113·9	7·6	55·9	−65·9	**610·3**
1958	390·3	111·6	120·5	9·3	60·0	−65·2	**628·2**
1959	400·1	118·3	124·3	5·7	68·1	−64·1	**648·1**
1960	418·6	120·4	133·8	14·8	81·3	−72·6	**694·5**
1961	443·5	126·2	148·4	10·0	85·4	−77·7	**732·8**
1962	474·9	132·1	161·0	12·5	86·9	−82·9	**781·7**
1963	507·6	136·6	175·1	9·0	93·1	−94·6	**823·5**
1964	536·2	142·3	193·5	16·7	99·3	−108·9	**877·1**
1965	557·7	146·8	207·0	11·0	110·7	−111·3	**919·0**
1966	584·6	150·8	220·0	16·2	118·0	−123·1	**967·0**
1967	614·4	157·2	235·4	13·9	126·6	−133·3	**1,012·3**
1968	638·9	166·1	248·4	15·8	138·5	−150·5	**1,055·4**
1969	677·4	172·9	271·2	26·1	160·3	−179·8	**1,129·2**
1970	706·3	180·1	283·7	26·6	186·2	−191·1	**1,193·9**
1971	753·0	186·4	303·9	16·4	206·7	−208·5	**1,258·5**
1972	798·7	191·3	325·9	22·0	233·4	−241·8	**1,332·7**
1973	844·7	197·4	345·9	27·9	261·0	−278·5	**1,404·2**
1974	869·3	199·7	349·1	28·9	288·0	−292·9	**1,449·6**
1975	898·8	209·1	337·9	−3·6	283·9	−273·7	**1,452·3**
1976	949·1	222·1	350·5	16·0	313·8	−329·3	**1,527·4**
1977	978·9	225·3	347·7	12·8	342·0	−338·7	**1,574·1**
1978	1,020·4	235·0	352·9	11·4	364·4	−356·9	**1,633·6**
1979	1,056·3	239·2	366·1	22·6	389·7	−396·4	**1,687·6**
1980	1,073·5	242·8	374·8	28·1	398·9	−424·1	**1,705·9**
1981	1,095·4	248·4	369·7	0·9	421·4	−432·3	**1,710·8**
1982	1,128·1	253·9	371·7	16·8	407·2	−449·7	**1,737·8**
1983	*1,136·3*	*258·7*	*366·6*	*9·3*	*421·0*	*−442·9*	***1,754·6***

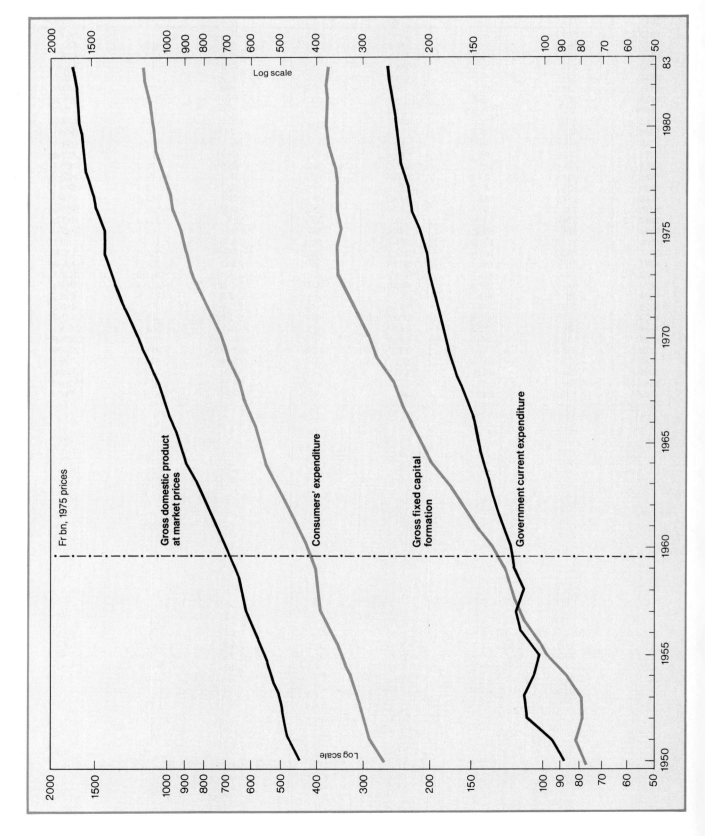

Chart F.1 Gross domestic product at constant prices, 1950–83

Fr bn, 1975 prices

Gross domestic product at market prices

Consumers' expenditure

Gross fixed capital formation

Government current expenditure

Log scale

Log scale

***Table* F.2** Industrial production, index and selected series, 1900–83

	Industrial production	Coal	Crude steel	Cars & commercial vehicles	Crude petroleum	Natural gas	Electricity
	Index nos., 1980 = 100	mn tons	mn tons	'000	'000 tons	mn cu m	bn KWh
1900	14·2	33·4	1·6	...	...	...	...
1901	13·4	32·3	1·4	...	...	...	0·34
1902	14·0	30·0	1·6	...	...	...	0·37
1903	14·2	34·9	1·8	...	...	...	0·43
1904	14·8	34·2	2·1	...	...	...	0·48
1905	15·2	35·9	2·3	14	...	...	0·53
1906	15·6	34·2	2·5	...	...	...	0·60
1907	16·6	36·8	2·8	...	...	...	0·67
1908	16·6	37·4	2·7	...	...	...	0·75
1909	17·8	37·8	3·0	...	...	...	0·85
1910	19·2	38·4	3·4	38	...	...	1·02
1911	19·8	39·2	3·8	...	...	...	1·23
1912	21·6	41·1	4·4	...	...	...	1·48
1913	21·6	40·8	4·7	45	...	...	1·80
1914	...	27·5	2·8	...	...	...	2·15
1915	...	19·5	1·1	...	...	...	1·90
1916	...	21·3	1·8	...	...	...	2·18
1917	...	28·9	2·0	...	...	...	2·40
1918	...	26·3	1·8	...	...	...	2·70
1919	12·3	22·4	1·3 / 2·2	...	47	...	2·90
1920	13·3	25·3	2·7	40	55	...	3·50 / 5·80
1921	11·9	29·0	3·1	55	56	...	6·50
1922	16·8	31·9	4·5	75	70	...	7·30
1923	19·0	38·6	5·2	110	70	...	8·17
1924	23·3	45·0	6·7	145	74	...	9·95
1925	23·1	48·1	7·5	177	65	...	11·14
1926	27·1	52·5	8·6	192	67	...	12·44
1927	23·7	52·9	8·3	191	73	...	12·58
1928	23·9	52·4	9·5	223	74	...	14·25
1929	26·3	55·0	9·7	254	75	...	15·60
1930	26·3	55·1	9·4	232	76	...	16·85
1931	22·7	51·0	7·8	201	74	...	15·67
1932	19·4	47·3	5·6	164	75	...	14·95
1933	21·2	48·0	6·6	189	79	...	16·40
1934	19·8	48·7	6·2	181	78	...	16·74
1935	19·0	47·1	6·3	165	76	...	17·47
1936	20·4	46·2	6·7	204	70	...	18·47
1937	21·6	45·4	7·9	202	70	...	20·08
1938	19·8	47·6	6·1	227	72	...	20·80
1939	...	50·2	8·0	...	70	...	22·10
1940	...	41·0	4·4	...	...	...	20·68
1941	...	43·9	4·3	55	58	...	20·28
1942	12·1	43·8	4·5	39	65	3	20·03
1943	10·7	42·4	5·1	19	68	46	21·07
1944	7·5	26·6	3·1	10	59	66	16·03
1945	9·9	35·0	1·7	35	29	85	18·37
1946	16·6	49·3	4·4	95	52	110	22·83
1947	19·6	47·3	5·7	136	50	147	25·81
1948	22·4	45·1	7·2	198	52	174	28·85
1949	24·1	53·0	9·2	286	58	228	29·93
1950	25·3	52·5	8·7	357	128	246	33·03
1951	28·3	55·0	9·8	447	291	282	38·15
1952	28·7	57·4	10·9	500	350	258	40·57
1953	28·9	54·5	10·0	498	367	233	41·46
1954	31·4	56·3	10·6	600	505	251	45·57
1955	34·0	57·4	12·6	725	878	256	49·63
1956	37·2	57·4	13·4	828	1,264	306	53·83
1957	40·3	59·1	14·1	928	1,410	439	57·43
1958	42·1	60·0	14·6	1,128	1,386	682	61·60
1959	43·5	59·8	15·2	1,283	1,618	1,645	64·51
1960	47·9	58·2	17·3	1,370	1,977	2,846	72·12
1961	50·2	55·3	17·6	1,245	2,163	4,010	76·49
1962	54·0	55·2	17·2	1,537	2,370	4,740	83·09
1963	55·2	50·2	17·6	1,737	2,522	4,861	88·25
1964	60·1	55·3	19·8	1,615	2,846	5,090	93·78
1965	61·3	54·0	19·6	1,616	2,988	5,048	101·44
1966	65·5	50·3	19·6	2,024	2,932	5,161	106·11
1967	67·1	47·6	19·7	2,010	2,832	5,563	111·64
1968	69·4	41·9	20·4	2,076	2,688	5,682	117·92
1969	77·1	40·6	22·5	2,459	2,496	6,506	131·52
1970	81·3	37·8	23·8	2,740	2,309	6,880	140·71
1971	85·6	33·0	22·8	3,010	1,861	7,149	149·00
1972	87·8	32·7	24·1	3,317	1,486	7,512	163·57
1973	93·5	28·5	25·3	3,581	1,254	7,536	174·70
1974	95·1	25·7	27·0	3,447	1,080	7,632	180·67
1975	89·4	25·6	21·5	3,287	1,028	7,356	178·51
1976	95·1	26·5	23·2	3,828	1,057	7,632	194·87
1977	95·9	24·4	22·1	3,998	1,037	8,924	202·56
1978	96·7	22·4	22·8	4,067	1,117	9,169	217·29
1979	100·0	21·1	23·4	4,184	1,197	9,037	231·06
1980	100·0	20·7	23·2	3,992	1,415	8,622	246·67
1981	97·4	26·3	21·3	3,426	1,676	8,267	264·54
1982	95·7	20·1	18·4	3,533	1,644	10,180	262·25
1983	96·6	19·6	17·6	3,816	1,656	11,315	297·20

Chart F.2   Industrial production, selected series, 1900–80

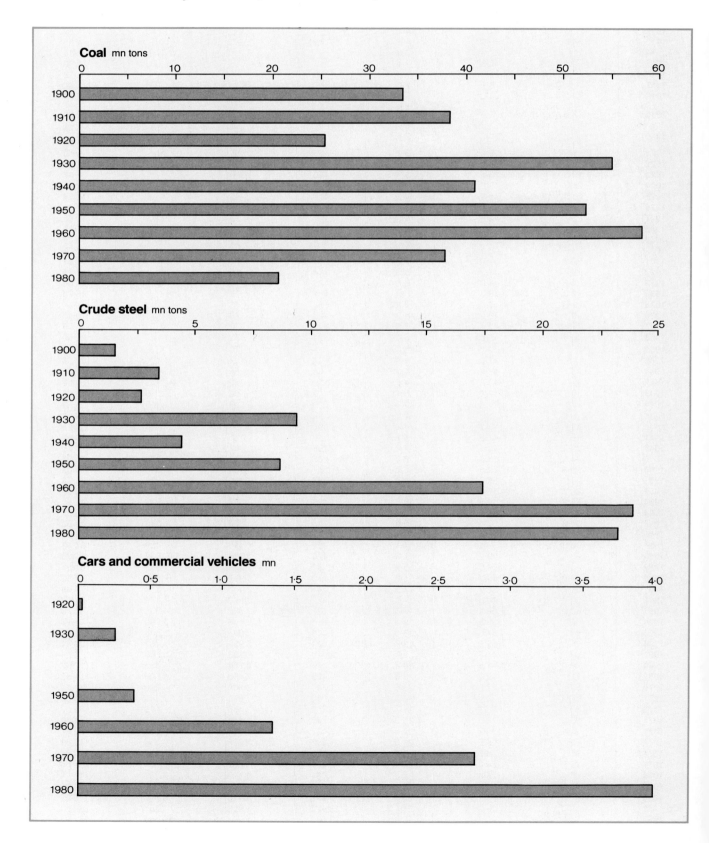

Table F.3 Prices and income, 1900–83

	Consumer prices		Wholesale prices		Compensation of employees	National income
	All items	Food	All items	Raw materials		
	Index nos., 1980 = 100				Fr bn	
1900	0·12	...	0·13	...	...	...
1901	0·12	...	0·12	...	...	...
1902	0·12	...	0·12	...	...	...
1903	0·12	...	0·12	...	...	...
1904	0·12	...	0·12	...	...	...
1905	0·12	...	0·13	...	...	...
1906	0·12	...	0·13	...	...	...
1907	0·12	...	0·14	...	...	...
1908	0·12	...	0·13	...	...	...
1909	0·12	...	0·13	...	...	...
1910	0·12	...	0·14	...	...	...
1911	0·13	...	0·15	...	...	...
1912	0·13	...	0·15	...	...	...
1913	0·13	...	0·15	...	...	...
1914	0·13	...	0·15	...	...	...
1915	0·15	...	0·21	...	...	...
1916	0·18	...	0·28	...	...	...
1917	0·21	...	0·40	...	...	...
1918	0·27	...	0·51	...	...	...
1919	0·34	...	0·54	...	...	...
1920	0·47	...	0·77	...	...	...
1921	0·41	...	0·52	...	...	...
1922	0·39	...	0·49	...	...	...
1923	0·44	...	0·63	...	...	...
1924	0·50	...	0·74	...	...	...
1925	0·53	...	0·83	...	...	...
1926	0·69	...	1·06	...	...	...
1927	0·72	...	0·93	...	...	...
1928	0·72	...	0·94	0·97	...	...
1929	0·77	0·87	0·92	0·94	...	...
1930	0·78	0·87	0·80	0·79	...	...
1931	0·75	0·87	0·68	0·61	...	...
1932	0·68	0·65	0·61	0·48	...	...
1933	0·65	0·65	0·58	0·48	...	...
1934	0·63	0·65	0·54	0·45	...	...
1935	0·58	0·65	0·51	0·45	...	...
1936	0·62	0·87	0·60	0·51	...	...
1937	0·78	0·87	0·83	0·68	...	...
1938	0·88	0·87	0·95	0·85	1·8	3·6
1939	0·94	0·87	0·95	0·85	...	...
1940	1·1	1·1	1·3	1·71	...	...
1941	1·3	1·3	1·6	1·99	...	...
1942	1·6	1·5	1·9	1·99	...	...
1943	2·0	2·0	2·2	2·85	...	...
1944	2·4	2·4	2·4	4·84	...	...
1945	3·5	3·3	3·5	6·83	...	...
1946	5·4	5·7	6·0	13·9	11·3	26·0
1947	8·1	9·4	9·1	17·1	16·8	33·0
1948	12·8	14·8	15·7	21·4	28·0	54·3
1949	14·4	15·9	17·5	32·2	34·9	65·4
1950	15·8	17·4	18·9	30·2	40·3	90·4
1951	18·5	20·3	24·2	28·5	51·6	109·9
1952	20·7	22·2	25·3	27·3	62·2	129·2
1953	20·3	21·8	24·2	28·5	65·0	135·4
1954	20·3	21·2	23·7	27·9	70·6	144·1
1955	20·5	21·5	23·7	28·5	76·6	155·0
1956	21·5	21·8	24·7	29·8	86·5	172·7
1957	22·1	22·4	26·2	31·0	96·8	194·2
1958	25·4	26·4	29·2	31·7	110·9	224·1
1959	27·0	27·0	30·6	34·2	121·5 / 119·8	244·4 / 241·2
1960	28·0	27·7	31·3	35·2	130·6	269·0
1961	28·8	28·9	32·0	36·4	146·1	293·2
1962	28·8	29·2	32·9	36·4	165·1	328·6
1963	30·4	30·7	34·1	37·4	188·2	368·4
1964	31·3	32·0	34·6	39·6	210·1	409·2
1965	32·2	32·6	35·1	40·1	226·5	440·1
1966	33·1	33·5	35·9	41·6	244·3	475·5
1967	33·9	33·8	35·6	40·6	236·7	513·5
1968	35·5	35·0	36·1	39·6	294·7	559·7
1969	37·8	37·0	39·2	45·1	337·1	639·3
1970	39·8	39·4	42·8	49·6	382·3	706·3
1971	42·2	41·7	43·7	48·1	432·1	796·7
1972	44·6	45·3	46·2	49·1	483·8	894·6
1973	47·8	49·6	52·1	61·9	558·1	1,014·8
1974	54·6	55·5	64·4	82·4	665·7	1,152·2
1975	60·9	62·2	65·0	67·8	783·7	1,297·6
1976	66·9	68·5	71·7	76·6	909·7	1,486·2
1977	72·9	77·2	76·6	82·7	1,036·4	1,680·1
1978	79·7	83·5	80·1	84·0	1,173·5	1,908·4
1979	88·0	91·3	89·8	94·9	1,330·0	2,179·1
1980	100·0	100·0	100·0	100·0	1,529·6	2,464·7
1981	113·5	114·0	113·9	111·1	1,735·4	2,753·0
1982	127·0	128·4	128·5	119·0	1,985·4	3,130·9
1983	139·2	140·3	...	...	2,193·0	3,477·6

	Total population	Males	Females	Age distribution		
				Under 15	15–64	65 & over
				mn		
1901	38·49	18·94	19·55	9·89	25·34	3·25
1906	38·84	19·10	19·75	9·99	25·55	3·30
1911	39·23	19·25	19·94	9·99	25·88	3·37
1921	38·78	18·45	20·35	8·69	26·52	3·57
1926	40·22	19·31	20·92	8·92	27·51	3·74
1931	41·26	19·93	21·33	9·34	27·97	3·94
1936	41·19	19·80	21·39	10·07	27·00	4·13
1946	40·13	19·12	21·01	8·59	27·10	4·44
1947	40·45	19·30	21·15	8·72	27·20	4·52
1948	40·91	19·59	21·32	8·94	27·31	4·60
1949	41·31	19·81	21·50	9·17	27·38	4·69
1950	41·65	20·00	21·64	9·38	27·45	4·73
	41·84	20·11	21·72	9·50	27·58	4·76
1951	42·16	20·29	21·87	9·72	27·62	4·81
1952	42·46	20·45	22·01	9·94	27·66	4·86
1953	42·75	20·61	22·14	10·15	27·69	4·91
1954	43·06	20·78	22·28	10·36	27·73	4·96
1955	43·43	20·97	22·46	10·62	27·79	5·02
1956	43·84	21·19	22·66	10·94	27·84	5·06
1957	44·31	21·44	22·88	11·27	27·94	5·11
1958	44·79	21·69	23·10	11·55	28·07	5·17
1959	45·24	21·93	23·31	11·80	28·19	5·25
1960	45·68	22·16	23·52	12·05	28·32	5·32
1961	46·16	22·52	23·75	12·20	28·55	5·41
1962	47·00	22·85	24·15	12·32	29·14	5·54
1963	47·85	22·31	24·55	12·41	29·78	5·66
1964	48·41	23·62	24·79	12·44	30·20	5·77
1965	48·76	23·74	25·02	12·48	30·37	5·91
1966	49·16	23·94	25·23	12·51	30·62	6·04
1967	49·55	24·13	25·42	12·52	30·84	6·18
1968	49·92	24·32	25·60	12·54	31·06	6·31
1969	50·32	24·54	25·78	12·57	31·33	6·42
1970	50·77	24·79	25·98	12·61	31·63	6·54
1971	51·25	25·05	26·20	12·66	31·94	6·66
1972	51·70	25·29	26·41	12·77	32·22	6·77
1973	52·12	25·52	26·60	12·74	32·50	6·88
1974	52·46	25·70	26·76	12·70	32·77	6·99
1975	52·71	25·82	26·89	12·60	33·01	7·10
1976	52·89	25·91	26·98	12·46	33·24	7·19
1977	53·08	26·00	27·08	12·33	33·46	7·28
1978	53·28	26·10	27·18	12·20	33·68	7·39
1979	53·48	26·20	27·28	12·07	33·52	7·49
1980	53·71	26·31	27·40	11·98	34·25	7·50
1981	53·96	26·43	27·53	11·91	34·67	7·38
1982	54·22	26·56	27·66	11·87	35·11	7·25

Table F.5   Labour market: employment, 1930–83

	Employed labour force[a]	Agriculture, forestry & fishing	Mining & quarrying	Mfg	Construction	Gas, electricity & water	Transport & communication	Distribution & services
				mn				
1930	(8·90)	...		(5·91)	...	...	...	...
1931	(8·24)	...		(5·47)	...	...	...	...
1932	(7·20)	...		(4·78)	...	...	...	...
1933	(7·07)	...		(4·69)	...	...	...	...
1934	(6·85)	...		(4·54)	...	...	...	...
1935	(6·54)	...		(4·34)	...	...	...	...
1936	(6·60)	...		(4·38)	...	...	...	...
1937	(7·00)	...	0·37	3·50	0·70	0·10	0·78	1·70
1938	(7·19)	...		(4·80)	...	...	...	...
1939	(7·28)	...		(4·93)	...	...	...	...
1940	...	...		...	...	...	...	...
1941	(6·44)	...		(4·22)	...	...	...	...
1942	(6·51)	...		(4·46)	...	...	...	...
1943	...	...		(4·23)	...	...	...	...
1944	...	...		(4·23)	...	...	...	...
1945	...	...		(4·28)	...	...	...	...
1946	(7·11)	...	0·45	3·43	0·75	0·11	0·81	1·56
1947	(7·41)	...	0·47	3·66	0·76	0·12	0·82	1·59
1948	(7·53)	...	0·47	3·77	0·78	0·12	0·81	1·60
1949	(7·60)	...	0·44	3·84	0·82	0·12	0·79	1·60
1950	(7·60)	...	0·42	3·86	0·83	0·12	0·76	1·61
1951	(7·70)	...	0·41	3·95	0·86	0·12	0·74	1·63
1952	(7·72)	...	0·41	3·93	0·90	0·12	0·72	1·64
1953	(7·65)	...	0·39	3·87	0·92	0·12	0·71	1·64
1954	(7·67)	...	0·39	3·88	0·95	0·12	0·69	1·65
	18·70	5·21	0·39	5·02	1·36	0·15	0·99	5·58
1955	18·72	5·04	0·38	5·04	1·43	0·15	0·99	5·69
1956	18·74	4·85	0·37	5·10	1·47	0·16	0·99	5·78
1957	18·87	4·64	0·37	5·25	1·53	0·16	1·01	5·89
1958	18·82	4·45	0·37	5·29	1·52	0·17	1·02	6·00
1959	18·67	4·34	0·36	5·21	1·53	0·17	1·03	6·04
1960	18·71	4·19	0·35	5·24	1·55	0·18	1·04	6·16
1961	18·72	4·04	0·33	5·29	1·58	0·18	1·05	6·25
1962	18·82	3·88	0·32	5·35	1·57	0·15	1·09	6·60
1963	19·13	3·74	0·31	5·49	1·66	0·15	1·13	6·81
1964	19·42	3·60	0·30	5·60	1·76	0·15	1·16	7·00
1965	19·54	3·47	0·29	5·41	1·85	0·15	1·18	7·21
1966	19·66	3·36	0·28	5·43	1·89	0·16	1·18	7·41
1967	19·74	3·23	0·26	5·41	1·90	0·16	1·19	7·62
1968	19·73	3·16	0·24	5·31	1·92	0·16	1·20	7·81
1969	20·06	2·97	0·25	5·53	2·00	0·17	1·19	7·95
1970	20·34	2·82	0·24	5·66	2·02	0·17	1·21	8·22
1971	20·44	2·67	0·22	5·73	2·00	0·17	1·20	8·45
1972	20·55	2·51	0·21	5·78	1·99	0·17	1·21	8·68
1973	20·81	2·36	0·20	5·89	2·01	0·17	1·22	8·96
1974	20·96	2·22	0·19	5·94	1·99	0·18	1·26	9·18
1975	20·71	2·10	0·17	5·78	1·90	0·17	1·26	9·33
1976	20·86	2·04	0·17	5·72	1·88	0·17	1·27	9·61
1977	21·04	1·98	0·17	5·70	1·88	0·18	1·30	9·83
1978	21·11	1·93	0·16	5·61	1·84	0·18	1·32	10·07
1979	21·12	1·89	0·15	5·52	1·82	0·18	1·33	10·23
1980	21·13	1·84	0·14	5·45	1·82	0·19	1·33	10·36
1981	20·95	1·79	0·14	5·27	1·79	0·19	1·33	10·44
1982	20·98	1·74	0·14	5·18	1·74	0·20	1·36	10·59
1983	20·84[b]	1·69		7·05			12·10	

a   For the years 1930–54 see notes on p. 83.
b   Estimated by OECD.

Table F.6 Labour market: other indicators, 1900–83

Year	Mfg Average weekly hrs worked	Mfg Average hourly wage rates Fr	Unemployment '000	Unemployment %	Industrial disputes Stoppages	Workers involved '000	Working days lost '000
1900	...	...	...	6·8	902	223	3,761
1901	...	...	...	7·8	523	111	1,862
1902	...	...	...	9·9	512	213	4,675
1903	...	...	...	9·4	567	123	2,442
1904	...	...	...	10·2	1,026	271	3,935
1905	...	...	...	9·0	830	178	2,747
1906	...	...	...	7·6	1,309	438	9,439
1907	...	...	...	7·0	1,275	198	3,562
1908	...	...	...	8·6	1,073	99	1,752
1909	...	...	...	7·3	1,025	167	3,560
1910	...	...	...	5·8	1,502	281	4,830
1911	...	...	...	5·7	1,471	231	4,096
1912	...	...	...	5·4	1,116	268	2,318
1913	...	...	...	4·7	1,073	220	2,224
1914	...	...	...	...	672	162	2,187
1915	...	...	...	...	98	9	55
1916	...	...	...	...	314	41	236
1917	...	...	...	...	696	294	1,482
1918	...	...	...	...	499	176	980
1919	...	...	...	...	2,026	1,151	15,478
1920	...	...	13	...	1,832	1,317	23,112
1921	...	...	28	...	475	402	7,027
1922	...	...	13	...	665	290	3,935
1923	...	...	10	...	1,068	331	4,172
1924	...	...	10	...	1,083	275	3,863
1925	...	...	12	...	931	249	2,046
1926	...	...	11	...	1,660	349	4,072
1927	...	...	47	...	396	111	1,046
1928	...	...	16	...	816	204	6,377
1929	...	3·83	10	...	1,213	240	2,765
1930	48·0	4·08	13	...	1,093	582	7,209
1931	46·7	4·08	64	...	286	48	950
1932	43·7	3·99	301	...	362	72	1,244
1933	45·3	3·89	305	...	343	87	1,199
1934	44·7	3·89	368	...	385	101	2,393
1935	44·5	3·80	464	...	376	109	1,182
1936	45·7	4·42	470	...	16,907	2,423	...
1937	40·2	5·60	380	...	2,616	1,133	...
1938	38·7	6·19	402	...	1,220	324	...
1939	40·7	...	418	...	...	...	...
1940	...	...	961	...	...	...	...
1941	...	...	395	...	...	...	...
1942	...	...	124	...	...	...	...
1943	...	...	42	...	...	...	...
1944	...	...	23	...	...	...	...
1945	...	...	68	...	...	...	...
1946	...	...	57	...	528	180	386
1947	...	...	46	...	2,285	2,998	22,673
1948	44·6	66·1	78	...	1,425	6,561	13,133
1949	43·8	73·9	131	...	1,426	4,330	7,129
1950	44·4	81·4	153	...	2,586	1,527	11,729
1951	44·8	104·3	120	...	2,514	1,754	3,495
1952	44·2	120·7	132	...	1,759	1,155	1,733
1953	44·1	124·2	180	...	1,761	1,784	9,722
1954	44·6	131·5	184 / 311	1·6	1,479	1,319	1,440
1955	44·9	141·6	283	1·4	2,672	1,061	3,079
1956	45·6	152·4	212	1·1	2,440	982	1,423
1957	46·1	164·4	161	0·8	2,623	2,964	4,121
1958	45·3	183·8	183	0·9	954	1,112	1,138
1959	45·0	195·1	254	1·3	1,512	940	1,938
1960	45·7	2·09	240	1·2	1,494	1,072	1,070
1961	46·0	2·25	212	1·1	1,963	2,552	2,601
1962	46·2	2·44	230	1·2	1,884	1,472	1,901
1963	46·3	2·65	273	1·4	2,382	2,646	5,991
1964	46·1	2·84	216	1·1	2,281	2,603	2,497
1965	45·6	3·00	269	1·3	1,674	1,237	980
1966	45·9	3·18	280	1·4	1,711	3,341	2,523
1967	45·4	3·37	365	1·8	1,675	2,824	4,204
1968	45·3	3·79	427	2·1	...	...	...
1969	45·4	4·21	477	2·3	2,480	1,444	2,224
1970	44·8	4·66	510	2·4	3,319	1,160	1,742
1971	44·5	5·18	569	2·6	4,358	3,235	4,388
1972	44·0	5·82	595	2·7	3,464	2,721	3,755
1973	43·6	6·92	576	2·6	3,731	2,246	3,915
1974	42·9	8·20	615	2·8	3,381	1,564	3,380
1975	41·7	9·66	902	4·1	3,888	1,827	3,869
1976	41·7	10·94	993	4·4	4,348	2,023	5,011
1977	41·3	12·40	1,073	4·7	3,281	1,920	3,666
1978	41·0	13·98	1,183	5·2	3,195	705	2,200
1979	40·8	15·78	1,355	5·9	3,121	967	3,657
1980	40·7	18·14	1,452	6·3	2,118	501	1,686
1981	40·3	20·72	1,694	7·3	2,442	329	1,496
1982	39·5	23·97	1,863	8·0	3,113	468	2,328
1983	38·9	26·70	1,864[a]	8·0[a]	3,360	454	1,484

a Estimated by OECD.

80

Table F.7   Value of exports and imports by country, 1900–83

	Total exports	Exports to: Germany	Exports to: Italy	Exports to: UK	Exports to: USA	Total imports	Imports from: Germany	Imports from: Italy	Imports from: UK	Imports from: USA
					Fr bn					
1900	4·11	0·47	0·16	1·23	0·26	4·70	0·43	0·15	0·68	0·51
1901	4·01	0·44	0·16	1·20	0·25	4·37	0·40	0·14	0·60	0·46
1902	4·25	0·49	0·18	1·28	0·25	4·39	0·42	0·15	0·57	0·43
1903	4·25	0·51	0·17	1·20	0·26	4·80	0·44	0·15	0·56	0·54
1904	4·45	0·56	0·19	1·22	0·25	4·50	0·43	0·15	0·52	0·48
1905	4·87	0·63	0·21	1·26	0·30	4·78	0·48	0·15	0·59	0·51
1906	5·27	0·64	0·25	1·30	0·40	5·63	0·58	0·18	0·75	0·59
1907	5·60	0·65	0·26	1·37	0·40	6·22	0·64	0·19	0·88	0·67
1908	5·05	0·62	0·24	1·18	0·32	5·64	0·61	0·17	0·79	0·66
1909	5·72	0·73	0·29	1·27	0·47	6·25	0·66	0·17	0·89	0·73
1910	6·23	0·80	0·34	1·28	0·46	7·17	0·86	0·19	0·93	0·61
1911	6·08	0·80	0·28	1·22	0·38	8·07	0·98	0·19	0·99	0·83
1912	6·71	0·82	0·30	1·37	0·43	8·23	1·00	0·21	1·05	0·89
1913	6·88	0·87	0·31	1·46	0·42	8·42	1·07	0·24	1·12	0·90
1914	4·87	0·51	0·22	1·17	0·38	6·40	0·61	0·17	0·86	0·80
1915	3·94	—	0·39	1·10	0·45	11·04	—	0·43	3·04	3·03
1916	6·21	—	0·78	1·12	0·62	20·64	—	0·72	5·97	6·16
1917	6·01	—	0·97	1·02	0·68	27·55	—	0·82	6·81	9·77
1918	4·72	—	0·78	1·08	0·42	22·31	—	0·82	6·40	7·14
1919	11·88	1·56	0·68	2·12	0·89	35·80	0·76	1·02	8·80	9·22
1920	26·89	1·50	1·25	4·24	2·26	49·91	2·67	1·28	10·32	10·87
1921	19·77	1·88	0·69	3·19	2·19	22·75	2·62	0·62	2·94	3·54
1922	21·38	1·97	0·80	3·98	2·01	24·28	1·45	0·77	3·27	3·85
1923	30·87	1·08	1·17	6·36	2·47	32·86	1·17	1·14	5·04	4·85
1924	42·37	3·96	1·48	7·90	3·15	40·16	2·05	1·48	4·77	5·59
1925	45·76	3·83	2·23	9·27	3·09	44·10	2·35	1·73	5·69	6·38
1926	59·68	4·38	2·62	10·59	3·67	59·60	4·93	2·23	6·14	7·82
1927	54·93	6·63	2·06	9·00	3·15	53·05	4·17	1·55	6·33	6·81
1928	51·38	5·62	2·13	7·94	3·03	53·44	5·00	1·53	5·31	6·18
1929	50·14	4·74	2·21	7·63	3·34	58·22	6·61	1·52	5·86	7·16
1930	42·84	4·16	1·68	6·89	2·44	52·51	7·94	1·53	5·30	6·15
1931	30·44	2·75	0·99	5·09	1·54	42·21	6·14	1·44	3·85	3·80
1932	19·71	1·70	0·60	1·98	0·96	29·81	3·61	0·63	2·46	2·90
1933	18·47	1·71	0·50	1·70	0·87	28·43	3·04	0·62	2·18	2·86
1934	17·85	1·99	0·55	1·57	0·84	23·10	2·23	0·48	1·65	2·19
1935	15·50	1·05	0·60	1·64	0·72	20·97	1·74	0·41	1·58	1·79
1936	15·49	0·67	0·14	1·96	0·88	25·41	1·77	0·22	1·80	2·53
1937	23·94	1·57	0·63	2·75	1·54	42·39	3·49	0·57	3·39	4·03
1938	30·59	1·85	0·49	3·56	1·68	46·06	3·15	0·58	3·24	5·28
1939	31·59	1·04	0·32	4·15	2·27	43·79	2·09	0·50	2·98	5·84
1940	17·51	0·65	0·26	2·14	1·21	45·77	0·10	0·82	3·68	8·49
1941	15·78	6·25	0·50	0·11	0·13	24·94	3·92	0·50	0·15	0·50
1942	29·66	17·80	0·30	0·14	—	25·95	7·52	0·42	—	0·14
1943	35·41	29·19	0·05	0·15	—	13·96	8·38	0·14	0·03	0·07
1944	25·56	22·42	—	0·08	—	9·77	4·81	0·03	0·03	1·41
1945	11·40	0·11	—	0·32	0·59	57·03	1·67	0·10	5·06	27·18
1946	101·4	2·34	0·65	5·34	6·40	264·7	12·79	2·35	15·10	83·86
1947	223·3	5·85	2·17	15·45	5·98	397·1	15·16	2·74	12·47	120·1
1948	434·0	23·38	4·61	31·83	15·81	672·7	35·96	11·38	18·83	118·7
1949	783·9	39·29	15·83	70·11	15·74	926·3	68·44	17·09	32·82	162·7
1950	1,078	84·31	28·01	98·81	43·69	1,073	69·79	37·25	39·95	131·6
1951	1,484	69·83	35·23	133·72	88·43	1,615	101·5	47·77	56·90	181·7
1952	1,416	78·89	37·96	85·19	54·84	1,592	114·7	33·91	60·11	159·7
1953	1,406	98·54	45·45	76·03	63·52	1,458	110·0	22·53	66·61	135·0
1954	1,510	123·3	57·53	84·42	54·06	1,522	120·3	27·59	70·03	133·4
1955	1,736	176·9	66·54	125·41	72·88	1,674	154·0	36·81	75·82	160·5
1956	1,623	166·2	65·36	97·24	78·27	1,978	199·0	49·84	108·45	238·6
1957	1,889	201·8	75·48	103·12	89·86	2,267	250·1	56·47	97·43	300·5
1958	2,153	224·5	72·76	105·15	126·4	2,357	274·2	55·45	84·31	236·7
1959	27·7	3·63	1·32	1·24	2·29	25·2	3·65	0·88	0·98	2·12
1960	33·9	4·66	1·98	1·71	1·95	31·0	4·89	1·25	1·13	1·95
1961	35·7	5·41	2·41	1·81	2·06	33·0	5·63	1·51	1·48	2·06
1962	36·3	6·28	2·73	1·72	2·10	37·1	6·54	2·05	1·92	3·83
1963	39·9	6·62	3·69	1·96	2·08	43·1	7·76	2·55	2·57	4·45
1964	44·4	7·73	3·43	2·26	2·32	49·7	9·11	3·13	2·68	5·61
1965	49·6	9·58	3·62	2·29	2·94	51·0	9·44	3·59	2·58	5·37
1966	53·8	10·37	4·44	2·46	3·26	58·6	11·27	4·69	2·88	5·92
1967	56·2	9·73	5·18	2·87	3·28	61·1	12·32	5·30	2·92	6·02
1968	62·6	11·63	5·77	2·98	3·78	68·8	14·73	6·56	3·04	6·51
1969	77·0	15·88	8·06	3·16	4·22	89·1	20·04	9·02	4·00	7·59
1970	98·5	20·49	11·11	3·83	5·30	105·1	23·43	9·81	4·80	10·53
1971	113·0	24·31	12·43	5·19	6·10	117·0	26·38	11·69	5·29	9·99
1972	131·5	27·79	15·11	7·04	6·97	135·7	30·20	13·84	6·65	11·02
1973	159·7	30·92	18·75	10·10	7·50	166·1	37·66	14·99	7·69	13·76
1974	220·2	37·92	25·69	14·35	10·74	254·7	48·87	19·01	10·82	19·76
1975	223·4	36·99	20·34	14·60	8·79	231·3	43·57	20·34	10·99	17·50
1976	266·2	46·01	29·06	16·07	12·06	308·0	59·16	27·50	15·06	22·57
1977	311·6	53·34	32·66	20·24	16·05	346·2	64·07	33·16	18·06	24·05
1978	344·6	59·82	37·64	24·96	19·25	368·4	70·01	37·38	20·30	26·88
1979	414·7	71·70	47·61	32·03	20·40	457·1	82·84	46·07	25·60	34·39
1980	469·7	75·35	58·63	32·74	20·78	570·8	92·16	53·41	30·78	45·35
1981	549·5	81·36	62·35	39·06	30·31	654·2	104·61	58·60	35·92	52·31
1982	607·0	89·56	68·45	43·92	34·33	758·3	127·66	72·78	46·06	59·73
1983	694·7	108·07	74·11	52·68	43·82	799·8	135·46	79·36	56·80	61·76

SOURCES

(For sources used in specific tables, see Notes.)

1 *Annuaire Statistique de la France*, Institut national de la statistique et des études économiques, Paris, 1983 and earlier years.

2 *Annuaire Statistique de la France, Résume Rétrospectif*, loc. cit. in no.**1**, 1966.

3 International Labour Office, *Technical Guide*, Vol. II. Geneva, 1972, 1976, 1980.

4 League of Nations, *Year Book of Labour Statistics*. Geneva.

5 Mitchell, B R, *European Historical Statistics, 1750–1975*, 2nd rev. edn. Macmillan, London, 1980.

6 Organisation for Economic Cooperation and Development (OECD), *Labour Force Statistics*. Paris, annual and quarterly.

7 OECD, *National Accounts, 1950 to 1978*. Paris, 1980.

8 OECD, *National Accounts, 1953 to 1982*. Paris, 1984, and quarterly accounts, 1984.

9 *Statistical Year Book of the League of Nations*. Geneva.

10 Supplements to the United Nations, *Statistical Year Book* and *Monthly Digest of Statistics*. New York, 1967, 1972 and 1977.

11 United Nations, *Monthly Bulletin of Statistics*. New York.

12 United Nations, *Statistics of National Income and Expenditure*, Series H, no. 7. New York, 1955.

13 United Nations, *Statistical Year Book*. New York.

14 *Year Book of Labour Statistics*. ILO, Geneva.

NOTES

Table F.1

Sources: **1, 2, 7, 8**

From 1950, OECD data have been used. There is a break in the series in 1959 when there was a change in the system of classification. The main differences in classification are explained in **8**.

For the years 1938 and 1949, constant price estimates published in **2** were linked to the OECD estimates at 1950 and roughly adjusted to 1975 prices. Figures for gross domestic product for the years 1930–37 and 1946–48 were obtained by using the volume index of national income given in **1**, 1983, p. 307.

Table F.2

Sources: **1, 5, 11, 13**

Industrial production: the current index covers mining, manufacturing (except the clothing industry), electricity and gas. It is a base weighted index. For further details of method, composition and linking, see notes to Table 3.03-2 and 3.08-1, pp. 308, 309 in **1**, 1983.

Coal: includes coal and lignite. For 1900–18 and 1939–44 parts of Alsace Lorraine are excluded.

Crude steel: includes Alsace Lorraine from 1919.

Cars and commercial vehicles: figures to 1938 are for years ended 30 September. Alsace Lorraine is excluded from 1941–44.

Natural gas: published figures are now given in terajoules. From 1977, the published figures have been converted to cubic metres using the conversion factor 33494 – see **11**.

Table F.3

Sources: **1, 5, 7, 8, 9, 11, 12, 13**

Consumer prices: the current series is a chain index, the weights being changed at the beginning of each calendar year. The coverage of the index has changed over the period to make it more comprehensive. For further details see **10**.

Wholesale prices: the 'All items' index is based on the series given in **1**, 1983, p. 307. For details of the way the index has been linked at successive periods see notes on p. 308 of **1**, 1983. The 'Raw materials' index is published in **13**; it includes both domestic and imported raw materials. For further details see **10**.

Compensation of employees: OECD data have been used from 1950; see **7** and **8**. The figures include wages and salaries in cash and in kind paid to employees, contributions on behalf of employees to social security schemes and private pension funds, as well as family allowances and private health insurance paid by employers. The 1938 figure and figures for 1946–49 are from **12**, converted to new francs.

National income: OECD data have been used from 1950. 'National income' is defined as the sum of compensation of employees received by residents, net entrepreneurial and property income of residents, and indirect taxes minus subsidies. Figures for 1938 and 1946–49 are from **12** but have been converted to new francs.

Two figures have been given for 1959 for the last two columns because of the change in classification; see notes to Table F.1.

Table F.4

Sources: **1, 6**

OECD data have been used from 1950 (second line); the figures are mid year estimates of resident population including armed forces temporarily stationed abroad.

For the period 1901–50 (first line), the figures are as at 1 January each year.

Alsace Lorraine is excluded from the figures before 1919.

Table F.5

Sources: **4, 6, 14**

OECD data have been used from 1954. The figures from 1954 (second line) are annual averages of those in civil employment and include employees, self employed and unpaid family workers working for at least one third of normal working time. The figures do not include the temporarily stopped or the unemployed.

The estimates are based on the French national industrial classification, which has been changed from time to time. From 1969, the estimates are more closely adjusted to the International Standard Industrial Classification. Figures for earlier years are not strictly comparable with those from 1969. For further details see **6**.

There have been revisions to the total in employment from time to time, but the industry data have not always been revised in detail. When this has occurred, the unrevised data have been given in the industry columns together with the *revised* figures for the employed labour force. Industry figures will not therefore always add to the total (cf. 1959–61 and 1966–68).

For 1930–54 (first line), the figures for the 'Employed labour force' are for wage and salary earners in mining, manufacturing, construction, transport, commerce, personal and public services. For the years 1930–36, fewer groups in transport and commerce are included. The figures for 1938 are for January–August. Figures available for the *total* labour force have been obtained from Census data covering the economically active population, which includes employers and self employed, employees and unemployed. For the years 1931 and 1936 (Census years), the economically active population numbered just over 21·5 and 20 mn, respectively.

The industry classification also covers wage earners and salaried employees only from 1930 to 1954. The figures are annual averages of the estimated number of employees in work on a specific date; no distinction is made between full and part time work. For the years 1930–36 and 1938–45, the figures given in the industry columns include wage earners and salaried employees in mining, manufacturing and transport. The economically active population in manufacturing in 1931 was returned as 5·9 mn and in 1936 as 5·1 mn. The figures for agriculture were 7·7 mn in 1931 and 7·2 mn in 1936. For further details see **4** and **14**.

Table F.6

Sources: **1, 4, 6, 14**

Manufacturing: average weekly hours worked: the current series is the average of scheduled working hours in the reporting establishments in a particular week. Thus, overtime is counted only when an entire establishment or a major section of it has extra working hours scheduled. When there is a temporary layoff, the figure of zero hours is included in the average figure. The series covers wage earners of both sexes over 18 years of age. Comprehensive revisions were made in 1954 and in 1972.

Figures for 1930–39 include mining and transport and communication. The figure for 1938 is for the period January to August.

Manufacturing: average hourly wage rates: Series refers to rates of pay in force on 1 January, 1 April, 1 July and 1 October; annual figure is an average of these four. Covers wage earners over 18 years of age of both sexes. Includes collective bonus payments but excludes overtime pay, individual bonuses or reimbursements. There was a change in the value of the franc in 1960: 1 new franc = 100 old francs. Since 1969, an average earnings figure has also been published. For further details of these series see **3, 4** and **14**.

Unemployment: OECD data have been used from 1954. The figures refer to persons available for work seeking employment and are based on Census results, annual labour force sample surveys and the Ministry of Labour series. The figures are therefore different from those published in United Nations publications. From June 1972, the figures exclude certain unemployed over the age of 60 (recipients of income maintenance benefits).

Before 1954, the figures are for job applicants still registered at the end of each month; annual figures are averages of monthly figures.

The percentage figure from 1954 is obtained by dividing the number of unemployed by the civilian labour force ($\times$ 100).

Table F.7

Sources: **1, 5**

For 1900–23, exports to and imports from the UK include trade with Cyprus, Malta, Gibraltar and Southern Ireland. For 1948–59, the Saarland is included as part of France. Alsace Lorraine became part of France from 1919. From 1948, trade with Germany refers to the Federal Republic of Germany.

The figures are in new francs from 1959 (100 old francs = 1 new franc). From 1934, statistics were collected on the basis of countries of origin or consumption and not on consignment and destination. There were also changes in the method of collection or of valuation in 1923 and in 1928 and 1956.

GERMANY

CONTENTS

Table G.1   Gross domestic product at constant prices, 1900–83

	Consumers' expenditure	Govt current expenditure	Gross fixed capital formation	Value of physical change in stocks	Exports of goods & services	Imports of goods & services	Gross domestic product at market prices
				Marks bn, 1975 prices			
1900	135·0	23·9	...	...	...	...	225·2
1901	136·9	24·7	...	...	...	...	219·5
1902	139·7	25·5	...	...	...	...	224·3
1903	145·3	25·5	...	...	...	...	237·3
1904	149·5	27·2	...	...	...	...	246·9
1905	151·9	29·6	...	...	...	...	252·2
1906	152·8	32·1	...	...	...	...	259·8
1907	160·3	32·9	...	...	...	...	271·2
1908	166·9	32·9	...	...	...	...	276·0
1909	168·3	35·2	...	...	...	...	281·2
1910	166·0	35·0	...	...	...	...	291·7
1911	172·0	35·4	...	...	...	...	301·8
1912	179·5	37·9	...	...	...	...	314·7
1913	179·1	42·0	...	...	...	...	328·9
1925	175·8	47·7	...	...	...	...	308·7
1926	173·0	50·2	...	...	...	...	296·2
1927	196·4	52·7	...	...	...	...	351·4
1928	199·2	55·1	...	...	...	...	359·5
1929	197·4	54·3	...	...	...	...	363·5
1930	189·4	53·5	...	...	...	...	341·0
1931	182·8	52·0	...	...	...	...	306·7
1932	179·1	51·7	...	...	...	...	278·0
1933	185·6	63·5	...	...	...	...	305·8
1934	197·4	80·4	...	...	...	...	334·9
1935	198·3	101·8	...	...	...	...	365·6
1936	201·1	129·2	...	...	...	...	403·5
1937	212·8	133·8	...	...	...	...	428·1
1938	221·3	184·9	...	...	...	...	461·2
1948a	55·9	29·3	17·6	3·8	3·4	−4·1	104·8
1949	126·2	63·6	44·9	3·8	10·3	−10·5	236·1
1950	144·4	64·2	56·8	5·7	20·9	−15·2	274·7
1951	155·8	70·4	59·7	5·7	28·4	−16·0	303·5
1952	170·0	77·4	64·9	7·2	32·1	−20·1	330·2
1953	188·4	77·5	76·0	2·7	37·1	−23·6	357·6
1954	199·8	79·5	85·5	3·9	45·9	−30·4	384·9
1955	220·5	83·1	103·3	6·8	53·6	−38·1	431·3
1956	240·0	83·6	112·3	4·4	61·6	−43·3	462·3
1957	255·0	87·7	112·1	7·0	71·3	−50·0	488·3
1958	267·7	95·0	116·9	5·2	73·7	−55·4	505·5
1959	283·0	103·5	130·6	5·5	82·6	−63·9	543·0
1960	305·8	109·8	143·8	11·5	93·3	−75·5	591·4
1961	324·1	116·7	153·6	9·3	96·9	−81·4	612·5
1962	341·8	127·7	160·0	7·0	101·0	−90·4	649·1
1963	351·3	135·4	162·2	4·5	109·0	−94·9	669·3
1964	369·8	137·7	180·3	9·8	118·1	−103·7	714·4
1965	395·2	144·5	189·0	15·3	125·8	−118·6	754·1
1966	407·3	149·0	191·2	7·4	138·6	−121·7	773·7
1967	411·8	154·4	178·0	−1·2	149·2	−120·2	773·0
1968	431·3	155·1	184·5	13·4	168·4	−136·5	818·8
1969	464·8	162·0	203·9	21·1	183·7	−158·9	879·9
1970	500·1	169·2	224·1	17·4	194·4	−182·9	925·1
1971	526·2	177·9	238·0	5·2	206·1	−200·8	953·7
1972	550·2	185·4	244·0	5·6	220·5	−213·6	993·3
1973	563·4	194·6	243·5	13·4	243·9	−222·4	1,038·6
1974	565·9	202·6	220·2	4·3	273·7	−223·6	1,044·2
1975	585·5	210·5	209·4	−6·5	257·0	−229·5	1,026·5
1976	607·9	213·8	219·1	10·6	284·6	−254·8	1,082·9
1977	630·7	215·9	227·5	7·9	296·0	−263·2	1,116·0
1978	653·5	224·4	238·5	6·2	305·9	−279·1	1,150·4
1979	674·1	232·2	255·8	19·4	320·2	−305·5	1,198·4
1980	683·7	238·2	264·0	13·3	337·5	−317·5	1,220·5
1981	675·5	241·9	253·0	−0·3	365·0	−315·3	1,219·5
1982	660·6	239·2	239·3	4·7	377·6	−314·9	1,206·8
1983	*668·0*	*239·2*	*246·6*	...	*372·9*	*−320·9*	*1,218·6*

a Six months only.

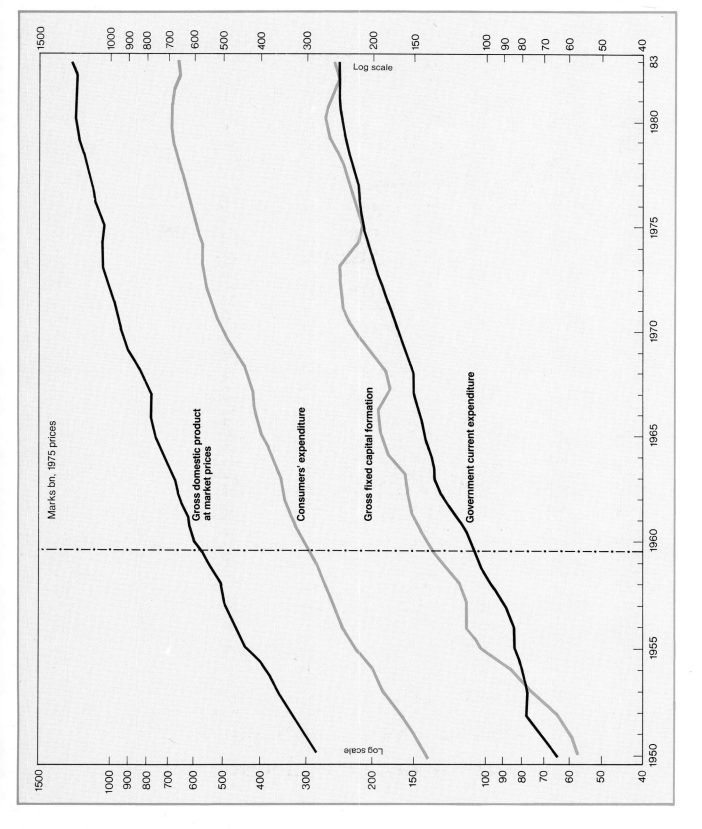

Chart G.1 Gross domestic product at constant prices, 1950–83

Marks bn, 1975 prices

Log scale

Gross domestic product at market prices

Consumers' expenditure

Gross fixed capital formation

Government current expenditure

87

	Industrial production	Coal	Crude steel	Cars & comm. veh.	Crude petroleum	Natural gas	Electricity
	Index nos., 1980 = 100	mn tons	mn tons	'000	'000 tons	mn cu m	bn KWh
1900	7·3	149·6	6·46	...	50	—	1·0
1901	7·1	152·7	6·14	...	44	—	1·3
1902	7·2	150·5	7·47	...	50	—	1·4
1903	7·8	162·3	8·43	...	63	—	1·6
1904	8·2	169·4	8·56	...	90	—	2·2
1905	8·4	173·8	9·67	...	79	—	2·6
1906	8·8	193·5	10·70	...	81	—	2·7
1907	9·5	205·7	11·62	4·3	106	—	3·2
1908	9·4	215·2	10·73	5·0	141	—	3·9
1909	9·8	217·5	11·52	7·9	137	—	4·8
1910	10·4	222·3	13·10	10·2	140	—	5·4
1911	11·0	234·5	14·30	13·1	137	—	6·0
1912	11·7	255·8	16·36	17·9	135	—	7·4
1913	12·0	277·3	17·61	...	121	—	8·0
1914	...	245·3	13·81	...	110	—	8·8
1915	...	234·8	12·28	...	99	—	9·8
1916	...	253·4	14·87	...	93	—	11·0
1917	...	263·2	15·50	...	91	—	12·0
1918	...	258·9	14·09	...	38	—	13·0
1919	...	210·3	8·71 / 7·85	...	37	—	13·5
1920	...	219·4	9·28	...	35	—	15·0
1921	...	237·0	10·00	...	38	—	17·0
1922	...	256·3	11·71	...	42	—	17·0
1923	...	180·4	6·31	...	51	—	15·4
1924	...	243·2	9·84	...	59	—	17·3
1925	12·4	272·5	12·20	49	79	—	20·3
1926	11·1	285·3	12·34	37	95	—	21·2
1927	14·3	304·2	16·31	97	97	—	25·1
1928	14·3	317·2	14·52	123 / 138	92	—	27·9
1929	14·4	337·9	16·25	128	103	—	30·7
1930	12·6	288·7	12·54	96	174	—	29·1
1931	10·2	251·9	8·29	78	229	—	25·8
1932	8·8	227·3	5·77	51	230	—	23·5
1933	9·9	236·5	7·62	105	239	—	25·7
1934	12·2	262·2	11·92	174	318	12	30·7
1935	14·4	290·1	16·45	247	427	14	35·7 / 36·7
1936	16·4	319·7	19·21	301	445	22	42·5
1937	18·3	369·2	19·85	331	451	21	49·0
1938	20·1	381·2	22·66	338	552	18	55·3
1939	...	400·1	23·73	741	...	30	61·4
1940	...	409·4	21·54	...	1,056	...	63·0
1941	...	422·6	20·84	...	901	...	70·0
1942	...	433·8	20·48	...	743	...	71·5
1943	...	443·9	20·76	...	710	...	73·9
1944	...	395·4	18·32	...	720	...	...
1945	...	59·8	...	...	543	71	...
1946	...	105·5	2·56	23	649	109	22·0
1947	...	129·8	3·06	23	577	78	27·8
1948	10·1	151·9	5·56	57	636	67	34·1
1949	14·9	177·0	9·16	159	842	54	40·7
1950	18·6	188·2	12·12	301	1,119	68	46·1
1951	22·3	203·8	13·51	370	1,367	84 / 57	53·7
1952	23·9	208·5	15·81	424	1,755	57	58·7
1953	25·5	210·7	15·42	484	2,189	58	62·9
1954	29·2	217·5	17·43	674	2,666	87	70·5
1955	32·9	222·9	21·34	902	3,147	240	78·9
1956	35·6	231·4	23·19	1,070	3,506	367	87·8
1957	37·7	231·9	24·51	1,206	3,960	357	94·7
1958	38·8	228·1	22·79	1,488	4,432	344	98·2
1959	41·5	237·2	29·44	1,711	5,103	388	106·2
1960	46·2	240·3	34·10	2,047	5,530	448	116·4 / 119·0
1961	49·4	241·7	33·46	2,139	6,204	481	127·3
1962	51·6	244·1	32·56	2,343	6,776	616 / 807	138·4
1963	53·1	250·6	31·60	2,654	7,383	1,171	150·4
1964	57·2	255·0	37·34	2,897	7,673	1,808	164·8
1965	61·3	238·7	36·82	2,963	7,884	2,639	172·3
1966	62·1	225·2	35·32	3,035	7,868	3,390	177·9
1967	60·5	209·7	36·74	2,468	7,927	4,338	184·7
1968	67·9	214·4	41·16	3,091	7,982	6,487	203·3
1969	76·0	219·8	45·32	3,711	7,876	8,912	226·1
1970	81·8	224·1	45·04	3,825	7,535	13,008	242·6
1971	83·4	220·8	40·31	3,957	7,420	15,720	259·6
1972	86·7	218·2	43·71	3,790	7,098	17,448	274·8
1973	92·4	221·7	49·52	3,920	6,638	18,984	299·0
1974	90·7	226·9	53·23	3,068	6,191	19,824	311·7
1975	84·7	220·1	40·41	3,153	5,741	18,804	301·8
1976	91·5	230·4	42·42	3,839	5,524	18,408	333·7
1977	94·1	214·3	38·99	4,104	5,401	19,143	335·3
1978	94·9	213·7	41·25	4,200	5,059	20,471	353·4
1979	100·0	223·9	46·04	4,260	4,774	20,742	372·2
1980	100·0	224·4	43·84	3,893	4,631	17,970	368·8
1981	98·3	219·1	42·16	3,902	4,459	19,334	368·8
1982	95·0	223·6	36·35	4,034	4,260	16,416	366·9
1983	95·8	209·2	36·11	4,162	4,116	17,882	371·8

Chart G.2   Industrial production, selected series, 1900–80

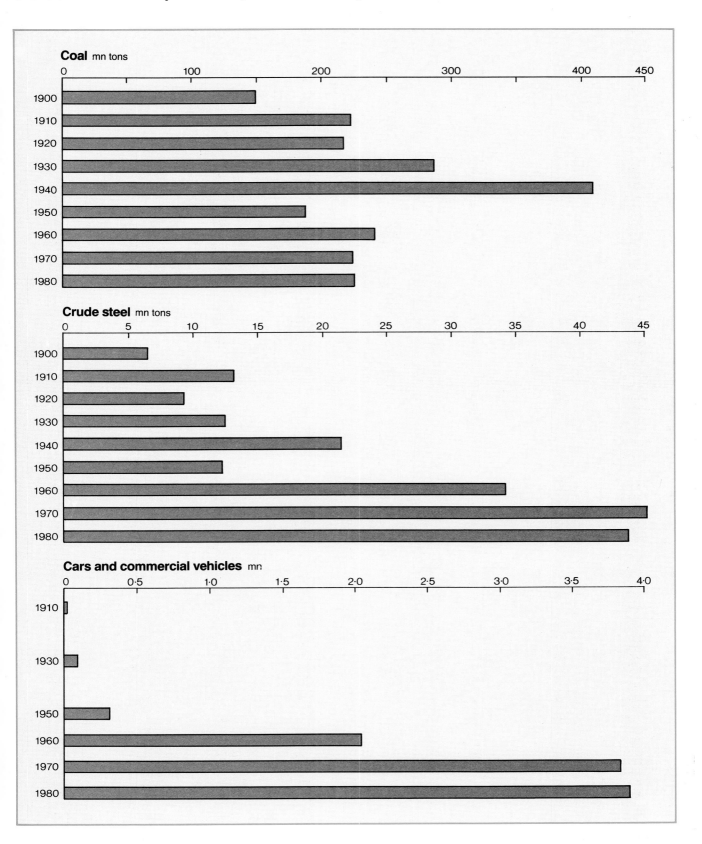

Coal mn tons

Crude steel mn tons

Cars and commercial vehicles mn

Table G.3 Prices and income, 1900–83

	Consumer prices		Producer prices		Compensation of employees	National income
	All items	Food	All items	Raw materials		
	Index nos., 1980 = 100[a]				Marks bn	
1900	15·2	...	1·2	...	20·39	28·86
1901	15·4	...	1·1	...	20·59	28·24
1902	15·4	...	1·1	...	20·90	29·13
1903	15·4	...	1·1	...	21·81	30·51
1904	15·6	...	1·1	...	22·80	32·02
1905	16·2	...	1·2	...	23·85	34·31
1906	17·2	...	1·3	...	25·45	36·17
1907	17·4	...	1·3	...	26·99	38·66
1908	17·4	...	1·2	...	27·27	38·54
1909	17·8	...	1·2	...	27·96	39·51
1910	18·2	...	1·3	...	29·43	41·89
1911	18·8	...	1·3	...	31·17	44·19
1912	19·8	...	1·4	...	32·82	47·30
1913	19·8	...	1·4	...	34·11	48·81
1914	20·4	...	1·4	...	...	...
1915	25·6	...	1·9	...	...	...
1916	33·6	...	2·1	...	...	...
1917	50·0	...	2·4	...	...	...
1918	59·8	...	3·0	...	...	...
1919	82·1	...	5·7	...	...	...
1920	201·7	...	20·3	...	...	...
1921	265·5	...	26·1	...	...	...
1922	b	...	b	...	...	...
1923	b	...	b	...	...	...
1924	25·3	...	1·7	...	...	...
1925	27·8	...	1·8	...	52·13	58·59
1926	28·1	...	1·8	...	52·27	57·56
1927	29·3	30·5	1·9	1937 = 100	60·77	71·99
1928	30·2	30·5	1·9	139	67·40	78·22
1929	30·5	31·1	2·0	137	70·91	80·10
1930	29·4	29·5	1·8	125	67·47	72·89
1931	27·0	25·8	1·6	107	57·06	57·83
1932	23·9	24·2	1·4	92	45·69	37·46
1933	23·4	22·9	1·3	92	45·30	45·73
1934	24·0	21·8	1·4	95	50·04	55·10
1935	24·4	22·6	1·4	95	53·40	64·05
1936	24·7	24·2	1·5	98	56·94	69·96
1937	24·8	26·6	1·5	100	61·05	79·10
1938	24·9	26·6	1·5	98	65·23	87·65
1939	25·0	...	1·5	99	...	...
1940	25·8	...	1·6	103	...	...
1941	26·4	...	1·6	104	...	...
1942	27·1	...	1·6	106	...	...
1943	27·4	...	1·7	106	...	...
1944	28·0	...	1·7	106	...	...
1945	29·1	30·0	...	...	...	...
1946	32·1	31·9	...	1980 = 100	...	...
1947	34·2	33·9	...	...	...	...
1948	39·3	39·7	33·1	40·3	...	...
1949	41·8	46·5	36·7	40·3	...	...
1950	39·3	43·1	43·3	39·8	44·89	89·78
1951	42·2	46·9	50·9	50·2	54·43	109·88
1952	43·0	49·4	52·5	54·9	60·66	125·45
1953	42·2	48·4	50·9	52·3	66·97	135·71
1954	42·2	48·9	49·9	51·3	73·19	145·95
1955	43·1	49·5	51·4	52·8	83·47	167·35
1956	43·6	50·7	51·9	54·4	93·53	184·71
1957	44·9	51·8	53·0	55·0	102·53	200·76
1958	45·9	53·0	52·5	54·4	110·70	214·71
1959	46·3	54·1	52·5	54·4	118·36	233·43
1960	46·8	54·7	53·0	54·4	132·92 / 143·16	260·43 / 279·37
1961	48·1	55·3	53·5	54·4	161·64	304·28
1962	49·4	55·8	54·0	54·4	178·84	329·27
1963	50·9	57·6	54·5	55·0	191·86	347·11
1964	51·9	58·7	55·0	56·0	209·93	380·64
1965	53·9	61·0	56·0	57·7	232·96	414·89
1966	56·0	62·7	57·6	58·3	250·83	439·63
1967	56·6	62·7	57·0	56·0	250·35	443·18
1968	57·8	62·2	57·0	53·8	268·84	480·05
1969	59·0	63·9	57·6	55·4	302·62	539·60
1970	60·9	65·2	60·5	56·6	360·64	607·67
1971	63·9	67·8	63·0	57·1	409·11	674·27
1972	67·6	71·7	64·8	58·8	450·26	739·74
1973	72·4	77·0	69·0	65·1	510·93	824·31
1974	77·3	80·9	78·1	77·7	563·12	879·14
1975	82·2	84·8	82·4	77·9	587·02	912·96
1976	85·2	88·7	85·4	83·1	631·24	999·02
1977	88·9	93·3	87·7	83·8	675·57	1,063·85
1978	91·3	94·6	88·7	81·6	720·89	1,147·20
1979	94·9	95·9	93·0	88·9	776·86	1,238·98
1980	100·0	100·0	100·0	100·0	842·05	1,312·38
1981	105·9	104·9	107·8	111·0	881·32	1,356·88
1982	111·6	111·4	113·8	114·6	900·20	1,399·59
1983	114·9	114·0	...	...	915·26	1,460·96

a For raw materials, 1937 = 100 until 1946.   b The years of hyperinflation.

Table G.4 Population, 1900–83

	Total population	Males	Females	Age distribution Under 15	15–64	65 and over
				mn		
1900	56·05	27·58	28·46	18·38	34·92	2·75
1901	56·87	...	...	...	...	...
1902	57·68	...	...	...	...	...
1903	58·63	...	...	...	...	...
1904	59·48	...	...	...	...	...
1905	60·31	...	...	...	...	...
1906	61·15	...	...	...	...	...
1907	62·01	...	...	...	...	...
1908	62·86	...	...	...	...	...
1909	63·72	...	...	...	...	...
1910	64·57	...	...	...	...	...
1911	65·36	32·26	33·10	20·98	41·11	3·27
1912	66·15	...	...	...	...	...
1913	66·98	...	...	...	...	...
1922	61·90	...	...	...	...	...
1923	62·31	...	...	...	...	...
1924	62·70	...	...	...	...	...
1925	62·41	30·20	32·21	14·79	44·00	3·62
1926	63·63	...	...	...	...	...
1927	64·02	...	...	...	...	...
1928	64·39	...	...	...	...	...
1929	64·74	...	...	...	...	...
1930	65·08	...	...	...	...	...
1931	65·42	...	...	...	...	...
1932	65·72	...	...	...	...	...
1933	65·22	31·69	33·53	15·00	45·66	4·56
1934	66·41	...	...	...	...	...
1935	66·87	...	...	...	...	...
1936	67·35	...	...	...	...	...
1937	67·83	...	...	...	...	...
1938	68·56	...	...	...	...	...
1939	69·31	33·91	35·40	14·97	48·93	5·41
1946	43·29	...	...	...	...	...
1947	44·68	...	...	...	...	...
1948	45·74	...	...	...	...	...
1949	46·51	...	...	...	...	...
1950	47·85	22·31	25·54	(10·43)	(32·97)	(4·45)
1951	48·37	22·58	25·79	...	...	...
1952	48·69	22·73	25·96	...	...	...
1953	49·14	22·96	26·18	...	...	...
1954	49·69	23·24	26·45	...	...	...
1955	50·19	23·49	26·69	(9·79)	(35·38)	(5·02)
1956	53·01	24·75	28·26	11·04	36·55	5·42
1957	53·66	25·07	28·58	11·23	36·83	5·59
1958	54·29	25·38	28·91	11·38	37·19	5·73
1959	54·88	25·67	29·21	11·55	37·45	5·88
1960	55·43	25·97	29·46	11·82	37·60	6·01
1961	56·18	26·41	29·76	12·18	37·74	6·26
1962	56·84	26·80	30·04	12·46	37·96	6·41
1963	57·39	27·10	30·29	12·73	38·06	6·59
1964	57·97	27·41	30·56	12·99	38·18	6·81
1965	58·62	27·79	30·83	13·24	38·35	7·03
1966	59·15	28·06	31·09	13·49	38·41	7·25
1967	59·29	28·05	31·24	13·69	38·14	7·46
1968	59·50	28·13	31·37	13·86	37·99	7·65
1969	60·07	28·48	31·59	14·01	38·22	7·84
1970	60·65	28·87	31·78	14·06	38·60	7·99
1971	61·30	29·26	32·04	14·12	38·97	8·22
1972	61·67	29·47	32·20	14·04	39·22	8·41
1973	61·98	29·65	32·33	13·87	39·51	8·60
1974	62·05	29·67	32·38	13·62	39·65	8·78
1975	61·83	29·50	32·33	13·29	39·61	8·94
1976	61·53	29·32	32·21	12·87	39·59	9·07
1977	61·40	29·24	32·16	12·45	39·73	9·22
1978	61·33	29·21	32·12	12·01	39·95	9·37
1979	61·36	29·25	32·11	11·57	40·29	9·50
1980	61·57	29·42	32·15	11·19	40·83	9·55
1981	61·68	29·50	32·18	10·80	41·43	9·45
1982	61·64	29·48	32·16	10·39	41·97	9·27
1983	61·42	...	...	...	...	...

Table G.5 Labour market: employment, 1929–83

	Employed labour force[a]	Agriculture, forestry & fishing	Mining & quarrying	Mfg	Construction	Gas, electricity & water	Transport & communication	Distribution & services
				mn				
1929	(17·60)	...		6·50		...	...	...
1930	(16·41)	...		5·66		...	...	...
1931	(14·34)	...		4·68		...	...	...
1932	(12·52)	...		3·86		...	...	...
1933	(13·02)	...		4·28		...	...	...
1934	(15·04)	...		5·41		...	...	...
1935	(15·95)	...		5·89		...	...	...
1936	(17·11)	...		6·39		...	...	...
1937	(18·39)	...		6·91		...	...	...
1938	(19·50)	...		7·35		...	...	...
1939	(20·60)	...		7·67		...	...	...
1940	(18·77)	...		7·01		...	...	...
1941	(18·77)	...		7·32		...	...	...
1942	(18·58)	...		7·08		...	...	...
1943	(19·13)	...		7·45		...	...	...
1944	(18·77)	...		7·64		...	...	...
1948	(11·88)			4·88		...	...	...
1949	(12·16)			5·15		...	...	...
1950	(12·59)			5·44		...	...	...
1950	20·37	5·02		8·73			6·62	
1951	20·90	4·85		9·12			6·93	
1952	21·29	4·70		9·37			7·23	
1953	21·80	4·54		9·77			7·50	
1954	22·38	4·40		10·27			7·71	
1955	23·21	4·29		10·89			8·04	
	23·79	4·18		11·36			8·26	
1956	24·75	4·18		11·68			8·89	
1957	25·21	4·11		11·95			9·16	
1958	25·36	3·98		12·08			9·30	
1959	25·57	3·82		12·36			9·39	
1960	25·95	3·62		12·66			9·67	
1961	26·24	3·45	0·51	10·15	2·02	0·29	1·47	8·36
1962	26·29	3·31	0·50	10·21	2·07	0·28	1·50	8·42
1963	26·32	3·14	0·48	9·91	2·16	0·28	1·52	8·83
1964	26·30	3·00	0·47	9·92	2·17	0·27	1·55	8·92
1965	26·42	2·88	0·45	10·11	2·21	0·26	1·58	8·93
1966	26·32	2·79	0·42	10·05	2·17	0·24	1·55	9·10
1967	25·46	2·64	0·38	9·55	1·99	0·22	1·52	9·16
1968	25·49	2·52	0·35	9·64	2·03	0·20	1·49	9·26
1969	25·87	2·40	0·34	10·07	2·07	0·19	1·48	9·32
1970	26·17	2·26	0·34	10·31	2·07	0·19	1·48	9·52
1971	26·32	2·13	0·43	9·84	2·27	0·21	1·55	9·89
1972	26·21	2·02	0·42	9·65	2·25	0·20	1·58	10·09
1973	26·41	1·92	0·40	9·70	2·25	0·21	1·61	10·32
1974	26·04	1·84	0·37	9·48	2·09	0·22	1·61	10·43
1975	25·29	1·77	0·36	9·01	1·88	0·24	1·58	10·45
1976	25·06	1·68	0·36	8·81	1·88	0·22	1·54	10·57
1977	25·01	1·59	0·33	8·77	1·84	0·23	1·52	10·73
1978	25·17	1·54	0·35	8·75	1·86	0·22	1·52	10·93
1979	25·51	1·48	0·34	8·81	1·94	0·23	1·53	11·18
1980	25·75	1·44	0·34	8·85	1·96	0·24	1·55	11·39
1981	25·57	1·41	0·36	8·60	1·93	0·24	1·54	11·49
1982	25·10	1·38	0·32	8·32	1·83	0·25	1·53	11·45
1983	24·65	1·37		10·35			12·93	

a For years 1929–50 see notes on p. 97.

	Mfg				Industrial disputes		
	Average weekly hrs worked	Average hourly earnings	Unemployment		Stoppages	Workers involved	Working days lost
		Marks	'000	%		'000	'000
1900	...	...	...	2·0	1,468	321	3,712
1901	...	...	...	6·7	1,091	149	2,427
1902	...	...	...	2·9	1,106	150	1,951
1903	...	...	...	2·7	1,444	251	4,158
1904	...	...	...	2·1	1,990	310	5,285
1905	...	...	...	1·6	2,657	966	18,984
1906	...	...	...	1·1	3,626	839	11,567
1907	...	...	...	1·6	2,512	575	9,017
1908	...	...	...	2·9	1,524	281	3,666
1909	...	...	...	2·8	1,652	291	4,152
1910	...	...	...	1·9	3,228	681	17,848
1911	...	...	...	1·9	2,798	896	11,466
1912	...	...	...	2·0	2,834	1,031	10,724
1913	...	...	...	2·9	2,464	655	11,761
1914	...	...	...	7·2	1,223	238	2,844
1915	...	...	...	3·3	141	48	46
1916	...	...	...	2·2	240	423	245
1917	...	...	...	1·0	562	1,468	1,862
1918	...	...	...	1·2	532	716	1,453
1919	...	...	...	3·7	3,719	2,761	33,083
1920	...	...	...	3·8	3,807	2,009	16,755
1921	...	...	...	2·8	4,455	2,036	25,874
1922	...	...	...	1·5	4,785	2,566	27,734
1923	...	...	...	9·6	2,046	1,917	12,344
1924	...	...	...	13·5	1,973	2,066	36,198
1925	...	...	...	6·7	1,708	1,115	2,936
1926	...	...	...	18·0	351	131	1,222
1927	...	...	...	8·8	844	686	6,144
1928	(45·36)	...	...	8·4	739	986	20,339
1929	46·02	96·8	1,899	9·3	429	268	4,251
1930	44·22	94·0	3,076	15·3	353	302	4,029
1931	42·48	86·9	4,520	23·3	463	297	1,890
1932	41·46	73·0	5,575	30·1	648	172	1,130
1933	42·96	70·7	4,804	26·3	(69)	(13)	...
1934	44·58	72·5	2,718	14·9	...	...	...
1935	44·46	73·6	2,151	11·6	...	...	...
1936	46·7	74·8	1,593	8·3	...	...	...
1937	47·6	76·4	912	4·6	...	...	...
1938	48·5	78·9	429	2·1	...	...	...
1939	48·7	81·2	119	...	...	...	...
1940	49·2	83·9	52	...	...	...	...
1948	44·6	1·05	592	4·2	...	...	...
1949	43·8	1·20	1,230	8·3	892	58	271
1950	44·4	1·28	1,580	10·2	1,344	79	380
1951	44·8	1·45	1,432	9·0	1,528	174	1,593
1952	44·2	1·56	1,379	8·4	2,529	84	443
1953	48·0	1·59	1,259	7·5	1,359	51	1,488
1954	48·7	1·63	1,221	7·0	538	116	1,587
1955	48·8	1·73	928	5·1	866	600	847
1956	47·8	1·90	761	4·0	268	52	1,580
1957	46·4	2·09	662	3·4	86	45	1,072
1958	45·5	2·23	683	3·5	1,484	202	782
1959	45·6	2·36	480	2·4	55	22	62
1960	45·6	2·62	237	1·2	28	17	38
1961	45·3	2·90	161	0·8	119	20	61
1962	44·7	3·23	142	0·7	195	79	451
1963	44·3	3·46	174	0·8	187	316	1,846
1964	43·6	3·74	157	0·7	34	6	17
1965	44·1	4·12	147	0·6	20	6	49
1966	43·7	4·42	161	0·7	205	196	27
1967	42·0	4·60	460	2·1	742	60	390
1968	43·0	4·79	324	1·5	36	25	25
1969	43·8	5·28	179	0·9	86	90	249
1970	43·8	5·96	149	0·7	...[a]	184	93
1971	43·0	6·66	185	0·8	...	536	4,484
1972	42·7	7·24	246	1·1	...	23	66
1973	42·8	8·03	274	1·2	...	185	563
1974	41·9	8·94	583	2·6	...	250	1,051
1975	40·4	9·69	1,074	4·7	...	36	69
1976	41·4	10·35	1,060	4·6	...	169	534
1977	41·7	11·14	1,030	4·5	...	34	24
1978	41·6	11·73	993	4·3	...	487	4,281
1979	41·8	12·36	876	3·8	...	77	483
1980	41·6	13·18	889	3·8	...	45	128
1981	41·1	13·92	1,272	5·5	...	253	58
1982	40·7	14·64	1,833	7·7	...	40	15
1983	40·5	15·14	2,264	9·2	...	94	41

a   Series discontinued.

Table G.7 Value of exports and imports by country, 1900–83

	Total exports	Exports to: France	Italy	UK	USA	Total imports	Imports from: France	Italy	UK	USA
					Marks bn					
1900	4·61	0·28	0·12	0·86	0·44	5·77	0·30	0·18	0·72	1·00
1901	4·43	0·25	0·12	0·91	0·39	5·42	0·27	0·18	0·55	0·99
1902	4·68	0·25	0·13	0·96	0·45	5·63	0·30	0·19	0·56	0·89
1903	5·02	0·27	0·13	0·98	0·47	6·00	0·33	0·20	0·59	0·94
1904	5·22	0·27	0·14	0·99	0·50	6·35	0·37	0·19	0·62	0·94
1905	5·73	0·29	0·16	1·04	0·54	7·13	0·40	0·21	0·72	0·99
1906	6·36	0·38	0·23	1·07	0·64	8·02	0·43	0·24	0·83	1·24
1907	6·85	0·45	0·30	1·06	0·65	8·75	0·45	0·29	0·98	1·32
1908	6·40	0·44	0·31	1·00	0·51	7·66	0·42	0·24	0·70	1·28
1909	6·60	0·46	0·29	1·02	0·61	8·52	0·49	0·29	0·72	1·26
1910	7·48	0·54	0·32	1·10	0·63	8·93	0·51	0·28	0·77	1·19
1911	8·11	0·60	0·35	1·14	0·64	9·68	0·52	0·29	0·81	1·34
1912	8·97	0·69	0·40	1·16	0·70	10·67	0·55	0·31	0·84	1·59
1913	10·10	0·79	0·39	1·44	0·71	10·75	0·58	0·32	0·88	1·71
1923	6·10	0·07	0·25	0·56	0·48	6·15	0·19	0·15	1·02	1·17
1924	6·67	0·11	0·24	0·61	0·49	9·13	0·69	0·37	0·83	1·71
1925	9·28	0·49	0·43	0·94	0·60	12·43	0·56	0·50	0·94	2·20
1926	10·42	0·67	0·49	1·16	0·74	9·98	0·38	0·39	0·58	1·60
1927	10·80	0·56	0·46	1·18	0·78	14·11	0·81	0·53	0·96	2·07
1928	12·06	0·69	0·55	1·18	0·80	13·93	0·74	0·47	0·89	2·03
1929	13·49	0·94	0·60	1·31	0·99	13·36	0·64	0·44	0·87	1·79
1930	12·04	1·15	0·48	1·22	0·69	10·35	0·52	0·37	0·64	1·31
1931	9·59	0·83	0·34	1·13	0·49	6·71	0·34	0·27	0·45	0·79
1932	5·74	0·48	0·22	0·45	0·28	4·65	0·19	0·18	0·26	0·59
1933	4·87	0·40	0·23	0·41	0·25	4·20	0·18	0·17	0·24	0·48
1934	4·18	0·28	0·25	0·38	0·16	4·45	0·18	0·19	0·21	0·37
1935	4·27	0·25	0·28	0·38	0·17	4·16	0·15	0·19	0·26	0·24
1936	4·78	0·26	0·24	0·41	0·17	4·23	0·10	0·21	0·26	0·23
1937	5·92	0·31	0·31	0·43	0·21	5·50	0·16	0·22	0·31	0·28
1938	5·26	0·23	0·35	0·37	0·16	5·45	0·16	0·28	0·31	0·46
1939	5·65	0·13	0·36	0·23	0·13	5·21	0·08	0·29	0·18	0·20
1940	4·89	—	0·72	—	0·01	5·01	—	0·51	—	0·02
1941	6·84	0·32	1·19	—	—	6·93	0·75	0·94	—	—
1942	7·56	0·55	1·31	—	—	8·69	1·40	1·02	—	—
1943	8·59	0·56	0·95	—	—	8·26	1·42	0·78	—	—
1948	1·82	0·22	0·07	0·26	0·10	3·16	0·01	0·07	0·13	1·57
1949	3·81	0·51	0·22	0·38	0·16	7·33	0·09	0·32	0·18	2·59
1950	8·36	0·61	0·49	0·36	0·43	11·37	0·69	0·51	0·49	1·74
1951	14·58	0·97	0·67	0·88	0·99	14·73	0·62	0·55	0·50	2·72
1952	16·91	1·08	0·63	0·96	1·04	16·20	0·61	0·64	0·53	2·51
1953	18·53	1·08	1·24	0·79	1·24	16·01	0·78	0·74	0·65	1·66
1954	22·04	1·19	1·34	0·86	1·23	19·34	0·97	0·84	0·85	2·23
1955	25·72	1·46	1·43	1·03	1·61	24·47	1·45	1·04	0·87	3·20
1956	30·86	1·95	1·66	1·26	2·07	27·96	1·35	1·22	1·15	3·97
1957	35·97	2·25	2·00	1·41	2·49	31·70	1·55	1·55	1·14	5·63
1958	37·00	2·16	1·85	1·46	2·64	31·13	1·60	1·70	1·36	4·19
1959	41·18	2·97	2·20	1·66	3·78	35·82	2·76	2·18	1·63	4·58
1960	47·95	4·20	2·85	2·15	3·72	42·72	4·00	2·63	1·96	5·97
1961	50·98	4·78	3·39	2·12	3·45	44·36	4·62	3·04	1·97	6·10
1962	52·98	5·44	4·11	1·95	3·86	49·50	5·27	3·74	2·35	7·03
1963	58·31	6·43	5·46	2·21	4·20	52·28	5·50	3·70	2·47	7·94
1964	64·92	7·42	4·59	2·72	4·79	58·84	6·27	4·47	2·78	8·07
1965	71·65	7·79	4·50	2·80	5·74	70·45	7·84	6·56	3·14	9·20
1966	80·63	9·22	5·66	3·13	7·18	72·67	8·62	6·68	3·16	9·18
1967	87·05	10·05	6·89	3·47	7·86	70·18	8·49	6·44	2·93	8·56
1968	99·55	12·24	7·57	4·03	10·84	81·18	9·78	8·07	3·41	8·85
1969	113·56	15·12	9·26	4·59	10·63	97·97	12·70	9·49	3·91	10·25
1970	125·28	15·48	11·17	4·46	11·44	109·61	13·90	10·84	4·26	12·07
1971	136·01	16·98	11·45	5·45	13·14	120·12	15·92	12·69	4·41	12·42
1972	149·02	19·41	12·56	7·05	13·80	128·74	18·16	13·90	4·58	10·76
1973	178·40	23·13	14·98	8·40	15·09	145·42	18·96	14·04	5·16	12·22
1974	230·58	27·34	18·73	11·01	17·34	179·73	20·90	14·98	6·27	13·97
1975	221·59	25·96	16·19	10·09	13·15	184·31	22·15	17·23	6·94	14·23
1976	256·64	33·67	19·00	12·18	14·41	222·17	25·83	18·90	8·54	17·56
1977	273·61	33·64	18·73	14·61	18·20	235·18	27·31	20·73	10·45	17·02
1978	284·91	34·90	19·43	16·88	20·18	243·71	28·28	23·18	12·07	17·43
1979	314·47	39·99	24·53	21·03	20·76	292·04	33·20	25·80	17·22	20·27
1980	350·33	46·62	29·94	22·92	21·48	341·38	36·59	27·08	22·86	25·69
1981	396·90	51·91	31·31	26·16	25·98	369·18	40·12	27·56	27·50	28·39
1982	427·74	60·13	32·38	31·32	28·12	376·46	42·88	28·71	27·00	28·21
1983	432·28	55·56	32·09	35·40	32·85	390·19	44·57	31·57	27·14	27·71

SOURCES

(For sources used in specific tables, see Notes.)

1 Hoffman, W H, *Das Wachstum der Deutschen Wirtschaft seit der Mitte des 19 Jahr Hunderts.* Springer-Verlag, Berlin and Heidelberg, 1965.

2 International Labour Office, *Technical Guide*, Vol. II. Geneva, 1972, 1976, 1980.

3 League of Nations, *Year Book of Labour Statistics.*

4 Mitchell, B R, *European Historical Statistics, 1750–1975*, 2nd rev. edn. Macmillan, London, 1980.

5 Organisation for Economic Cooperation and Development (OECD), *Labour Force Statistics.* Paris, annual and quarterly.

6 OECD, *National Accounts 1950 to 1978.* Paris, 1980.

7 OECD, *National Accounts 1953 to 1982.* Paris, 1984, and quarterly accounts, 1984.

8 *Statistisches Jahrbuch.* W Kohlhammer GmH, Stuttgart and Mainz, annual.

9 *Statistical Year Book of the League of Nations.* Geneva.

10 Supplements to the United Nations, *Statistical Year Book* and *Monthly Digest of Statistics.* New York, 1967, 1972 and 1977.

11 United Nations, *Monthly Bulletin of Statistics.* New York.

12 United Nations, *Statistics of National Income and Expenditure,* Series H, no. 7. New York, 1955.

13 United Nations, *Statistical Year Book.* New York.

14 *Year Book of Labour Statistics.* ILO, Geneva.

NOTES

Table G.1

Sources: **1, 6, 7, 12**

From 1950, OECD data have been used. There is a break in the series in 1960 when there was a change in the system of classification. The main differences in classification are explained in **7**.

For 1948–49, constant price estimates published in **12** were linked to OECD data at 1950 and roughly adjusted to 1975 prices. The figure for 1948 is for six months only. For 1900–38, the figures are for prewar Germany and are based on estimates made by Hoffmann, **1**, roughly adjusted to 1975 prices.

The figures for gross domestic product have been obtained by using an index of output (based on Hoffmann's estimates) and extrapolating the 1936 figure published in **12** and grossed up to include the whole of Germany. Hoffmann's figures are for *net* national product and were not, therefore, used for this column. Similarly, Hoffmann's estimates for capital formation have not been used as they are net and not gross figures.

Table G.2

Sources: **4, 8, 9, 11, 13**

Industrial production: a combined base weighted index of output in manufacturing, mining and electricity and gas industries. The current index is based on 1970 weights. The Saar is included from 1950. Figures from 1938 are for the Federal Republic of Germany; 1900–37 covers the whole of Germany. For further details of method of construction and weights see **10**.

Coal: includes brown and hard coal.

Cars and commercial vehicles: the figures for 1946–48 are for the British and American occupation zones only. For 1900–28 (first line), chassis production for export is excluded from the figures.

Natural gas: published figures are now given in terajoules. From 1977, the published figures have been converted to cubic metres using the conversion factor 35169 – see **11**. From 1951 (second line) to 1962 (first line), natural gas from oil wells is included.

Electricity: the Saar is included from 1960 (second line).

The following boundary changes affect the figures in this table.

1900–18	parts of Alsace Lorraine included
1921–34	the Saar excluded
1945–58	the Saar excluded
From 1945	Federal Republic of Germany only for most of the series

Table G.3

Sources: **1, 4, 6, 7, 9, 13**

Consumer prices: base weighted indices measuring fluctuations in prices of selected items. The current weights and selected items were derived from a family expenditure survey conducted among private households of all types of consumers. The index is for the Federal Republic of Germany for all items from 1945 and for food from 1938. From 1960 the Saar and from 1962 West Berlin, are included.

In the prewar period, the index for 'All items' covered the whole of prewar Germany. Commodity coverage would not have been so comprehensive but would have covered food, heating and lighting, clothing and rent.

For details of methods of collection and coverage of current series, see **10**.

Producer prices: the official title of the 'All items' index is 'Index of producers' prices of industrial products'. It is a base weighted index, and the commodity coverage has been widened considerably in recent years. From 1968, value added tax has been excluded from the prices making up the index. In 1924, prices for the index were based on gold following the 'great inflation' and from 1925, a new series was spliced on to the old index. From 1948, the series is for the Federal Republic of Germany and excludes the Saar before 1960 and West Berlin before 1962.

The official title of the 'Raw materials' index is 'Price index of basic materials'. It is a base weighted index relating to basic materials purchased by goods producing sectors (excluding agriculture and forestry). The price relatives include customs duties (imported goods) and turnover compensation tax.

The series for 1928–44 is for the whole of Germany based on 1937 = 100. It includes some semi-manufactured goods.

For further details of the current series see **10**.

Compensation of employees: OECD data have been used from 1950. The figures include wages and salaries in cash and in kind paid to employees, together with contributions on behalf of employees to social security schemes and private pension funds as well as family allowances and private health insurance paid by employers. Two figures are given for 1960 because of the change in classification (see notes to Table 1). See also **7**.

For 1900–38 Hoffmann's estimates of *arbeitseinkommen* have been given; see **1** for composition of the series. These cover pre-war Germany, whereas the figures from 1950 are for the Federal Republic of Germany.

National income: OECD data have been used from 1950. National income is defined as the sum of compensation of employees, net entrepreneurial and property income of residents and indirect taxes less subsidies. Two figures have been given for 1960 because of the change in classification (see notes to Table G.1). For further details, see **7**.

Estimates by Hoffmann, **1**, for pre-war Germany have been given for the period 1900–38. They refer to Netto-sozialprodukt and may not be comparable with the figures from 1950. For further details of composition, see **1**. Hoffman's estimates show a minus figure for income from capital in some years and for factor incomes from abroad for the years 1926–38.

Table G.4

Sources: **1, 5**

OECD data have been used from 1950. From 1956, the figures are annual averages of the resident (*de jure*) population. For 1950–55, they are mid year estimates and exclude West Berlin. The figures for 1900–49 are taken from Hoffman, **1**, and are mid year estimates. The figures for 1900, 1911, 1925, 1933 and 1939 are Census data. Federal Republic only from 1946.

Age distribution: for the years 1900–55 the population distribution relates to those under 14 years and 14–64 years. The years 1950 and 1955 have been estimated by the author on the basis of data in **1**.

Table G.5

Sources: **3, 5, 13, 14**

OECD data have been used from 1950. The figures are annual averages of those in civil employment and include employees, self employed and unpaid family workers working for at least one third of normal working time. The unemployed and temporarily stopped are not included.

From 1948, the figures are for the Federal Republic of Germany; the Saar is included from 1950 (second line) and West Berlin from 1956 (second line). The classification of industrial activity was changed in 1960. From 1972, the data are not strictly comparable with earlier years because of a change in the way in which national data were converted to the International Standard Industrial Classification.

'Distribution and services' includes wholesale and retail trades, restaurants and hotels, finance, insurance, real estate and business services, commercial, social and personal services.

For 1929–50 (first line), the figures for the 'Employed labour force' are for wage earners and salaried employees only in mining, manufacturing, construction, commerce, personal and public services and agriculture. The numbers are based on sickness insurance statistics published in **3** and from 1936 have been extrapolated by means of an index published in **13**, 1948, and **14**, 1954. The figures include the Saar from 1935 and Austria and Sudetenland for 1939–44. Figures available for the *total* labour force are from Census data covering the economically active population which includes employers and self employed, employees and unemployed. For the years 1933 (excluding the Saar) and 1939 (1937 territory), the economically active population numbered just over 32 mn and 34·5 mn, respectively.

The figures given for this period in the industry classifications are for wage earners and salaried employees in manufacturing. For 1939–44 they include employees in the mining and building industries. The economically active population in manufacturing was 9·97 mn in 1933 and 11·51 mn in 1939. For further details see **3**.

Table G.6

Sources: **4, 14**

Manufacturing: average weekly hours worked: the current series is of average weekly hours *paid for* in the reporting week. This comprises, in addition to hours actually worked, hours not worked but paid for, such as annual vacation, paid public holidays and paid sick leave. It covers wage earners of both sexes including foremen but excluding apprentices. The sample was revised in 1973. Construction workers and public utilities are included for 1953–56, building workers for 1936–40 and mining in 1939 and 1940.

The figures are for the Federal Republic of Germany from 1948; the Saar is included from 1960 and West Berlin from 1964.

Manufacturing: average hourly earnings: the current series is of average hourly earnings per wage earner, both sexes, without distinction as to age, and including foremen (but not apprentices). Earnings include cash payments before deduction of taxes and social security contributions payable by workers; payment for normal working hours, overtime pay, holiday pay, sick leave, bonuses and gratuities, cost of living allowances and special premiums are included; also includes family allowances paid directly by the employer. The figures are for the Federal Republic of Germany from 1948; the Saar is included from 1960 and West Berlin from 1964.

For the period 1929–41, the series includes mining and transport.

For further details of these series see **2** and **3**.

Unemployment: the figures refer to the unemployed registered at employment offices at the end of each month; the annual figure is the average of months. For 1948–60, the figures are for a specific date: 30 June for 1948–54 and 30 September for 1955–60. The figures for 1900–28 are for the unemployed in trade unions. From 1949, the figures refer to the Federal Republic of Germany. For further details see **2**.

The percentage figure is obtained by dividing the number of unemployed by the number of employees (employed and unemployed) derived from the latest one per cent sample population census (× 100).

Industrial disputes: for 1933 the figures are for the first quarter only. For 1949 and 1950, the figures are for the American and British zones. From 1950, coverage is of the Federal Republic of Germany including West Berlin from 1960.

Table G.7

Sources: **4, 8, 14**

Figures refer to the Federal Republic of Germany from 1948. For 1923–35 and 1945–59, the Saar is excluded. Austria became part of Germany in 1938. Trade with UK included Southern Ireland up to 1923. Alsace Lorraine is included to 1918.

Figures from 1923 are post inflation values.

From 1906, figures refer to countries of origin and consumption; German free ports are not included in customs area before this date.

ITALY

CONTENTS

Table It.1   Gross domestic product at constant prices, 1900–83

	Consumers' expenditure	Govt current expenditure	Gross fixed capital formation	Value of physical change in stocks	Exports of goods & services	Imports of goods & services	Gross domestic product at market prices
				L bn, 1975 prices			
1900	...	...	...	...	...	...	15,659
1901					...	...	16,687
1902					...	...	16,344
1903					...	...	17,105
1904					...	...	17,051
1905	12,960	1,516	2,442	388	...	...	17,822
1906					...	...	18,122
1907					...	...	19,900
1908					...	...	19,490
1909					...	...	20,843
1910					...	...	19,365
1911					...	...	20,885
1912					...	...	21,357
1913					...	...	21,828
1914					...	...	21,250
1915					...	...	22,621
1916	15,423	7,811	2,375	− 394	...	...	24,313
1917					...	...	24,591
1918					...	...	23,370
1919					...	...	22,406
1920					...	...	23,734
1921	...	...	...	...	...	...	22,856
1922	...	...	...	...	...	...	24,206
1923	...	...	...	...	...	...	25,341
1924	...	...	...	...	...	...	25,341
1925	...	...	...	...	...	...	26,948
1926	18,682	3,656	4,862	− 242		204	27,162
1927	18,968	3,837	4,640	− 903		341	26,883
1928	19,471	3,961	5,040	1,303		− 321	29,454
1929	19,874	3,950	5,306	879		− 127	29,882
1930	19,467	4,083	5,151	− 1,182		328	27,847
1931	18,914	5,005	4,374	− 848		− 197	27,248
1932	19,439	5,292	3,974	485		− 850	28,340
1933	19,831	5,613	4,196	− 364		− 743	28,533
1934	19,399	5,665	4,706	− 576		− 811	28,383
1935	19,756	6,621	5,794	939		− 1,814	31,296
1936	19,144	8,594	6,327	− 1,000		− 2,540	30,525
1937	20,307	8,272	6,239	1,242		− 2,836	33,224
1938	20,889	7,710	5,839	727		− 2,241	32,924
1939	21,192	8,808	6,549	1,394		− 3,091	34,852
1940	21,127	9,842	6,383	− 848		− 3,066	33,438
1941	19,852	11,230	6,039	− 1,090		− 3,792	32,239
1942	18,569	15,024	5,195	− 1,575		− 6,281	30,932
1943	15,833	18,815	3,996	− 1,909		− 8,931	27,804
1944	13,490	10,857	2,375	− 818		− 4,590	21,314
1945	11,926	7,527	2,065	− 970		− 2,726	17,822
1946	16,350	8,605	4,973	697		− 3,356	27,269
1947	19,510	6,691	6,350	2,606		− 2,404	32,753
1948	21,438	7,092	5,950	− 212		− 1,515	32,753
1949	22,913	7,396	5,905	394		− 1,692	34,916
1950	24,102	7,431	6,527	758		− 1,695	37,123
1951	25,098	7,979	7,060	1,212	2,190	− 2,963	39,308
1952	26,744	8,313	8,052	17	2,143	− 3,294	41,050
1953	28,395	8,496	9,105	344	2,630	− 3,754	44,130
1954	28,830	8,860	10,145	54	2,885	− 3,874	45,734
1955	30,058	9,015	11,397	989	3,220	− 4,249	48,794
1956	31,478	9,318	12,151	780	3,743	− 4,836	51,074
1957	32,774	9,477	13,248	635	4,540	− 5,369	53,782
1958	34,083	9,996	13,598	712	5,112	− 5,558	56,389
1959	35,782	10,433	14,776	952	6,014	− 6,198	60,068
1960	37,977	10,855	16,596	1,792	7,206	− 8,547	63,870
1961	40,818	11,330	18,515	2,075	8,268	− 9,721	69,112
1962	43,733	11,772	20,324	1,679	9,125	− 11,173	73,400
1963	47,789	12,276	21,966	1,100	9,717	− 13,690	77,517
1964	49,372	12,795	20,688	514	10,767	− 12,849	79,685
1965	50,983	13,302	18,948	795	12,918	− 13,105	82,290
1966	54,634	13,828	19,767	1,004	14,363	− 14,944	87,215
1967	58,668	14,434	22,087	1,356	15,392	− 16,959	93,476
1968	61,700	15,183	24,472	52	17,527	− 17,957	99,593
1969	65,770	15,607	26,369	1,036	19,587	− 21,421	105,666
1970	70,772	16,008	27,169	2,651	20,728	− 24,851	111,278
1971	72,849	16,914	26,294	980	22,173	− 25,491	113,106
1972	75,326	17,814	26,534	1,017	24,525	− 28,288	116,728
1973	79,750	18,244	28,585	5,339	25,339	− 31,188	124,936
1974	81,853	18,756	29,542	5,381	27,481	− 31,573	130,110
1975	80,571	19,362	25,776	− 352	28,529	− 28,508	125,378
1976	83,341	19,785	26,381	4,591	32,075	− 32,701	132,740
1977	84,511	20,339	26,288	2,223	34,813	− 32,690	135,259
1978	86,814	20,807	26,261	1,691	38,348	− 35,345	138,892
1979	91,094	21,141	27,792	3,318	41,976	− 40,130	145,704
1980	95,475	21,587	30,403	7,643	40,052	− 43,496	151,404
1981	96,262	22,255	30,600	1,167	41,690	− 41,269	151,616
1982	96,242	22,660	28,986	1,691	42,588	− 42,200	151,087
1983	95,661	23,712	27,455	...	43,510	− 42,601	149,303

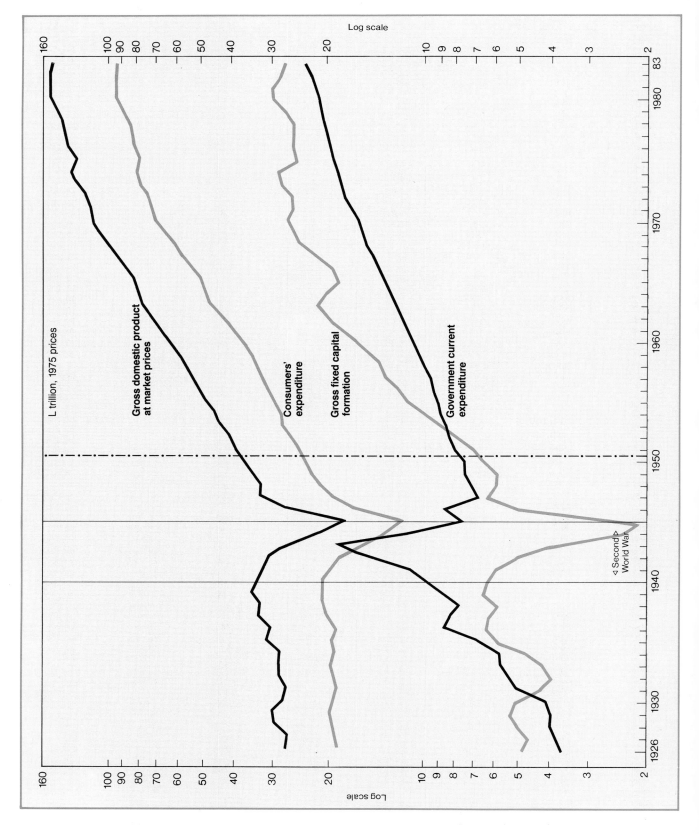

Chart It.1   Gross domestic product at constant prices, 1926–83

Log scale

L trillion, 1975 prices

Gross domestic product at market prices

Consumers' expenditure

Gross fixed capital formation

Government current expenditure

◁ Second ◁
World War

Table It.2   Industrial production, index and selected series, 1900–83

	Industrial production	Coal	Crude steel	Cars & commercial vehicles	Crude petroleum	Natural gas	Electricity
	Index nos., 1980 = 100	mn tons	mn tons	'000	'000 tons	mn cu m	bn KWh
1900	4·3	0·5	0·12	...	2	1	0·16
1901	4·3	0·4	0·13	...	2	1	0·22
1902	4·7	0·4	0·14	...	3	2	0·30
1903	4·7	0·3	0·19	...	3	2	0·40
1904	4·9	0·3	0·20	...	4	3	0·45
1905	5·2	0·4	0·27	...	6	3	0·55
1906	5·8	0·5	0·39	...	8	6	0·70
1907	6·3	0·4	0·43	...	8	6	0·95
1908	6·5	0·5	0·54	...	7	7	1·15
1909	6·7	0·6	0·66	...	6	8	1·30
1910	6·7	0·6	0·73	...	7	9	1·50
1911	6·7	0·6	0·74	...	10	9	1·80
1912	7·2	0·7	0·92	...	8	7	2·00
1913	7·0	0·7	0·93	...	7	6	2·20
1914	6·7	0·8	0·91	...	6	6	2·58
1915	8·7	0·9	1·01	...	6	6	2·93
1916	8·7	1·3	1·27	...	7	6	3·43
1917	7·8	1·7	1·33	...	6	7	4·00
1918	7·5	2·1	0·93	...	5	7	4·30
1919	7·3	1·1	0·73	...	5	9	4·00
1920	7·3	1·6	0·77	...	5	8	4·69
1921	6·7	1·0	0·70	...	5	8	4·54
1922	7·5	0·9	0·98	...	4	7	4·73
1923	8·1	1·1	1·14	...	5	7	5·61
1924	9·0	1·0	1·36	...	5	7	6·45
1925	10·2	1·2	1·79	50	8	7	7·26
1926	10·2	1·4	1·78	64	5	6	8·39
1927	9·9	1·1	1·60	55	6	6	8·74
1928	10·8	0·8	1·96	58	6	6	9·63
1929	11·1	1·0	2·12	55	6	7	10·38
1930	10·5	0·8	1·74	47	8	9	10·67
1931	9·5	0·6	1·41	29	16	12	10·47
1932	9·5	0·7	1·40	30	27	13	10·59
1933	10·1	0·7	1·77	42	27	14	11·65
1934	9·9	0·8	1·85	45	20	15	12·60
1935	10·6	0·9	2·21	51	16	12	13·80
1936	10·6	1·6	2·03	53	16	13	13·65
1937	12·3	2·1	2·09	77	14	15	15·43
1938	12·3	2·3	2·32	71	13	17	15·54
1939	13·4	3·1	2·28	69	12	20	18·42
1940	13·6	4·4	2·26	48	11	28	19·43
1941	12·7	4·4	2·06	39	12	42	20·76
1942	11·0	4·9	1·93	30	13	55	20·23
1943	8·5	3·3	1·73	21	11	55	18·25
1944	5·2	1·1	1·03	14	7	49	13·55
1945	3·6	1·6	0·40	10	7	42	12·65
1946	8·7	2·7	1·15	29	11	64	17·49
1947	11·2	3·3	1·69	42	10	94	20·57
1948	12·2	1·9	2·13	59	9	117	22·69
1949	13·2	2·0	2·06	86	9	249	20·78
1950	15·3	1·8	2·36	129	8	510	24·68
1951	17·4	2·1	3·06	148	18	966	29·22
1952	17·6	2·0	3·54	139	64	1,433	30·84
1953	19·4	1·9	3·50	165	85	2,280	32·62
1954	21·1	1·8	4·21	217	72	2,967	35·57
1955	23·3	1·5	5·40	270	204	3,627	38·12
1956	24·9	1·6	5·91	316	570	4,466	40·59
1957	26·6	1·5	6·79	352	1,262	4,987	42·73
1958	28·1	1·5	6·27	403	1,546	5,175	45·49
1959	30·7	1·9	6·76	501	1,695	6,118	49·35
1960	35·4	1·5	8·23	645	1,998	6,447	56·24
1961	39·3	2·2	9·12	760	1,972	6,862	60·57
1962	43·2	2·5	9·49	947	1,808	7,113	64·86
1963	46·9	1·9	10·16	1,180	1,784	7,223	71·34
1964	47·8	1·7	9·79	1,091	2,669	7,638	76·74
1965	50·2	1·4	12·68	1,176	2,207	7,758	82·97
1966	55·8	1·6	13·64	1,366	1,757	8,765	89·99
1967	60·0	2·9	15·89	1,543	1,615	9,340	96·83
1968	63·8	2·1	16·96	1,664	1,506	10,405	104·01
1969	65·7	2·2	16·43	1,596	1,479	11,927	110·45
1970	70·8	1·7	17·28	1,848	1,405	13,135	117·42
1971	70·8	1·4	17·45	1,817	1,291	13,383	124·86
1972	73·8	1·0	19·81	1,833	1,152	14,185	135·26
1973	80·8	1·3	20·99	1,951	1,047	15,320	145·52
1974	84·6	1·2	23·80	1,758	1,031	15,294	148·91
1975	76·9	1·2	21·84	1,448	1,071	14,578	147·33
1976	86·2	1·2	23·45	1,579	1,102	15,663	163·55
1977	87·7	1·1	23·33	1,570	1,083	13,685	166·54
1978	89·2	1·9	24·28	1,644	1,478	13,681	175·04
1979	95·4	2·1	24·25	1,621	1,632	12,549	181·25
1980	100·0	1·9	26·50	1,597	1,800	12,421	186·30
1981	97·7	2·0	24·78	1,432	1,466	13,998	181·76
1982	96·2	1·9	23·99	1,452	1,740	14,490	183·72
1983	90·8	1·9	21·68	1,565	2,196	13,000	180·71

Chart It.2   Industrial production, selected series, 1900–80

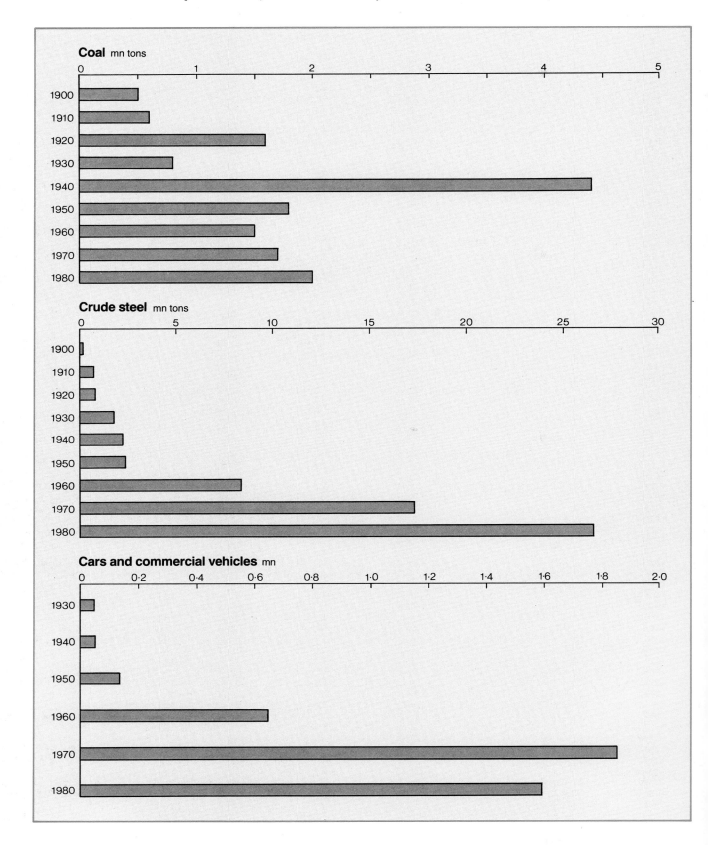

	Consumer prices		Producer prices		Compensation of employees	National income
	All items	Food	All items	Producers' goods		
	Index nos., 1980 = 100				L bn	
1900	0·05	...	0·07	...	...	...
1901	0·05	...	0·06	...	...	...
1902	0·05	...	0·06	...	...	...
1903	0·05	...	0·06	...	...	...
1904	0·05	...	0·06	...	...	...
1905	0·05	...	0·06	...	...	...
1906	0·06	...	0·06	...	...	...
1907	0·06	...	0·07	...	...	...
1908	0·06	...	0·07	...	...	...
1909	0·06	...	0·07	...	...	...
1910	0·06	...	0·07	...	...	...
1911	0·06	...	0·07	...	...	...
1912	0·06	...	0·08	...	...	...
1913	0·06	...	0·08	...	...	...
1914	0·06	...	0·07	...	...	...
1915	0·07	...	0·09	...	...	...
1916	0·09	...	0·14	...	...	...
1917	0·12	...	0·21	...	...	...
1918	0·17	...	0·31	...	...	...
1919	0·17	...	0·34	...	...	...
1920	0·23	...	0·44	...	...	...
1921	0·27	...	0·41	...	...	...
1922	0·27	...	0·41	...	...	...
1923	0·27	...	0·41	...	...	...
1924	0·28	...	0·41	...	...	...
1925	0·31	...	0·46	...	...	...
1926	0·34	...	0·47	...	...	...
1927	0·31	0·22	0·39	...	...	...
1928	0·29	0·22	0·38	0·37	...	...
1929	0·30	0·23	0·36	0·36	...	...
1930	0·29	0·21	0·33	0·31	...	...
1931	0·26	0·19	0·28	0·26	...	...
1932	0·25	0·18	0·26	0·25	...	...
1933	0·24	0·17	0·24	0·22	...	...
1934	0·23	0·16	0·24	0·22	...	...
1935	0·23	0·16	0·26	0·24	...	...
1936	0·25	0·18	0·29	0·28	...	...
1937	0·27	0·18	0·34	0·33	...	...
1938	0·29	0·18	0·36	0·34	...	...
1939	0·31	0·36	0·38	0·36	...	...
1940	0·36	0·36	0·44	0·41	...	...
1941	0·41	0·36	0·49	0·48	...	...
1942	0·48	0·53	0·55	0·52	...	...
1943	0·80	0·89	0·83	...	...	...
1944	3·4	4·2	3·1	...	...	...
1945	6·7	8·0	7·4	...	...	...
1946	8·0	9·6	10·4	9·2	...	...
1947	12·9	15·4	18·7	17·2	...	...
1948	13·7	16·2	19·7	18·0	...	...
1949	13·9	16·2	18·6	18·2	...	...
1950	13·7	15·6	17·6	18·2	...	...
1951	15·0	16·6	20·1	20·2	4,075	9,714
1952	15·6	17·3	18·9	19·8	4,503	10,475
1953	16·0	17·7	18·9	19·6	4,953	11,673
1954	16·4	18·3	18·8	19·2	5,417	12,455
1955	16·8	18·9	18·9	20·0	5,941	13,766
1956	17·3	19·7	19·3	20·4	6,480	15,010
1957	17·5	19·7	19·5	20·9	7,049	16,094
1958	18·0	20·3	19·1	20·0	7,569	17,314
1959	18·0	19·9	18·6	19·8	8,104	18,404
1960	18·3	20·1	18·8	20·0	8,977 / 9,855	19,971 / 21,370
1961	18·8	20·1	18·8	20·2	10,954	23,787
1962	19·6	21·0	19·3	20·4	12,745	26,724
1963	21·1	22·9	20·3	21·3	15,506	30,580
1964	22·3	24·0	21·0	21·9	17,348	33,378
1965	23·4	25·4	21·4	21·7	18,313	35,977
1966	23·8	25·9	21·6	21·9	19,585	39,117
1967	24·9	26·3	21·4	21·9	21,663	43,162
1968	25·2	26·3	21·6	22·2	23,555	46,851
1969	25·7	27·0	22·2	23·6	25,954	51,735
1970	27·1	28·1	24·0	26·2	30,349	57,999
1971	28·5	29·2	24·6	26·5	34,727	63,222
1972	30·1	31·2	25·6	27·2	38,753	69,264
1973	33·3	34·8	30·2	33·3	47,080	82,418
1974	39·6	41·0	42·5	46·6	58,606	100,366
1975	46·3	48·3	46·1	50·1	71,204	111,917
1976	54·2	56·8	56·7	58·6	86,953	140,270
1977	64·2	67·4	66·5	68·0	106,501	170,221
1978	71·8	76·4	72·1	75·2	124,315	199,752
1979	82·4	86·5	83·3	85·4	148,895	244,355
1980	100·0	100·0	100·0	100·0	184,154	306,569
1981	119·5	118·0	116·6	119·4	225,544	358,478
1982	139·2	137·4	132·8	137·1	263,910	418,675
1983	159·6	154·2	...	...	303,762	474,915

Table It.4   Population, 1901–82

	Total population	Males	Females	Age distribution		
				Under 15	15–64	65 & over
				mn		
1901	32·48	16·16	16·32	11·16	19·35	1·97
1911	34·67	17·02	17·65	11·73	20·57	2·36
1921	37·97	18·73	19·25	11·79	23·43	2·75
1931	41·18	20·13	21·04	12·24	25·92	3·02
1936	42·92	21·07	21·85	13·17	26·59	3·20
1950	46·77	23·05	24·05	12·47	30·86	3·78
1951	47·10	23·21	24·21	12·43	31·12	3·86
1952	47·35	23·34	24·33	12·39	31·34	3·94
1953	47·61	23·48	24·48	12·32	31·62	4·02
1954	47·07	22·93	24·14	12·26	31·93	4·12
1955	47·39	23·08	24·31	12·19	32·23	4·22
1956	47·66	23·20	24·45	12·17	32·46	4·29
1957	47·93	23·31	24·62	12·21	32·61	4·36
1958	48·32	23·51	24·81	12·25	32·77	4·46
1959	48·60	23·67	24·93	11·42	32·93	4·24
1960	48·97	23·85	25·12	11·47	33·10	4·41
1961	49·16	23·87	25·28	11·40	33·27	4·49
1962	49·56	24·10	25·47	11·34	33·59	4·63
1963	49·94	24·28	25·66	11·45	33·76	4·72
1964	50·44	24·55	25·89	11·52	34·06	4·86
1965	50·84	24·72	26·12	11·72	34·12	5·00
1966	51·23	24·92	26·31	11·56	34·34	5·33
1967	51·66	25·18	26·49	11·81	34·56	5·29
1968	52·04	25·37	26·67	11·78	34·84	5·42
1969	52·38	25·52	26·86	12·16	34·79	5·42
1970	52·77	25·70	27·07	12·11	35·10	5·56
1971	53·12	25·89	27·23	12·32	35·13	5·68
1972	53·55	26·10	27·45	12·34	35·24	5·97
1973	53·98	26·30	27·68	12·33	35·56	6·10
1974	54·54	26·59	27·95	12·33	35·98	6·23
1975	54·97	26·80	28·16	12·34	36·25	6·37
1976	55·33	26·99	28·33	12·45	36·45	6·43
1977	55·58	27·10	28·47	12·40	36·65	6·53
1978	55·81	27·22	28·59	12·15	36·99	6·66
1979	56·02	27·32	28·70	11·86	37·30	6·85
1980	56·12	27·37	28·75	11·48	37·43	7·21
1981	56·29	27·46	28·84	11·31	37·70	7·28
1982	56·45	27·54	28·91	10·85	38·19	7·41

Table It.5 Labour market: employment, 1929–83

	Employed labour force	Agriculture, forestry & fishing	Mining & quarrying	Mfg	Construction	Gas, electricity & water	Transport & communication	Distribution & services
				mn				
1929	...	...	...	1·11	...	...	...	...
1930	...	...	...	...	...	...	...	...
1931	17·26	8·08		5·31		...	0·79	3·08
1932	...	...		...		...	...	...
1933	...	...		...		...	...	...
1934	...	...		0·85		...	...	...
1935	...	...		1·00		...	...	...
1936	18·75	8·84	0·13	3·98	0·98	0·07	0·70	4·06
1937	...	...		1·16		...	...	...
1938	...	...		1·22		...	...	...
1939	...	...		1·26		...	...	...
1940	...	...		1·35		...	...	...
1941	...	...		1·36		...	...	...
1942	...	...		1·35		...	...	...
1947	...	...		1·73		...	...	...
1948	...	...		1·70		...	...	...
1949	...	...		1·68		...	...	...
1950	...	...		1·67		...	...	...
1951	20·14	8·06		7·04[a]		...	...	4·39
1952	...	...		1·67		...	...	...
1953	...	...		1·68		...	...	...
1954	...	...		1·70		...	...	...
1954	18·57	8·00	0·14	4·15	1·24	0·13	0·66	4·25
1955	19·34	7·96	0·15	4·42	1·32	0·14	0·73	4·62
1956	19·93	7·45	0·15	4·97	1·59	0·11	0·70	4·96
1957	19·97	7·11	0·15	5·17	1·62	0·11	0·72	5·09
1958	20·00	6·97	0·14	5·18	1·65	0·11	0·73	5·22
1959	19·99	6·85	0·14	5·25	1·67	0·11	0·75	5·22
1960	20·00	6·57	0·15	5·35	1·78	0·11	0·80	5·24
1961	20·02	6·21	(0·15)	5·54	1·82	(0·13)	0·86	5·31
1962	19·86	5·82	(0·15)	5·61	1·95	(0·13)	0·91	5·29
1963	19·48	5·29	(0·15)	5·69	2·01	(0·15)	0·92	5·27
1964	19·29	4·94	(0·14)	5·56	2·10	(0·16)	1·02	5·37
1965	18·82	4·90	(0·13)	5·44	1·94	(0·15)	1·00	5·26
1966	18·99	4·81		7·06			7·12	
1967	19·21	4·71		7·20			7·29	
1968	19·29	4·42		7·29			7·58	
1969	19·11	4·20		7·44			7·46	
1970	19·22	3·88		7·59			7·75	
1971	19·18	3·88		7·62			7·68	
1972	18·88	3·59		7·48			7·81	
1973	19·06	3·49		7·47			8·10	
1974	19·47	3·41		7·64			8·42	
1975	19·59	3·27		7·67			8·65	
1976	19·74	3·24		7·57			8·93	
1977	19·95	3·15	0·21[b]	5·48	1·98	...	1·13	8·00
1978	20·04	3·09	0·20[b]	5·43	2·01	...	1·13	8·18
1979	20·27	3·01	0·21[b]	5·41	2·02	...	1·13	8·49
1980	20·55	2·93	0·22[b]	5·49	2·06	...	1·15	8·70
1981	20·62	2·76	0·22[b]	5·39	2·12	...	1·16	8·97
1982	20·54	2·55	0·22[b]	5·28	2·10	...	1·14	9·26
1983	20·56	2·54		7·41			10·61	

a Including transport.
b Including gas, electricity and water.

	Mfg				Industrial disputes		
	Average hrs worked per month	Average hourly earnings	Unemployment		Stoppages	Workers involved	Working days lost
		L	'000	%		'000	'000
1900	...	...			1,053	350	...
1901	...	...	...	...	617	136	...
1902	...	...	...	...	847	215	...
1903	...	...	...	...	715	155	...
1904	...	...	...	...	1,649	382	...
1905	...	...	...	...	2,268	581	...
1906	...	...	...	...	1,674	324	...
1907	...	...	...	...	1,071	189	...
1908	...	...	...	...	1,109	196	...
1909	...	...	...	...	1,255	386	...
1910	...	...	...	...	1,090	241	...
1911	...	...	...	...	907	465	...
1912	...	...	...	...	905	217	...
1913	...	...	...	...	599	174	...
1914	...	...	...	...	905	217	...
1915	...	...	...	...	608	180	...
1916	...	...	...	...	577	138	...
1917	...	...	...	...	470	175	...
1918	...	...	...	...	313	159	...
1919	...	...	...	...	1,871	1,555	...
1920	...	...	...	...	2,070	2,314	...
1921	...	...	...	...	1,134	724	...
1922	...	...	...	...	575	448	...
1923	...	...	...	...	201	66	...
1924	...	...	...	...	368	187	...
1925	...	...	110	...	618	308	...
1926	...	...	114	...	...	...	...
1927	...	...	278	...	169	19	...
1928	180[a]	...	324	...	77	3	...
1929	182	2·11	301	...	83	3	...
1930	175	2·13	425	...	82	3	...
1931	171	1·99	734	...	67	4	...
1932	169	1·93	1,006	...	23	0·6	...
1933	174	1·88	1,019	...	34	0·8	...
1934	172	1·81	964	...	38	0·6	...
1935	158	1·76	...	...	43	0·6	...
1936	157	1·84	...	...	...	...	...
1937	163	2·17	874	4·6	...	...	...
1938	159	2·23	810	4·3	...	...	...
1939	157[b]	2·50	706	3·8[c]	...	...	...
	Average hrs worked per day						
1946	...	...	1,324	...	...	...	...
1947	...	...	1,620	...	...	...	...
1948	7·95	134	1,742[d]	8·9	...	...	...
1949	7·97	142	1,673	8·6	1,159	2,894	16,578
1950	7·97	143	1,615	8·3	1,250	3,537	7,761
1951	8·07	157	1,721	8·8	1,178	2,135	4,515
1952	8·07	165	1,850	9·5	1,558	1,472	3,531
1953	8·10	169	1,947	10·0	1,412	4,679	5,828
1954	8·12	175	1,959	10·0	1,990	2,045	5,377
1955	8·12	185	1,481	7·6	1,981	1,403	5,622
1956	8·02	198	1,847	9·4	1,904	1,678	4,137
1957	8·03	207	1,643	8·2	1,731	1,227	4,619
1958	8·02	216	1,322	6·6	1,937	1,283	4,172
1959	8·05	221	1,117	5·6	1,925	1,900	9,190
1960	8·07	232	836	4·2	2,471	2,338	5,786
1961	8·08	248	710	3·5	3,502	2,698	9,891
1962	8·00	286	611	3·0	3,652	2,910	22,717
1963	8·00	334	504	2·5	4,145	3,694	11,395
1964	7·92	371	549	2·7	3,841	3,246	13,089
1965	7·87	386	714	3·6	3,191	2,310	6,993
1966	7·88	401	759 / 1,192	3·9 / 5·8	2,387	1,888	14,474
1967	7·92	426	1,106	5·3	2,658	2,244	8,568
1968	7·92	445	1,172	5·6	3,377	4,862	9,240
1969	7·83	489	1,160	5·6	3,788	7,507	37,825
1970	7·80	606	1,111	5·3	4,162	3,722	20,887
1971	7·73	703	1,109	5·3	5,598	3,891	14,799
1972	7·78	788	1,297	6·3	4,765	4,405	19,497
1973	7·67	966	1,305	6·2	3,769[e]	6,133	23,419
1974	7·67	1,209	1,113	5·3	5,174[e]	7,824	19,467
1975	7·68	1,794	1,230	5·8	3,601	14,110	27,189
1976	7·67	2,133	1,426	6·6	2,706	11,898	25,378
1977	7·70	2,673	1,545	7·0	3,308	13,803	16,566
1978	7·72	3,244	1,571	7·1	2,479	8,774	10,177
1979	7·65	3,849	1,698	7·5	2,000	16,237	27,530
1980	7·73	4,684	1,698	7·6	2,238	13,825	16,457
1981	7·75	5,742	1,913	8·4	2,204	8,227	10,527
1982	7·70	6,635	2,068	9·1	1,747	10,483	18,563
1983	...	...	2,278	9·9	1,565	6,844	14,003

a Average for February – December.   b Average for first four months.   c December figure.
d Excluding third quarter.   e Excluding political strikes.

	Total exports	Exports to:				Total imports	Imports from:			
		France	Germany	UK	USA		France	Germany	UK	USA
					L bn					
1900	1·34	0·17	0·22	0·15	0·12	1·70	0·17	0·20	0·36	0·23
1901	1·37	0·18	0·24	0·15	0·14	1·72	0·18	0·21	0·28	0·23
1902	1·46	0·17	0·25	0·14	0·18	1·72	0·18	0·22	0·29	0·21
1903	1·48	0·17	0·23	0·13	0·17	1·81	0·19	0·24	0·28	0·21
1904	1·56	0·17	0·21	0·13	0·19	1·88	0·19	0·25	0·32	0·24
1905	1·69	0·18	0·22	0·13	0·23	2·02	0·21	0·29	0·35	0·24
1906	1·89	0·21	0·25	0·13	0·24	2·51	0·23	0·39	0·45	0·31
1907	1·94	0·20	0·30	0·16	0·24	2·88	0·26	0·53	0·52	0·39
1908	1·72	0·20	0·25	0·13	0·20	2·91	0·28	0·52	0·50	0·41
1909	1·86	0·20	0·31	0·17	0·27	3·11	0·33	0·50	0·49	0·39
1910	2·07	0·22	0·29	0·21	0·26	3·25	0·33	0·53	0·48	0·36
1911	2·19	0·21	0·30	0·22	0·25	3·39	0·33	0·55	0·51	0·42
1912	2·38	0·22	0·33	0·26	0·26	3·70	0·39	0·63	0·58	0·52
1913	2·50	0·23	0·34	0·26	0·27	3·65	0·28	0·61	0·59	0·52
1914	2·20	0·17	0·32	0·31	0·26	2·92	0·21	0·50	0·51	0·44
1915	2·51	0·44	0·20	0·39	0·28	4·70	0·24	0·23	0·85	1·75
1916	3·05	0·74	—	0·45	0·32	8·39	0·60	0·01	1·98	3·42
1917	3·28	0·91	—	0·48	0·24	13·99	0·99	0·02	2·17	6·19
1918	3·31	1·21	—	0·73	0·17	16·04	1·23	0·02	2·67	6·64
1919	6·00	1·40	0·09	0·77	0·63	16·62	0·76	0·09	2·44	7·35
1920	11·63	1·70	0·57	1·38	0·94	26·82	1·90	1·10	4·61	8·69
1921	8·04	0·97	0·81	0·80	1·08	16·91	1·07	1·29	1·68	5·71
1922	9·16	1·37	0·97	1·12	1·02	15·74	1·15	1·25	2·02	4·40
1923	10·95	1·58	0·70	1·21	1·52	17·16	1·32	1·31	2·20	4·61
1924	14·27	1·82	1·57	1·49	1·24	19·37	1·47	1·52	2·17	4·65
1925	18·17	2·02	2·03	1·85	1·90	26·20	2·36	2·25	2·73	6·20
1926	18·54	2·11	2·22	1·76	1·93	25·88	2·14	2·96	1·88	5·61
1927	15·52	1·28	2·23	1·53	1·64	20·38	1·80	2·11	1·83	3·96
1928	14·44	1·36	1·86	1·40	1·52	21·92	1·36	2·30	1·79	4·01
1929	14·77	1·30	1·78	1·46	1·72	21·30	1·30	2·74	2·04	3·56
1930	12·12	1·23	1·56	1·19	1·33	17·35	1·50	2·26	1·68	2·54
1931	10·21	1·12	1·09	1·20	1·05	11·64	0·83	1·59	1·10	1·33
1932	6·81	0·52	0·78	0·74	0·69	8·27	0·48	1·15	0·74	1·11
1933	5·99	0·46	0·73	0·69	0·53	7·43	0·41	1·14	0·73	1·12
1934	5·22	0·35	0·83	0·53	0·39	7·68	0·44	1·25	0·71	0·96
1935	5·24	0·31	0·85	0·43	0·42	7·79	0·47	1·43	0·57	0·88
1936	5·54	0·19	1·09	0·16	0·55	6·04	0·13	1·62	0·05	0·90
1937	10·44	0·44	1·50	0·64	0·78	13·94	0·49	2·59	0·56	1·54
1938	10·50	0·33	2·20	0·59	0·78	11·27	0·25	3·02	0·73	1·34
1939	10·82	0·24	1·90	0·52	0·77	10·31	0·15	3·03	0·57	0·98
1940	11·52	0·29	3·56	0·28	0·39	13·22	0·13	5·14	0·42	1·22
1941	14·51	0·22	7·11	—	—	11·47	0·21	6·89	—	0·09
1942	16·05	0·18	7·64	—	—	14·04	0·12	8·37	—	0·02
1947	341	...	...	...	...	937	...	...	...	...
1948	576	23·1	16·6	45·5	51·3	844	7·9	17·6	27·8	317·7
1949	641	36·2	54·3	67·0	26·4	883	21·5	39·7	34·6	311·0
1950	753	65·3	73·8	85·8	47·7	926	41·8	75·9	51·1	217·9
1951 .	1,030	92·7	80·2	138·6	70·5	1,355	58·5	99·9	50·1	284·5
1952	867	56·7	88·0 / 86·7	71·2	87·2	1,460	58·9	136·7 / 135·5	83·4	307·5
1953	942	49·1	103·9	67·8	90·1	1,513	75·9	179·6	116·9	202·8
1954	1,024	60·4	115·2	81·0	80·2	1,524	97·5	203·7	102·6	186·5
1955	1,160	67·5	145·7	84·1	99·6	1,695	108·4	214·7	90·5	253·1
1956	1,341	95·9	180·0	86·6	125·9	1,984	100·2	247·6	107·2	325·4
1957	1,595	101·1	224·7	99·2	161·9	2,296	121·4	281·2	121·8	427·1
1958	1,611	84·6	226·9	109·2	177·5	2,010	94·7	243·3	109·9	358·0
1959	1,821	112·1	295·1	135·7	216·0	2,105	162·1	292·9	116·7	234·1
1960	2,280	172·1	375·8	156·3	239·7	2,953	248·7	418·8	151·9	418·4
1961	2,614	199·7	465·5	175·7	238·8	3,265	299·5	509·4	179·2	539·7
1962	2,918	269·1	562·0	174·8	275·6	3,797	334·3	642·1	239·9	553·3
1963	3,159	328·1	564·2	169·1	298·2	4,745	460·6	813·2	290·9	651·6
1964	3,724	406·5	707·2	207·8	316·9	4,533	446·5	738·5	248·1	615·8
1965	4,500	463·9	953·3	210·6	386·7	4,611	451·5	681·4	213·8	620·9
1966	5,024	582·6	1,007·1	238·6	465·2	5,368	542·2	857·9	251·5	656·6
1967	5,441	675·6	959·7	263·0	539·8	6,142	654·8	1,060	271·0	665·0
1968	6,366	801·2	1,189	281·2	681·3	6,429	728·2	1,148	272·8	748·4
1969	7,330	1,061	1,440	263·9	795·3	7,792	968·4	1,462	313·0	886·0
1970	8,254	1,065	1,780	313·3	846·1	9,356	1,235	1,861	352·9	967·1
1971	9,362	1,267	2,129	362·2	918·4	9,901	1,396	1,994	360·0	890·4
1972	10,849	1,536	2,487	463·0	1,062	11,265	1,772	2,286	395·5	930·8
1973	12,989	1,881	2,821	648·2	1,111	16,343	2,443	3,302	559·7	1,352
1974	19,826	2,498	3,662	1,025	1,504	26,714	3,510	4,734	808·9	2,038
1975	22,866	3,017	4,243	1,041	1,487	25,200	3,334	4,296	831·9	2,184
1976	31,167	4,684	5,884	1,495	2,010	36,731	4,975	6,231	1,284	2,983
1977	39,968	5,715	7,413	2,106	2,666	42,429	5,895	7,140	1,582	2,950
1978	47,505	6,773	9,037	2,876	3,385	47,868	6,966	8,310	1,912	3,239
1979	59,926	8,873	11,336	3,916	3,877	64,597	9,032	11,107	2,613	4,381
1980	66,719	10,101	12,211	4,064	3,544	85,564	11,856	14,178	3,784	5,940
1981	86,040	11,686	13,351	4,999	5,841	103,674	12,938	16,191	4,012	7,032
1982	99,231	15,103	15,491	6,219	6,999	116,216	14,531	18,658	4,601	7,864
1983	110,537	16,254	18,331	7,019	8,526	122,002	15,362	19,372	4,750	7,246

Sources

(For sources used in specific tables, see Notes.)

1 *Annuario Statistico Italiano*. Istituto Centrale di Statistica, Rome.

2 *Basic Statistics of the Community*. Statistical Office of the European Communities, Brussels, 1982.

3 International Labour Office, *Technical Guide*, Vol. II. Geneva, 1972, 1976, 1980.

4 League of Nations, *Yearbook of Labour Statistics*.

5 Mitchell, B R, *European Historical Statistics 1750–1975*, 2nd rev. edn. Macmillan, London, 1980.

6 Organisation for Economic Cooperation and Development (OECD), *Labour Force Statistics*. Paris, annual and quarterly.

7 OECD, *National Accounts 1950 to 1978*. Paris, 1980.

8 OECD, *National Accounts 1953 to 1982*. Paris, 1984.

9 *Sommario di Statistiche storiche dell'Italia 1861–1975*. Istituto Centrale di Statistica, Rome, 1976.

10 *Statistical Year Book of the League of Nations*. Geneva.

11 Supplements to the United Nations, *Statistical Year Book* and *Monthly Bulletin of Statistics*. New York, 1967, 1972 and 1977.

12 United Nations, *Monthly Bulletin of Statistics*. New York.

13 United Nations, *Statistical Year Book*. New York.

14 *Year Book of Labour Statistics*. ILO, Geneva.

Notes

Table It.1

Sources: **7, 8, 9**

From 1951, OECD data have been used. There is a break in the series in 1960 when there was a change in the system of classification. The main differences in classification are explained in **8**.

For 1926–50 the OECD figures are linked to a constant price series published in **9** and roughly converted to 1975 prices. Each category of expenditure has been re-referenced to 1975 prices independently. The final column is for gross *national* product for this period. Net imports or exports of goods and services shown in the table from 1926 to 1950 are residual figures and therefore include any statistical discrepancy caused by the independent re-referencing of the component categories.

Table It.2

Sources: **2, 5, 12, 13**

Industrial production index: the current base weighted index was introduced in 1973 with base weights of 1970. The index includes mining, manufacturing (except for some subgroups of miscellaneous manufactures), electricity and gas. Before the introduction of the revised index in 1973, the index for manufacturing, which forms part of the combined index, excluded printing and publishing and repair shops.

For 1929–38, the series includes building and public works; mining is excluded for 1929–32.

Coal: includes both coal and lignite.

Natural gas: published figures are now given in terajoules. From 1977, the published figures have been converted to cubic metres using the conversion factor 38309; see **12**.

Table It.3

Sources: **5, 7, 8, 10, 12, 13**

Consumer prices: the indices are weighted arithmetic averages with fixed base weights. The national index represents a weighted arithmetic average of indices relating to four major areas of the country (North West, North East, Central and Southern, and Insular). The index for 'Food' includes tobacco.

Producer prices: the current series was revised in 1976 and now includes 344 commodities. It is a base weighted index. The current series for raw materials is called a 'Producers goods' index and is part of the 'All items' index. It was linked to the raw materials index in 1953.

For further details of these price series see **11**.

Compensation of employees: OECD data have been used from 1951. The figures include wages and salaries in cash and in kind paid to employees together with contributions on behalf of employees to social security schemes and private pension funds. Two figures are given for 1960 because of the change in classification (see notes to Table It.1).

National income: OECD data have been used from 1951. National income is defined as the sum of compensation of employees, net entrepreneurial and property income of residents and indirect taxes less subsidies. Two figures are given for 1960 because of the change in classification (see notes to Table It.1).

Table It.4

Sources: **6, 9**

OECD data have been used from 1950. From 1954, the figures are annual averages of the present-in-area (*de facto*) population. Permanent inmates of institutions (religious communities, old people's homes, prisons, etc.) are excluded; these numbered about 605,000 in 1971.

For the period 1950–53, the estimates are for mid year and the breakdown by sex is of the resident population (i e, includes those working abroad). The figures for 1901–36 are Census figures. The figure for 1921 includes the territories acquired by Italy after the First World War.

Age distribution: figures for 1950–58 are based on resident population estimates (i e, they include Italians working abroad) and do not, therefore, add up to total population figures given in the table. Up to and including 1958, the age distribution is for under 15 years and 15–64 years; from 1959 it is under 14 years and 14–64 years.

Table It.5

Sources: **4, 6**

OECD data have been used from 1954. The figures are annual averages of those in civilian employment and include employees, self employed and unpaid family workers working for at least one third of normal working time. The unemployed and temporarily stopped are not included. Up to 1968, permanent inmates of institutions were excluded from the figures. In 1977, definitions and classifications were revised. The figures from 1966 are on the revised basis; previous years are not strictly comparable. Figures for 1966 on the previous classification are:

Employed labour force 18·46 mn
Agriculture 4·59 mn
Industry 7·53 mn
Other activities 6·34 mn

The figures were also revised in 1956.

'Distribution and services' includes the wholesale and retail trades, restaurants and hotels, finance, insurance, real estate and business services, community, social and personal services (including, since 1969, permanent inmates of institutions).

For 1930–54 (first line), the figures are for wage earners only in manufacturing industries and are based on the Ministry of Corporations index. The annual figure is an average of the figures for the last week of each month. The 1931, 1936 and 1951 figures are from Census data and refer to the economically active population (employers, self employed, employees and unemployed).

For further details see **4**.

Table It.6

Sources: **4, 5, 6, 14**

Manufacturing: average hours worked per month: the current series is an average of hours actually worked per *day* including overtime in the reporting week. Covers wage earners of both sexes including apprentices. Data are based on quarterly surveys covering all establishments employing ten or more workers during the last week of each quarter. The scope of the series was revised in 1965 and in 1978.

For 1928–38, the figures are for average hours of work per month.

Manufacturing: average hourly earnings: the current series is an average of earnings of hourly paid workers including overtime and other bonus payments. Covers wage earners of both sexes including apprentices. For

1948–74 the figures exclude payments for annual vacation and public holidays. Data are based on quarterly surveys as above. The scope of the series was revised in 1965 and in 1978.

Unemployment: the current series includes all persons aged 14 years and over looking for work during the reference week including school leavers. From 1977, the definition was widened to include housewives, students, pensioners, etc, who stated that they were looking actively for work. The figures have been revised on this basis back to 1966; two figures are given for 1966. From 1955, the figures are based on labour force sample surveys, the coverage of which has varied.

For 1932–54, the figures refer to numbers unemployed on the register at the end of the month. For 1925–32, the figures are for insured workers only.

The percentage figure is obtained by dividing the number of unemployed by the civilian labour force ($\times$ 100).

For further details of all these series see **3, 14**.

Table It.7

Sources: **1, 9**

Changes in definition affected the trade figures in 1907 and 1930. Trade with Germany included Austria for 1937–45. From 1952 (second line) the figures for Germany refer to the Federal Republic of Germany. Trade with the UK included Southern Ireland up to 1923.

JAPAN

CONTENTS

Table J.1 Gross domestic product at constant prices, 1930–83

	Consumers' expenditure	Govt current expenditure	Gross fixed capital formation	Value of physical change in stocks	Exports of goods & services	Imports of goods & services	Gross domestic product at market prices
			Y bn, 1975 prices				
1930	11,578	3,894	1,193		...	...	14,485
1931	11,471	5,269	1,272		...	...	14,914
1932	11,471	5,727	1,193		...	...	15,129
1933	11,471	5,956	1,431		...	...	15,773
1934	11,790	5,727	2,385		...	...	17,382
1935	11,365	5,956	2,465		...	...	17,811
1936	11,684	5,956	2,703		...	...	18,455
1937	12,215	9,621	3,657		...	...	22,747
1938	12,109	12,600	3,816		...	...	23,498
1939	11,471	10,767	4,771		...	...	23,713
1940	10,303	11,225	4,691		...	...	22,318
1941	9,984	13,974	4,850		...	...	22,640
1942	9,560	14,890	5,248		...	...	22,962
1943	9,028	16,952	4,612		...	...	22,962
1944	7,435	16,723	5,168		...	...	22,103
1945	...	...	...		...	...	...
1946	7,223	2,520	3,260		...	...	12,446
1947	7,860	1,833	3,896		...	...	13,519
1948	8,922	3,207	3,975		...	...	15,236
1949	9,878	3,665	3,260		...	...	15,558
1950	10,728	4,123	3,021		...	...	17,275
1951	11,684	4,582	3,737		...	...	19,528
1952	13,702	5,498	3,263	633	1,020	− 1,055	21,674
1953	15,417	5,578	3,767	89	1,178	− 1,389	23,269
1954	16,179	5,711	4,055	288	1,291	− 1,547	24,587
1955	17,457	5,684	4,138	995	1,483	− 1,638	26,695
1956	18,816	5,661	5,019	871	1,813	− 2,161	28,706
1957	19,996	5,628	5,943	1,187	1,988	− 2,729	30,801
1958	21,436	5,884	6,221	508	1,988	− 2,006	32,600
1959	23,105	6,192	7,115	804	2,511	− 2,809	35,573
1960	25,416	6,470	9,302	1,010	2,798	− 3,486	40,237
1961	27,562	6,864	11,891	2,416	2,991	− 4,433	46,095
1962	30,185	7,443	13,236	680	3,494	− 4,402	49,349
1963	33,083	8,093	14,615	1,542	3,749	− 5,194	54,532
1964	36,928	8,575	17,060	1,893	4,538	− 5,928	61,737
1965	39,000	9,119	17,607	1,278	5,563	− 6,346	64,906
1966	42,146	8,904	18,235	1,214	5,380	− 6,555	69,291
1967	46,247	9,419	20,684	1,469	6,212	− 7,368	76,633
1968	50,631	9,865	24,454	2,572	6,568	− 9,172	84,890
1969	54,832	10,431	29,352	3,204	8,087	− 10,159	95,730
1970	60,367	10,960	34,903	3,034	9,670	− 11,454	107,474
1971	64,547	11,581	40,811	3,745	11,295	− 13,961	118,016
1972	68,337	12,203	42,548	1,782	13,197	− 14,614	123,452
1973	74,849	12,842	46,972	1,849	13,885	− 16,065	134,336
1974	81,841	13,480	53,409	2,449	14,881	− 19,907	146,158
1975	81,275	13,948	48,551	3,528	18,253	− 20,912	144,641
1976	84,568	14,890	48,017	494	18,982	− 18,919	148,031
1977	87,406	15,502	49,438	1,051	22,626	− 20,150	155,880
1978	90,717	16,105	51,832	1,153	25,408	− 21,157	164,075
1979	94,993	16,919	56,721	966	25,408	− 22,692	172,327
1980	100,632	17,641	60,294	1,809	26,438	− 25,653	181,170
1981	101,899	18,151	60,948	1,637	31,359	− 23,899	190,128
1982	102,456	18,994	63,403	1,177	35,964	− 24,257	197,785
1983	106,774	19,658	64,540	989	37,095[a]	− 25,006[a]	204,098[a]
	110,330	20,134	64,685	...	38,868	− 23,453	210,303

a Estimated by OECD Secretariat.

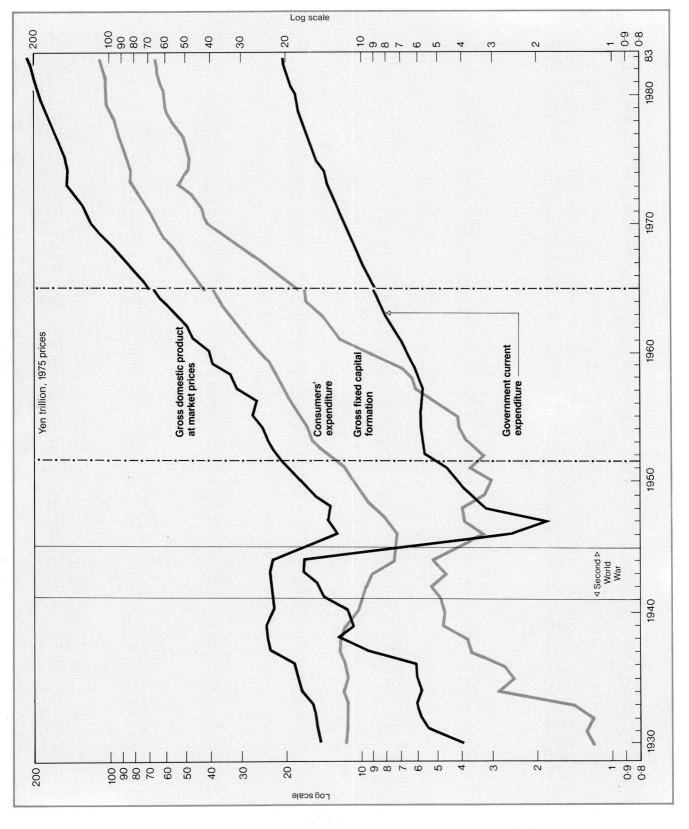

Chart J.1 Gross domestic product at constant prices, 1930–82

Log scale

Yen trillion, 1975 prices

Gross domestic product at market prices

Consumers' expenditure

Gross fixed capital formation

Government current expenditure

◁ Second ▷
World
War

200
100
90
80
70
60
50
40
30
20
10
9
8
7
6
5
4
3
2
1
0·9
0·8

1930   1940   1950   1960   1970   1980   83

Log scale

113

	Industrial production	Coal	Crude steel	Cars & commercial vehicles	Crude petroleum	Natural gas	Electricity
	Index nos., 1980 = 100	mn tons	'000 tons	'000	'000 tons	mn cu m	bn KWh
1900	0·89	7·4	...	—	116	...	...
1901	0·92	8·9	1	—	149	...	...
1902	0·89	9·7	2	—	159	...	...
1903	0·90	10·1	2	—	161	...	...
1904	0·89	10·7	2	—	189	...	...
1905	0·92	11·5	6	—	196	...	...
1906	1·0	13·0	6	—	229	...	...
1907	1·1	13·8	7	—	267	...	...
1908	1·1	14·8	3	—	276	...	...
1909	1·1	15·0	7	—	252	...	...
1910	1·2	15·7	9	—	258	...	...
1911	1·3	17·6	12	—	221	...	...
1912	1·4	19·6	15	—	223	...	...
1913	1·6	21·3	17	—	259	...	...
1914	1·5	22·3	19	—	365	...	...
1915	1·7	20·5	20	—	416	...	...
1916	2·0	22·9	371	—	419	14·0	2·2
1917	2·3	26·4	773	—	386	25·4	2·6
1918	2·5	28·0	813	—	340	25·8	3·1
1919	2·6	31·3	814	—	326	28·7	3·5
1920	2·4	29·2	811	—	290	38·2	3·8
1921	2·6	26·2	932	—	298	33·1	5·1
1922	2·7	27·7	909	—	285	31·8	5·6
1923	2·7	28·9	959	—	251	26·2	6·1
1924	2·8	30·1	1,100	—	252	20·1	7·8
1925	3·1	31·5	1,300	—	266	23·2	9·1
1926	3·3	31·4	1,506	0·2	248	22·3	10·6
1927	3·5	33·5	1,685	0·3	248	28·1	12·1
1928	3·6	33·9	1,906	0·3	270 / 261	27·4	13·7
1929	3·9	34·3	2,294	0·4	278	28·7	15·1
1930	3·9	31·4	2,289	0·5	282	43·4	15·8
1931	3·6	28·0	1,883	0·4	273	76·6	16·0
1932	3·8	28·1	2,398	0·9	226	51·3	17·4
1933	4·6	32·5	3,198	1·7	202	46·9	19·5
1934	4·9	35·9	3,844	2·8	256	47·1	21·8
1935	5·2	37·8	4,705	5·1	316	41·5	24·7
1936	5·9	41·8	5,223	12·2	352	41·1	27·1
1937	6·9	45·3	5,801	18·1	353	53·1	30·2
1938	7·1	48·7	6,472	24·4	353	50·6	32·4
1939	7·8	51·1	6,696	34·5	334	54·7	34·1
1940	8·2	56·3	6,856	46·0	301	56·7	34·6
1941	8·5	56·5	6,844	46·5	275	53·6	37·7
1942	8·2	53·5	7,044	37·2	236	54·1	36·1
1943	8·3	55·5	7,650	25·9	247	45·5	37·7
1944	8·5	52·9	6,729	21·8	229	44·3	36·1
1945	3·7	29·9	1,963	8·2	221	40·9	21·9
1946	1·7	20·4	557	14·9	192	35·9	30·3
1947	2·1	27·2	952	11·3	183	39·2	32·8
1948	2·7	33·7	1,715	20·4	159	51·0	37·8
1949	3·5	38·0	3,111	28·7	194	57·8	41·5
1950	4·2	38·5	4,839	31·6	293	68·8	46·3
1951	5·7	43·3	6,502	38·5	336	82·8	47·9
1952	6·1	43·3	6,988	39·0	306	91·1	52·0
1953	7·4	46·5	7,662	49·8	296	110·5	57·5
1954	8·0	42·7	7,750	70·1	300	141·0	60·0
1955	9·0	42·4	9,408	68·9	314	155·5	65·2
1956	11·1	46·6	11,106	111·1	310	176·8	73·6
1957	12·9	51·7	12,570	182·0	321	243·6	81·3
1958	12·8	49·7	12,118	188·3	367	367·9	85·4
1959	15·3	47·3	16,629	262·8	406	506·8	99·1
1960	18·9	51·1	22,138	481·6	526	731·4	115·5
1961	22·3	54·5	28,268	813·8	657	950·3	132·0
1962	24·2	54·4	27,546	990·7	760	1,209	140·4
1963	26·6	52·1	31,501	1,284	785	1,695	160·2
1964	31·1	50·9	39,799	1,704	657	1,859	179·6
1965	32·6	49·5	41,161	1,876	671	1,727	190·3
1966	36·8	51·3	47,784	2,287	782	1,777	215·3
1967	43·9	47·5	62,154	3,147	788	1,859	244·9
1968	51·5	46·6	66,893	4,086	744	2,016	273·3
1969	65·2	44·7	82,167	4,675	749	2,157	316·3
1970	66·6	39·7	93,322	5,290	770	2,359	359·5
1971	68·4	33·4	88,557	5,811	752	2,434	385·6
1972	73·4	28·1	96,901	6,294	716	2,475	428·5
1973	86·3	22·4	119,322	7,083	700	2,595	470·2
1974	81·1	20·3	117,131	6,552	672	2,572	459·0
1975	72·6	19·1	102,313	6,942	606	2,436	475·8
1976	80·6	18·4	107,399	7,842	580	2,493	511·8
1977	83·9	18·3	102,405	8,514	592	2,804	532·6
1978	89·3	19·0	102,105	9,269	542	2,641	564·0
1979	95·6	17·7	111,748	9,636	482	2,414	589·6
1980	100·0	18·1	111,395	11,043	428	2,197	577·5
1981	101·0	17·7	101,676	11,180	396	2,386	583·2
1982	101·4	17·6	99,540	10,193	396	2,285	581·1
1983	105·1	17·1	96,984	11,122	420	2,311	555·5

Chart J.2   Industrial production, selected series, 1900–80

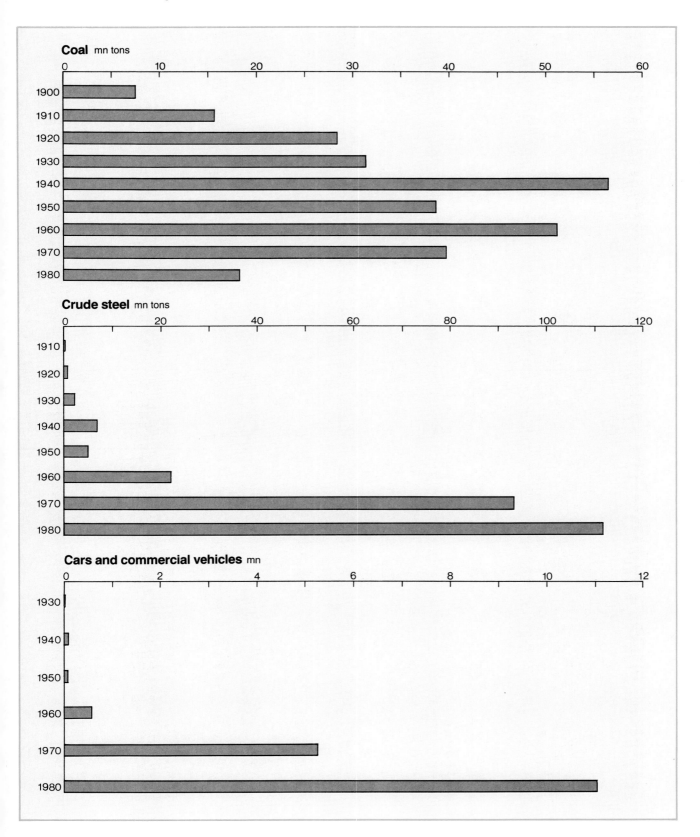

Table J.3 Prices and income, 1900–83

	Consumer prices		Wholesale prices		Compensation of employees	National income
	All items	Food	All items	Producers' goods		
	Index nos., 1980 = 100				Y bn	
1900	...	...	0·06	...	...	...
1901	...	...	0·06	...	...	...
1902	...	...	0·06	...	...	...
1903	...	...	0·06	...	...	...
1904	...	...	0·06	...	...	...
1905	...	...	0·07	...	...	...
1906	...	...	0·07	...	...	...
1907	...	...	0·08	...	...	...
1908	...	...	0·07	...	...	...
1909	...	...	0·07	...	...	...
1910	...	...	0·07	...	...	...
1911	...	...	0·07	...	...	...
1912	...	...	0·08	...	...	...
1913	...	...	0·08	...	...	...
1914	...	...	0·07	...	...	...
1915	...	...	0·07	...	...	...
1916	...	...	0·09	...	...	...
1917	...	...	0·11	...	...	...
1918	...	...	0·15	...	...	...
1919	...	...	0·18	...	2·6	12·5
1920	...	...	0·20	...	3·1	11·6
1921	...	...	0·16	...	3·7	12·4
1922	0·28	...	0·15	...	4·1	11·8
1923	0·26	...	0·16	...	4·4	11·4
1924	0·26	...	0·16	...	4·4	12·9
1925	0·26	...	0·16	...	4·3	13·6
1926	0·23	...	0·14	...	4·4	12·9
1927	0·22	...	0·13	...	4·6	13·1
1928	0·22	...	0·13	...	4·7	13·9
1929	0·21	...	0·12	...	4·5	13·0
1930	0·18	...	0·11	...	5·0	11·7
1931	0·16	...	0·09	...	4·5	10·5
1932	0·16	...	0·10	...	4·6	11·3
1933	0·17	...	0·11	...	4·8	12·4
1934	0·17	...	0·12	...	5·3	13·1
1935	0·18	...	0·12	...	5·5	14·4
1936	0·19	...	0·12	...	6·0	15·5
1937	0·20	...	0·15	...	6·8	18·6
1938	0·23	...	0·16	...	7·8	20·0
1939	0·26	...	0·18	...	9·6	25·4
1940	0·30	...	0·20	...	11·4	31·0
1941	0·31	...	0·21	...	13·8	35·8
1942	0·32	...	0·23	...	16·2	42·1
1943	0·34	...	0·25	...	20·8	48·4
1944	0·4	...	0·28	...	26·6	56·9
1945	0·6	...	0·42	...	...	...
1946	3·4	4·2	2·0	1·9	111	361
1947	7·3	8·5	5·8	4·9	315	968
1948	13·3	14·2	15·5	12·0	828	1,962
1949	17·5	17·8	25·3	18·3	1,144	2,737
1950	16·3	15·9	29·6	23·6	1,415	3,382
1951	19·0	18·4	41·4	36·3	1,819	4,525
1952	19·9	19·1	42·2	37·4	2,222	5,084
					2,330	5,567
1953	21·3	20·2	42·5	37·4	2,878	6,448
1954	22·6	21·8	42·2	35·9	3,189	7,231
1955	22·4	21·2	41·5	35·2	3,474	7,868
1956	22·5	20·9	43·3	38·4	3,956	8,670
1957	23·2	21·7	44·6	39·5	4,537	10,130
1958	23·1	21·5	41·7	35·9	4,953	10,544
1959	23·3	21·6	42·1	36·6	5,509	11,729
1960	24·2	22·4	42·6	36·6	6,406	14,128
1961	25·4	23·8	43·0	37·0	7,598	16,722
1962	27·2	25·7	42·3	36·3	9,061	19,025
1963	29·2	28·3	43·1	36·7	10,661	21,776
1964	30·4	29·4	43·2	36·7	12,332	24,883
1965	32·4	31·9	43·5	36·7	14,317	27,856
					14,233	27,796
1966	34·1	33·1	44·5	37·8	16,281	32,287
1967	35·4	34·7	45·4	38·9	18,729	38,143
1968	37·3	37·0	45·7	38·5	22,081	44,793
1969	40·8	39·7	44·4	39·6	25,592	52,440
1970	42·3	42·7	48·4	41·1	31,224	63,346
1971	42·0	45·3	51·3	40·1	37,096	69,209
1972	42·3	47·3	53·3	40·5	43,035	79,789
1973	49·0	52·9	60·2	49·1	54,081	98,232
1974	65·2	67·8	73·7	67·3	68,411	115,836
1975	72·9	76·6	75·9	68·8	79,648	127,891
1976	79·7	83·6	79·7	73·4	90,292	144,459
1977	86·1	89·2	81·2	74·9	100,867	158,919
1978	89·4	92·3	79·1	71·7	108,819	174,758
1979	92·6	94·3	84·9	79·4	117,682	188,943
1980	100·0	100·0	100·0	100·0	128,224	204,828
1981	104·9	105·3	101·4	101·0	138,794	215,283
1982	107·7	107·2	103·2	102·6	147,072	226,246
1983	109·7	109·4	...	...	155,455[a]	234,145[a]

a Estimated by OECD secretariat.

Table J.4 Population, 1900–83

	Total population	Males	Females	Age distribution Under 15	15–64	65 & over
			mn			
1900	43·85	22·05	21·80	...	...	...
1901	44·36	22·30	22·06	...	...	...
1902	44·96	22·61	22·36	...	...	...
1903	45·55	22·90	22·65	15·26	27·92	2·37
1904	46·14	23·20	22·94	...	...	...
1905	46·62	23·42	23·20	...	...	...
1906	47·04	23·60	23·44	...	...	...
1907	47·42	23·79	23·63	...	...	...
1908	47·97	24·04	23·92	16·40	29·02	2·54
1909	48·55	24·33	24·23	...	...	...
1910	49·18	24·65	24·53	...	...	...
1911	49·85	24·99	24·86	...	...	...
1912	50·58	25·37	25·21	...	...	...
1913	51·31	25·74	25·57	17·91	30·53	2·85
1914	52·04	26·11	25·93	...	...	...
1915	52·75	26·47	26·29	...	...	...
1916	53·50	26·84	26·66	...	...	...
1917	54·13	27·16	26·98	...	...	...
1918	54·74	27·45	27·29	19·21	32·41	3·12
1919	55·03	27·60	27·43	...	...	...
1920	55·96	28·04	27·92	20·42	32·60	2·94
1921	56·67	28·41	28·26	...	...	...
1922	57·39	28·80	28·59	...	...	...
1923	58·12	29·18	28·94	...	...	...
1924	58·88	29·57	29·31	...	...	...
1925	59·74	30·01	29·73	21·92	34·80	3·02
1926	60·74	30·52	30·22	...	...	...
1927	61·66	30·98	30·68	...	...	...
1928	62·60	31·45	31·15	...	...	...
1929	63·46	31·89	31·57	...	...	...
1930	64·45	32·39	32·06	23·58	37·81	3·06
1931	65·46	32·90	32·56	...	...	...
1932	66·43	33·36	33·07	...	...	...
1933	67·43	33·85	33·58	...	...	...
1934	68·31	34·29	34·02	...	...	...
1935	69·25	34·73	34·52	25·55	40·47	3·23
1936	70·11	35·10	35·01	...	...	...
1937	70·63	35·13	35·50	...	...	...
1938	71·01	35·13	35·88	...	...	...
1939	71·38	35·23	36·15	...	...	...
1940	71·93	35·39	36·54	26·37	42·11	3·45
1941	72·22	...	...	...	...	...
1942	72·88	...	...	...	...	...
1943	73·90	...	...	...	...	...
1944	74·43	...	...	...	...	...
1945	72·15	...	...	26·48	41·97	3·70
1946	75·75	...	...	...	...	...
1947	78·10	38·13	39·97	27·57	46·79	3·74
1948	80·00	39·13	40·87	...	...	...
1949	81·77	40·06	41·71	...	...	...
1950	83·20	40·81	42·39	29·43	49·66	4·11
1951	84·54	41·49	43·05	...	...	...
1952	85·81	42·13	43·68	...	...	...
1953	86·98	42·72	44·26	...	...	...
1954	88·24	43·34	44·90	...	...	...
1955	89·28	43·86	45·42	29·80	54·73	4·75
1956	90·17	44·30	45·87	...	...	...
1957	90·93	44·67	46·26	...	...	...
1958	91·77	45·08	46·69	...	...	...
1959	92·64	45·50	47·14	...	...	...
1960	93·42	45·88	47·54	28·07	60·00	5·35
1961	94·29	46·30	47·99	...	...	...
1962	95·18	46·73	48·45	...	...	...
1963	96·17	47·21	48·96	...	...	...
1964	97·18	47·71	49·47	...	...	...
1965	98·28	48·24	50·04	25·17	66·93	6·18
1966	99·04	48·61	50·43	...	...	...
1967	100·20	49·18	51·02	...	...	...
1968	101·33	49·74	51·59	...	...	...
1969	102·54	50·33	52·21	...	...	...
1970	103·72	50·92	52·80	24·82	71·57	7·33
1971	105·15	51·61	53·54	...	...	...
1972	107·60	52·82	54·78	...	...	...
1973	109·10	53·61	55·49	...	...	...
1974	110·57	54·38	56·19	...	...	...
1975	111·94	55·09	56·85	27·22	75·85	8·87
1976	113·09	55·67	57·42	27·49	76·40	9·20
1977	114·15	56·20	57·95	27·65	76·95	9·55
1978	115·17	56·70	58·47	27·71	77·54	9·92
1979	116·13	57·18	58·95	27·66	78·16	10·31
1980	117·06	57·59	59·47	27·51	78·90	10·65
1981	117·88	58·00	59·88	27·60	79·27	11·01
1982	118·69	58·40	60·29	27·25	80·09	11·35
1983	119·48	58·79	60·69	26·91	80·90	11·67

Table J.5 Labour market: employment, 1900–83

	Employed labour force	Agriculture, forestry & fishing	Mining	Mfg	Gas, electricity & water	Construction	Transport & communication	Distribution & services
				mn				
1900	24·77	17·33		2·93			4·51	
1901	24·96	17·29		3·04			4·63	
1902	25·12	17·24		3·13			4·75	
1903	25·30	17·19		3·23			4·88	
1904	25·44	17·11		3·32			5·01	
1905	25·60	17·04		3·37			5·19	
1906	25·73	16·94		3·42			5·37	
1907	25·86	16·85		3·56			5·46	
1908	25·97	16·74		3·69			5·54	
1909	26·09	16·63		3·75			5·71	
1910	26·17	16·49		3·89			5·79	
1911	26·26	16·35		3·98			5·92	
1912	26·35	16·21		4·08			6·06	
1913	26·42	16·06		4·17			6·19	
1914	26·47	15·88		4·25			6·34	
1915	26·53	15·72		4·32			6·49	
1916	26·56	15·52		4·44			6·59	
1917	26·59	15·33		4·55			6·71	
1918	26·62	15·13		4·63			6·86	
1919	26·62	14·91		4·68			7·03	
1920	27·26	14·85		4·59			7·82	
1921	27·50	14·84		4·64			8·02	
1922	27·73	14·82		4·71			8·20	
1923	27·97	14·81		4·75			8·41	
1924	28·21	14·80		4·82			8·59	
1925	28·44	14·79		4·87			8·79	
1926	28·68	14·77		4·91			8·99	
1927	28·91	14·76		4·95			9·20	
1928	29·15	14·75		4·99			9·41	
1929	29·38	14·73		4·87			9·78	
1930	29·62	14·72		5·07			9·83	
1931	28·99	14·80		4·74			9·45	
1932	29·18	14·83		4·92			9·42	
1933	29·78	14·79		5·26			9·72	
1934	30·79	14·78		5·85			10·16	
1935	31·40	14·77		6·22			10·41	
1936	30·86	14·57		6·20			10·09	
1937	31·16	14·53		6·47			10·17	
1938	31·47	14·49		6·74			10·25	
1939	31·78	14·45		7·08			10·25	
1940	32·48	14·40		7·66			10·42	
1941	32·58	14·28		8·11			10·19	
1942	32·60	14·17		8·59			9·84	
1947	34·66	17·65	...	6·69[a]	...	1·37	1·67	7·28
1948	34·93	17·09	0·61	6·33	...	1·36	1·64	7·88[a]
1949	36·12	18·58	0·45	6·65	...	1·25	1·78[a]	7·41
1950	36·48	18·53	0·47	6·04	...	1·35	1·59[a]	8·49
1951	36·74	17·18	0·54	6·25	...	1·44	1·85[a]	9·38
1952	37·56	17·19	0·62	6·31	...	1·52	1·93[a]	10·00
1953	39·36	16·69	0·60	7·19	0·16	1·63	(1·74)	11·35
1954	39·89	16·19	0·57	7·44	0·17	1·70	(1·69)	12·10
1955	41·19	16·54	0·49	7·56	0·18	1·81	(1·74)	12·84
1956	41·97	16·15	0·43	8·05	0·19	1·83	(1·85)	13·47
1957	42·81	14·67	0·50	8·53	0·22	2·17	1·89	14·83
1958	42·98	14·08	0·45	8·98	0·22	2·23	1·96	15·06
1959	43·35	13·48	0·48	8·96	0·23	2·43	2·07	15·70
1960	44·36	13·40	0·43	9·46	0·23	2·53	2·16	16·15
1961	44·98	13·03	0·38	10·11	0·23	2·74	2·25	16·24
1962	45·56	12·67	0·41	10·66	0·24	2·90	2·36	16·32
1963	45·95	11·94	0·33	11·08	0·25	2·90	2·43	17·02
1964	46·55	11·49	0·30	11·29	0·25	3·08	2·61	17·53
1965	47·30	11·13	0·29	11·50	0·26	3·28	2·68	18·16
1966	48·27	10·72	0·26	11·78	0·26	3·50	2·85	18·90
1967	49·20	10·36	0·26	12·52	0·27	3·59	2·89	19·29
1968	50·02	9·88	0·27	13·05	0·27	3·70	3·02	19·77
1969	50·40	9·46	0·24	13·45	0·27	3·71	3·11	20·11
1970	50·94	8·86	0·20	13·77	0·28	3·94	3·24	20·56
1971	51·21	8·15	0·19	13·83	0·29	4·14	3·33	21·22
1972	51·26	7·55	0·16	13·83	0·29	4·33	3·27	21·74
1973	52·59	7·05	0·13	14·43	0·34	4·67	3·37	22·48
1974	52·37	6·75	0·14	14·27	0·33	4·64	3·31	22·82
1975	52·23	6·61	0·16	13·46	0·32	4·79	3·32	23·48
1976	52·71	6·43	0·18	13·45	0·33	4·92	3·41	23·90
1977	53·42	6·34	0·19	13·40	0·31	4·99	3·41	24·67
1978	54·08	6·33	0·15	13·26	0·32	5·20	3·42	25·30
1979	54·79	6·13	0·12	13·33	0·33	5·36	3·49	25·94
1980	55·36	5·77	0·11	13·67	0·30	5·48	3·50	26·39
1981	55·81	5·57	0·10	13·85	0·31	5·44	3·44	26·98
1982	56·38	5·48	0·10	13·80	0·34	5·41	3·49	27·77
1983	57·33	5·31		19·93			32·09	

a Including gas, electricity and water.

118

Table J.6 Labour market: other indicators, 1923–83

	Mfg				Industrial disputes		
	Average hrs worked per month	Average monthly earnings	Unemployment		Stoppages	Workers involved	Working days lost
		Y	'000	%		'000	'000
1923	283·0	46·26	...	...	...	...	...
1924	278·0	47·48	...	...	333	55	638
1925	278·6	47·14	...	...	293	40	361
1926	279·7	46·18	...	...	495	67	722
1927	276·0	52·64	...	...	383	47	1,177
1928	273·6	54·73	...	...	397	46	584
1929	272·8	55·52	...	...	576	77	572
1930	266·3	53·05	369	5·3	907	81	1,085
1931	264·0	49·37	423	6·1	998	65	980
1932	265·3	50·59	486	6·8	893	55	619
1933	271·7	50·55	409	5·6	410	49	385
1934	272·0	50·87	373	5·0	626	50	446
1935	272·8	50·49	356	4·6	590	38	301
1936	273·8	51·30	338	4·3	547	31	163
1937	275·6	53·03	295	3·7	628	124	338
1938	276·6	55·46	237	3·0	262	18	41
1939	276·3	54·69	...	...	358	73	35
1940	278·0	61·73	...	...	271	33	54
1941	280·0	69·12	...	...	159	11	...
1942	282·1	76·62	...	...	173	10	...
1943	282·9	88·56	...	...	292	11	...
1944	298·9	100·76	...	...	216	7	...
1945	204·9	88·47	...	...	95	36	...
1946	...	437·5	...	...	702	517	6,266
		Y'000					
1947	183·4	1·8	370	...	464	219	5,036
1948	184·1	4·9	240	0·7	744	2,304	6,995
1949	182·8	8·4	380	1·0	554	1,122	4,321
1950	186·8 / 195·6	8·6 / 10·6	440	1·2	584	763	5,468
1951	192·8	11·7	390	1·1	576	1,163	6,015
1952	194·4	13·5	470	1·2	590	1,624	15,075
1953	196·7	15·3	450	1·1	611	1,341	4,279
1954	195·9	16·3	590	1·5	647	928	3,836
1955	198·0	16·7	680 / 760	1·6 / 1·8	659	1,033	3,467
1956	204·4	18·3	710	1·7	646	1,098	4,562
1957	202·9	19·3	590	1·4	827	1,557	5,634
1958	201·4	19·2	630	1·4	903	1,279	6,052
1959	204·7	20·8	650	1·5	887	1,216	6,020
1960	207·0	22·6	500	1·1	1,063	918	4,912
1961	203·4	24·8	440	0·9	1,401	1,680	6,150
1962	198·4	27·3	400	0·9	1,299	1,518	5,400
1963	196·9	30·2	400	0·9	1,079	1,183	2,770
1964	195·7	33·1	370	0·8	1,234	1,050	3,165
1965	191·8	36·1	390	0·8	1,542	1,682	5,669
1966	193·0	40·5	440	0·9	1,252	1,132	2,742
1967	193·9	45·6	630	1·3	1,214	733	1,830
1968	193·0	52·7	590	1·2	1,546	1,163	2,841
1969	190·0	61·8	570	1·1	1,783	1,412	3,634
1970	187·4	71·4	590	1·2	2,260	1,720	3,915
1971	184·3	81·0	640	1·4	2,527	1,896	6,029
1972	183·3	93·6	730	1·3	2,498	1,544	5,147
1973	182·0	116·3	680	1·3	3,326	2,236	4,604
1974	173·2	146·5	730	1·4	5,211	3,621	9,663
1975	167·8	163·7	1,000	1·9	3,391	2,732	8,016
1976	173·9	183·6	1,080	2·0	2,720	1,356	3,254
1977	174·5	200·8	1,100	2·0	1,712	692	1,519
1978	175·6	214·6	1,240	2·2	1,517	660	1,358
1979	177·9	227·8	1,170	2·1	1,153	450	930
1980	178·2	244·6	1,140	2·0	1,133	563	1,001
1981	177·4	259·7	1,260	2·2	955	247	554
1982	177·0	269·6	1,360	2·4	944	216	538
1983	178·0	279·1	1,560	2·7	893	224	507

Table J.7 Value of exports and imports by country, 1900–83

	Total exports	Exports to: France	Germany	UK	USA	Total imports	Imports from: France	Germany	UK	USA
					Y bn					
1900	0·21	0·019	0·004	0·011	0·053	0·29	0·008	0·029	0·072	0·063
1901	0·26	0·027	0·005	0·012	0·072	0·26	0·004	0·028	0·051	0·043
1902	0·27	0·027	0·005	0·017	0·080	0·28	0·005	0·026	0·050	0·049
1903	0·30	0·034	0·005	0·017	0·083	0·33	0·005	0·027	0·049	0·046
1904	0·33	0·036	0·004	0·018	0·101	0·38	0·003	0·029	0·075	0·058
1905	0·34	0·027	0·004	0·013	0·094	0·50	0·005	0·043	0·115	0·104
1906	0·44	0·040	0·008	0·023	0·126	0·44	0·005	0·043	0·101	0·070
1907	0·45	0·043	0·011	0·022	0·131	0·51	0·007	0·048	0·116	0·081
1908	0·40	0·034	0·008	0·026	0·122	0·46	0·005	0·046	0·108	0·078
1909	0·44	0·042	0·008	0·027	0·132	0·43	0·006	0·040	0·086	0·054
1910	0·50	0·045	0·011	0·026	0·144	0·52	0·005	0·044	0·095	0·055
1911	0·52	0·044	0·012	0·024	0·143	0·58	0·006	0·057	0·111	0·081
1912	0·62	0·044	0·014	0·030	0·169	0·68	0·005	0·061	0·116	0·127
1913	0·72	0·060	0·013	0·033	0·185	0·80	0·006	0·068	0·123	0·122
1914	0·67	0·031	0·010	0·033	0·197	0·67	0·004	0·045	0·092	0·097
1915	0·79	0·042	—	0·069	0·204	0·64	0·004	0·006	0·058	0·103
1916	1·23	0·064	—	0·103	0·340	0·88	0·005	0·004	0·082	0·204
1917	1·75	0·098	—	0·203	0·479	1·20	0·004	0·003	0·093	0·360
1918	2·16	0·142	—	0·143	0·530	1·90	0·004	0·003	0·066	0·626
1919	2·38	0·067	—	0·112	0·828	2·50	0·009	—	0·128	0·766
1920	2·20	0·072	0·001	0·098	0·565	2·68	0·015	0·012	0·235	0·873
1921	1·50	0·035	0·002	0·033	0·496	1·94	0·012	0·048	0·184	0·574
1922	1·88	0·079	0·004	0·054	0·732	2·22	0·019	0·111	0·232	0·596
1923	1·69	0·026	0·003	0·040	0·606	2·39	0·022	0·120	0·237	0·512
1924	2·11	0·086	0·009	0·061	0·745	2·97	0·033	0·145	0·313	0·671
1925	2·67	0·059	0·012	0·060	1·006	3·11	0·033	0·124	0·227	0·665
1926	2·41	0·042	0·008	0·060	0·861	2·92	0·025	0·145	0·170	0·680
1927	2·38	0·054	0·011	0·065	0·834	2·71	0·027	0·131	0·153	0·674
1928	2·40	0·063	0·013	0·059	0·826	2·74	0·024	0·134	0·165	0·626
1929	2·60	0·045	0·013	0·063	0·914	2·76	0·026	0·157	0·153	0·654
1930	1·87	0·027	0·011	0·062	0·506	2·01	0·017	0·106	0·093	0·433
1931	1·48	0·016	0·008	0·053	0·425	1·69	0·012	0·073	0·063	0·342
1932	1·80	0·022	0·009	0·061	0·445	1·94	0·021	0·072	0·079	0·510
1933	2·35	0·039	0·012	0·089	0·492	2·46	0·022	0·096	0·083	0·621
1934	2·79	0·038	0·020	0·109	0·399	2·97	0·018	0·110	0·070	0·769
1935	3·28	0·043	0·027	0·120	0·536	3·27	0·020	0·121	0·082	0·810
1936	3·59	0·043	0·035	0·147	0·594	3·64	0·020	0·116	0·073	0·847
1937	4·19	0·047	0·043	0·168	0·639	4·77	0·028	0·177	0·106	1·270
1938	3·94	0·037	0·033	0·135	0·425	3·79	0·014	0·171	0·063	0·915
1939	5·16	0·026	0·025	0·132	0·642	4·17	0·014	0·141	0·024	1·002
1940	5·42	0·024	0·075	0·057	0·569	4·65	0·012	0·083	0·011	1·241
1941	4·38	—	0·035	0·004	0·278	4·07	0·001	0·070	0·005	0·572
1942	3·51	—	0·039	—	—	2·92	—	0·040	0·002	0·014
1943	3·06	—	0·015	—	—	2·94	—	0·121	—	0·005
1944	...	—	—	—	—	...	—	—	—	—
1945	...	—	—	—	—	...	—	—	—	—
1946	2·26	—	—	0·028	1·5	4·07	—	0·050	—	3·5
1947	10·15	0·004	0·021	0·624	1·8	20·27	—	0·159	—	17·6
1948	52·02	0·821	0·159	3·2	16·9	60·29	—	0·183	0·185	37·6
1949	169·8	1·8	0·315	12·6	30·7	284·5	1·2	2·3	1·5	176·8
1950	298·0	3·8	3·7	9·4	64·5	348·2	1·4	3·0	2·4	150·6
1951	488·8	7·0	7·8	19·4	66·6	737·2	8·0	6·1	12·0	250·1
1952	458·2	10·1	5·8	26·3	84·4	730·4	3·1	8·1	13·2	276·6
1953	458·9	4·2	5·7	11·9	84·2	867·5	9·6	13·6	17·6	273·5
1954	586·5	4·2	6·5	18·4	101·7	863·8	7·4	15·9	13·4	305·5
1955	723·8	4·2	9·1	21·9	164·2	889·7	5·5	16·6	13·7	278·6
1956	900·2	5·1	13·1	22·7	198·1	1,162·7	7·8	20·2	24·0	384·2
1957	1,028·9	6·5	21·4	26·5	217·6	1,542·1	10·4	51·6	35·5	584·3
1958	1,035·6	3·2	15·8	37·9	248·6	1,091·9	7·5	32·5	21·4	380·2
1959	1,244·3	4·3	17·0	37·2	376·8	1,295·8	9·0	37·3	37·3	401·6
1960	1,459·6	5·6	23·9	43·4	396·6	1,616·8	11·6	44·3	35·7	559·3
1961	1,524·8	6·3	30·0	41·3	384·1	2,091·8	14·1	69·5	49·4	754·5
1962	1,769·8	8·3	37·5	69·2	504·1	2,029·1	16·7	76·6	52·5	651·2
1963	1,962·8	11·3	41·6	56·1	542·5	2,425·1	18·2	79·1	53·7	747·8
1964	2,402·3	14·9	53·6	71·2	663·0	2,857·5	25·4	89·8	66·7	841·0
1965	3,042·6	17·6	77·4	73·8	892·5	2,940·8	22·5	80·2	58·5	851·9
1966	3,519·5	25·3	88·8	81·2	1,069·0	3,428·2	23·1	85·3	77·2	956·8
1967	3,759·0	27·9	77·4	106·5	1,084·3	4,198·7	31·4	131·0	92·6	1,156·3
1968	4,669·8	33·9	103·5	131·3	1,471·1	4,675·4	45·8	144·2	92·6	1,269·9
1969	5,756·4	43·2	141·4	125·4	1,784·8	5,408·5	53·8	160·3	118·9	1,472·4
1970	6,954·4	45·8	198·1	172·8	2,138·3	6,797·2	67·1	222·1	142·3	2,001·4
1971	8,392·8	66·7	229·3	200·0	2,621·9	6,910·0	69·6	212·9	146·2	1,748·0
1972	8,806·1	87·3	286·5	301·6	2,725·1	7,229·0	92·6	209·8	154·3	1,802·3
1973	10,031	98·1	344·7	368·6	2,568·2	10,404	145·9	303·2	206·2	2,518·4
1974	16,208	214·7	436·7	446·3	3,734·7	18,076	172·4	422·8	255·1	3,694·3
1975	16,545	207·5	492·3	436·7	3,312·1	17,170	148·5	337·6	240·4	3,441·5
1976	19,935	286·1	664·2	415·2	4,653·8	19,229	159·6	364·5	250·3	3,505·2
1977	21,648	269·9	747·5	524·4	5,292·2	19,132	151·0	403·8	258·0	3,357·4
1978	20,556	232·0	764·2	490·6	5,259·0	16,728	157·8	421·4	290·2	3,108·7
1979	22,532	305·3	933·0	674·5	5,772·8	24,245	235·0	563·6	366·1	4,456·9
1980	29,382	456·8	1,300·6	857·9	7,118·1	31,995	293·8	570·1	440·0	5,558·1
1981	33,469	485·9	1,308·9	1,054·1	8,518·7	31,464	256·9	532·5	594·1	5,552·2
1982	34,433	575·2	1,241·0	1,189·5	9,015·2	32,656	300·0	583·2	457·9	5,990·5
1983	34,909	477·0	1,396·4	1,184·1	10,178·6	30,015	309·5	573·3	461·3	5,855·3

Sources

(For sources used in specific tables, see Notes.)

1 Bank of Japan, *100 Year Statistics of the Japanese Economy*. Tokyo, 1966.

2 Bank of Japan, Explanatory notes and Supplement to **1**.

3 International Labour Office, *Technical Guide*, Geneva. Vol. II. 1972, 1976, 1980.

4 *Japan Statistical Year Book*. Statistics Bureau, Prime Minister's Office, Tokyo.

5 League of Nations, *Year Book of Labour Statistics*.

6 Mitchell, B R, *International Historical Statistics Africa and Asia*. New York University Press, 1982.

7 Organisation for Economic Cooperation and Development (OECD), *Labour Force Statistics*. Paris, annual and monthly.

8 OECD, *National Accounts 1950 to 1978*. Paris, 1980.

9 OECD, *National Accounts 1953 to 1982*. Paris, 1984.

10 *Statistical Year Book of the League of Nations*. Geneva.

11 Supplements to the United Nations, *Statistical Year Book* and *Monthly Bulletin of Statistics*. New York, 1967, 1972 and 1977.

12 United Nations, *Monthly Bulletin of Statistics*. New York.

13 United Nations, *Statistical Year Book*. New York.

14 *Year Book of Labour Statistics*. ILO, Geneva.

Notes

Table J.1

Sources: **1, 8, 9**

From 1952, OECD data have been used. There is a break in the series in 1965 when there was a change in the system of classification; two figures are given for 1965. The main differences in classification are explained in **9**.

For 1930–51 the figures are based on estimates published in **1**. Further details on the compilation of these estimates can be found in **2**. For 1946–51, the figures refer to fiscal years (beginning 1 April) and not calendar years. Figures for 1930–51 have been roughly adjusted to 1975 prices. Each category of expenditure has been re-referenced independently and this means that the total for gross domestic product may not equal the sum of components.

Table J.2

Sources: **1, 4, 6, 12, 13**

Industrial production: the index includes mining, manufacturing, and electricity and gas. The series is linked at 1930 to estimates made by Kasushi Ohkawa published in **1** and at 1929 to estimates given in **6**. For further details of method and coverage see **2**.

Coal: from 1975, the figures are for coal and lignite.

Cars and commercial vehicles: includes chassis for buses and trucks.

Crude petroleum: includes Formosa up to 1928 (first line).

Electricity: public supply only up to 1965. Includes electricity generated by industrial establishments (primarily for their own use) from 1966. Figures are for fiscal years (1 April) until 1982.

Table J.3

Sources: **1, 8, 9, 12, 13**

Consumer prices: base weighted indices measuring fluctuations in prices that affect the consumption standards of non-farm households residing in cities. For 1900–45, the 'All items' index is the retail price index for Tokyo compiled by the Bank of Japan. This index has been linked to the consumer price index at 1946.

Wholesale prices: up to 1955, referred to as the 'Tokyo wholesale price index'. It was considerably revised in 1952 and in 1955 the word 'Tokyo' was dropped, although the price data are still obtained mainly from Tokyo. The current series is linked to an earlier series compiled by the Bank of Japan.

The 'Producers' goods' index covers those commodities which are consumed in production. The current index includes raw materials, semi-finished goods, fuel and energy and building materials, but coverage has varied. From December 1982, substantial changes have been made in the presentation of data for the component categories of the wholesale price index. For details see **4**, 1984.

For further details of coverage and weights used see **2** and **11**.

Compensation of employees: OECD data have been used from 1952. The series includes wages and salaries in cash and in kind paid to employees together with contributions on behalf of employees to social security schemes and private pension funds. Two figures are given for 1965 because of the change in classification (see notes to Table J.1).

For 1930–52 (first line), Japan Economic Planning Agency estimates published in **1** have been used; for 1919–29, estimates made by Yuzo Yamada published in **1** were used.

The figures for 1946–50 are for fiscal years (starting on 1 April).

National income: OECD data have been used from 1952. National income is defined as the sum of compensation of employees, net entrepreneurial and property income of residents and indirect taxes less subsidies.

Two figures are given for 1965 because of the change in classification (see notes to Table J.1).

For 1919–52, estimates made by Yuzo Yamada and the Japan Economic Planning Agency (see above) have been used. The figures for 1946–50 are for fiscal years.

For further details of these two series see **2** and **9**.

Table J.4

Sources: **1, 2, 7**

Current figures are for the *de facto* population at 1 October each year. For 1900–19 the figures are at 1 January each year and cover the population of Hokkaido, Honshu, Shikoku, Kyushu and Okinawa. The total population figure for 1920 on this basis is 55·47 mn. The 1945 figures are from a Population Survey taken on 1 November.

For 1945–71 Okinawa is excluded. For other territorial changes in the postwar period see **4**.

Age distribution: for the period up to 1921, the estimates of population by age are based on estimates published in **2**. These early estimates are for the permanently domiciled population and have not been adjusted to the 1920 Census results. The figures in the table have been calculated by obtaining the percentage in each age group in the early estimates and applying these percentages to the total population figure shown in the table to get a rough estimate of the numbers in the different age groups consistent with the total population figure. For further details see **2**.

Table J.5

Sources: **1, 5, 7**

From 1953, OECD data have been used. Figures are annual averages of those in employment and currently cover employees, self employed, unpaid family workers working for at least one third of normal working time and the armed forces (national self defence forces). The temporarily stopped and the unemployed are not included.

From 1967, coverage of the survey on which the figures are based was changed. Figures were adjusted to the new definitions by the Japanese Bureau of Statistics back to 1957. Figures for 1957 on the previous basis are:

Employed labour force	43·03 mn
Agriculture	15·80 mn
Manufacturing	8·53 mn

For 1953–68, employment in gas, electricity and water industries has been estimated by the OECD Secretariat.

'Distribution and services' includes wholesale and retail trades, restaurants and hotels, finance, insurance, real estate and business services, commercial social and personal services and the national self defence forces.

Okinawa is included in the figures from 1973.

For 1947–52, the data are taken from **5**. A new industrial classification was introduced in 1950 and earlier figures are therefore not strictly comparable. For the period 1900–42, the figures are for the gainfully employed population based on estimates made by Kazushi Ohkawa published in 1. The figures for this period in the third column include mining, manufacturing (excluding public and government owned companies) and gas and electricity industries. The figures in the fourth column include civil engineering and construction, transport and communication, commerce and the government sector.

Table J.6

Sources: **1, 4, 5, 6, 14**

Manufacturing: average hours worked and earnings per month: average hours worked include overtime. Average earnings include overtime and bonus payments as well as marriage allowances paid by employers. Data are based on surveys of establishments with 30 or more employees including administrative, technical, clerical and production workers. The sample design was revised in 1982.

The industrial classification was changed in 1950 and the figures are not strictly comparable before and after that date. The second figure given for 1950 is the average for October–December and this is consistent with the years that follow; the first figure is the average for January–September on the previous classification. From 1965, the tobacco industry is excluded from the figures. There were revisions in the industry coverage in 1926, 1930, 1939 and 1946.

For 1926–38, public utilities, civil engineering and construction industries are included in the figures. Figures for hours worked for 1923–38 refer to normal working hours and not average hours worked.

For further details see **2**.

Unemployment: figures are annual averages. In 1955 there was a change in the coverage of the official statistics. For further details see **3**. The percentage figure is the number of unemployed expressed as a percentage of the civilian labour force.

Table J.7

Sources: **4, 6**

From 1952, the figures for Germany are for the Federal Republic of Germany. For 1900–45, Japan includes South Sakhalin and Taiwan, and for 1910–45, Korea. Southern Ireland is included in the UK up to 1923.

Part IV

Analytical tables and charts

CONTENTS

The tables and charts in this section bring together some of the data from the tables in Parts II and III so that an idea of comparative movements in different countries can be obtained. The tables should be used in conjunction with the country tables, as the data are subject to the same qualifications pointed out in the notes to the tables.

The section also includes tables analysing the external trade of the UK and the USA.

Table IV.1   Rates of growth of total output, six countries, 1900–83

	UK	USA	France	Germany	Italy	Japan
	annual averages, per cent					
1900–13	1·53	3·98	2·63[b]	2·91	2·59	...
1920–29	1·74	3·76[a]	5·91	4·08[c]	2·59	...
1929–38	1·88	0·13[a]	−1·91	2·66	1·08	6·23[e]
1950–60	2·66	3·26	4·56	7·97	5·54[d]	8·82
1960–73	2·28	4·17	5·56	4·43	5·30	10·43
1973–83	2·22	2·04	2·23	1·64	1·80	3·70
1900–38	1·05	2·65[a]	1·26[b]	1·89	1·97	...
1950–83	2·37	3·25	4·24	4·63	4·26[d]	7·87

a   1920–28 and 1929–39; 1900–39.
b   1901–13 and 1901–38.
c   1925–29.
d   1951–60 and 1951–83.
e   1930–38.

Chart IV.1   Rates of growth of total output

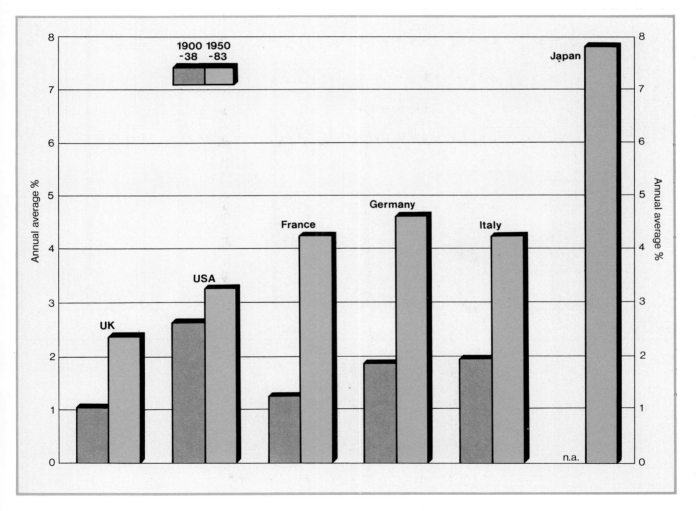

Note: See notes to Table IV.1.

***Table* IV.2** Rates of growth of productivity, six countries, 1900–83

	UK		USA		France	Germany	Italy	Japan
	Output per person employed		Output per manhour		Output per person employed			
	Whole economy	Mfg	Whole economy[a]	Mfg				
				annual averages, per cent				
1900–13	0·81	...	1·68	2·25	...	...	...	...
1920–29	1·98	3·40	2·76	5·57	...	...	...	...
1929–38	0·79	2·08	1·31	1·61	...	...	...	...
1950–60	2·11	2·07	2·51	1·96	4·88[b]	5·25	4·37[b]	6·52
1960–73	2·59	3·59	2·91	3·42	4·64	3·34	5·55	8·65
1973–83	1·33	1·62	0·86[c]	1·52[c]	2·15	3·44	1·04	2·78
1950–83	2·04	2·50	2·19[c]	2·40[c]	3·81[b]	3·95	3·73[b]	6·20

a Gross private domestic product.
b 1954–60 and 1954–83.
c To 1982.

Chart IV.2 *Rates of growth of productivity, 1950–83*

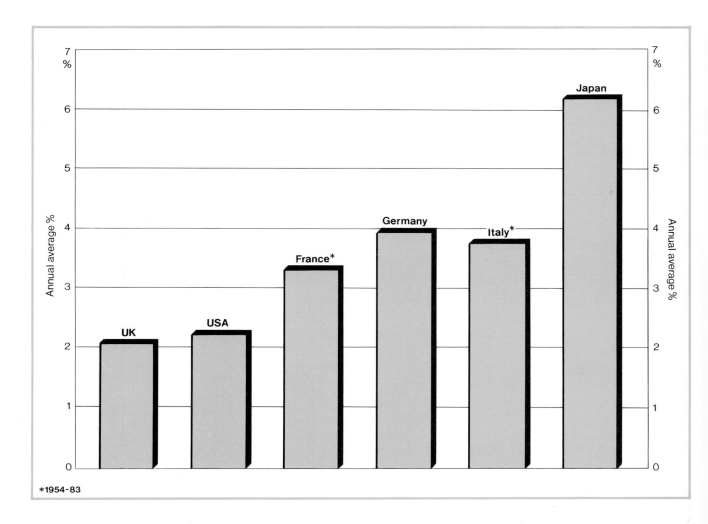

*1954-83

***Table* IV.3** Gross domestic product per head, at constant prices, six countries, selected periods, 1900–82

	UK	USA	France	Germany[a]	Italy	Japan
	£ (1980)	$ (1972)	Fr (1975)	DM (1975)	L'000 (1975)	Y'000 (1975)
1900	1,249	1,518	...	3,984	513·8	...
1920	1,267	2,082	...	4,597[b]	601·9	...
1938	1,611	2,286	9,155	7,255	767·1	330·9
1950	1,888	3,511	10,624	5,741	793·7	207·6
1970	3,003	5,293	23,516	15,253	2,108·7	1,137·8
1982	3,555	6,377	31,761[c]	19,578	2,697·9[c]	1,719·6

a Before 1950, figures for Germany refer to the pre-1948 territory.
b 1925.
c 1980.

***Table* IV.4** Output per head, selected commodities, six countries, selected periods, 1900–80

	UK	USA	France[a]	Germany	Italy[a]	Japan
Coal (tons)						
1900	5·56	2·53	0·84	2·67	0·012	0·169
1920	5·33	4·84	0·75	4·14[b]	0·026	0·522
1940	4·73	3·15				0·783
1960	3·76	2·09	1·27	4·51	0·031	0·547
1980	2·29	3·28	0·39	3·64	0·034	0·155
Crude steel (tons)						
1900	0·121	0·134	0·036	0·115	0·004	...
1920	0·211	0·393	0·080	0·189	0·018	0·014
1940	0·273	0·458	0·209	...	...	0·095
1960	0·472	0·499	0·379	0·641	0·169	0·237
1980	0·202	0·445	0·432	0·712	0·472	0·952
Cars & commercial vehicles						
1910	0·0003	0·0020	0·0010	0·0002	—	—
1920	0·0017	0·0179	0·0014	—	—	—
1930	0·0052	0·0226	0·0049	0·0015	0·0011	—
1960	0·0346	0·0369	0·0300	0·0385	0·0133	0·0052
1980	0·0235	0·0281	0·0741	0·0625	0·0285	0·0943

a Figures refer to 1901 and 1921.
b 1922.

***Table* IV.5** Expenditure per head, selected items, UK and USA, selected periods, 1900–80

	Food		Clothing & footwear		Cars & motorcycles		Other consumer durables	
	UK	USA	UK	USA	UK	USA	UK	USA
	£ (1980)	$ (1972)	£ (1980)	$ (1972)	£ (1980)	$ (1972)	£ (1980)	$ (1972)
1900	249·5	353·4[a]	77·0	143·2	0·78	...	37·5[b]	92·0[d]
1910	240·8	406·9[a]	72·8	171·0	1·42	...	35·0[b]	106·1[d]
1920	255·3	422·5[a]	81·2	164·3	4·71	...	24·5	117·4[d]
1930	315·4	389·1	80·8	173·5	9·35	49·8	36·5	81·2
1940	280·5	528·7	72·3	190·0	...	68·6	120·0[c]	91·3
1950	382·4	600·1	88·4	201·6	6·64	135·9	42·7	143·8
1960	387·9	639·7	109·2	202·5	40·9	135·0	68·1	149·4
1970	399·7	731·3	141·9	240·9	75·9	186·2	71·4	248·2
1980	408·8	794·9	176·3	342·1	112·7	238·9	125·3	364·5

a Perishables – see notes to Table US.6.
b Including other non-durable items – see notes to Table UK.6.
c Including cars and motorcycles.
d Including cars, etc.

***Table* IV.6** Distribution of employment, UK and USA, selected periods, 1900–80

	Agriculture		Mfg		Distribution & services[c]	
	UK[a]	USA[b]	UK[a]	USA[b]	UK[a]	USA[b]
	% employment in:					
1900	13	41	33	20	36	17
1910	12	33	33	23	36	19
1920	9	27	35	27	32	20
1930	8	23	32	21	39	23
1950	3	11	37	26	31	28
1960	3	8	35	26	35	33
1970	2	4	34	25	40	38
1980	1	3	27	20	48	44

a Figures are for 1901 and 1911 and after 1930 refer to employees only; this affects the percentages, particularly in agriculture and distribution and services.
b US figures for agriculture include all those employed; other figures are for employees.
c Distribution and services excludes transport and communication but includes (in UK) public administration.

Chart IV.6   *Distribution of employment, UK and USA, 1900 and 1980*

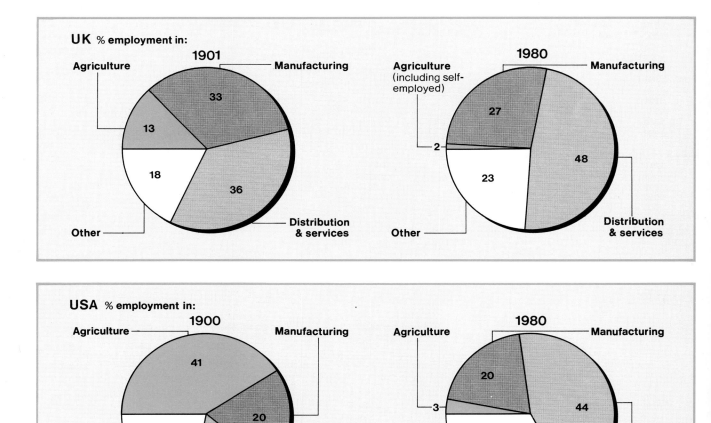

130

Table **IV.7**   Distribution of employment, Japan and Germany, selected periods, 1900–80

| | % employment in: | | | | | |
| | Agriculture | | Industry[a] | | Distribution & services[b] | |
	Japan	Germany	Japan[c]	Germany	Japan[c]	Germany
1900	70·0	...	11·8	...	18·2	...
1910	63·0	...	14·9	...	22·1	...
1920	54·5	...	16·8	...	28·7	...
1930	49·7	...	17·1	...	33·2	...
1940	44·3	...	23·6	...	32·1	...
1950	50·8	24·6	21·5[d]	42·8	27·6[d]	32·5
1960	30·2	15·8	28·5	48·8	41·3	37·3
1970	17·4	8·6	35·7	49·3	46·7	42·0
1980	10·4	5·6	35·3	44·2	54·0	50·3

a Comprising manufacturing, mining and quarrying, construction, public utilities.   b Including transport and communication.
c Before 1950, construction included in distribution and services.   d Public utilities included in distribution and services.

Chart IV.7   *Distribution of employment, Japan and Germany, 1900, 1950 and 1980*

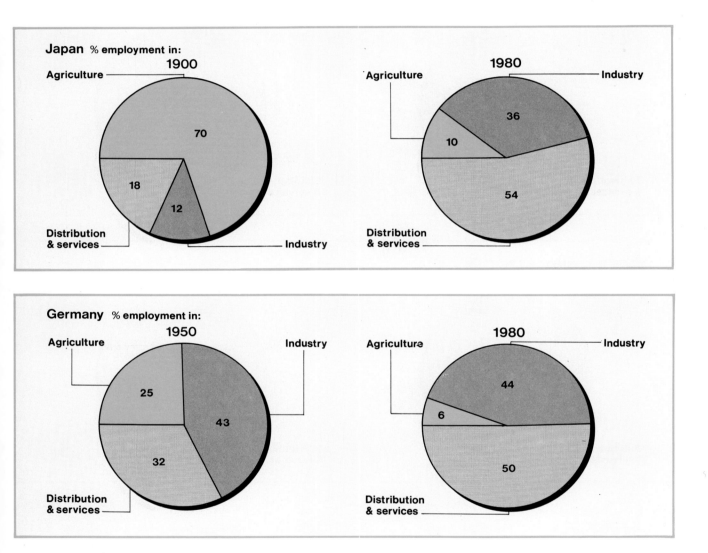

***Table* IV.8** Distribution of employment, Italy and France, selected periods, 1954–80

	% employment in:					
	Agriculture		Industry[a]		Distribution & services[b]	
	Italy	France	Italy	France	Italy	France
1954	43·1	27·9	30·4	37·0	26·4	35·1
1960	32·9	22·4	36·9	39·1	30·2	38·5
1970	20·2	13·9	39·5	39·8	40·3	46·4
1980	14·3	8·7	37·8	36·0	47·9	55·2

a Manufacturing, mining and quarrying, construction, public utilities.
b Including transport and communication.

Chart* IV.8   *Distribution of employment, Italy and France, 1954 and 1980

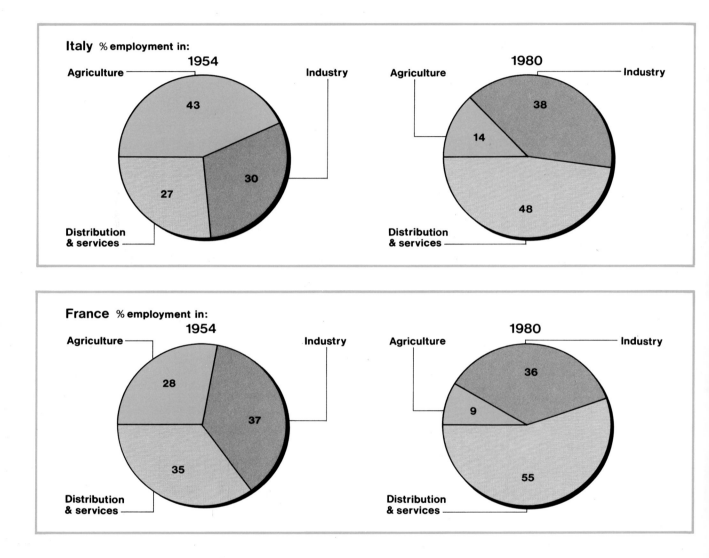

Table IV.9 Population trends, six countries, selected periods, 1900–80

	UK	USA	France	Germany	Italy	Japan
Total population growth (1950 = 100)						
				1938 = 100		
1900	81·4	50·0	92·0[a]	80·9	69·4[a]	52·7
1920	86·5	69·9	92·7[b]	90·0[d]	81·2[b]	67·3
1938	93·9	85·2	98·4[c]	100·0	91·8[c]	85·3
				1950 = 100		
1950	100·0	100·0	100·0	100·0	100·0	100·0
1970	109·6	134·7	121·3	126·8	112·8	124·7
1980	111·3	149·5	128·4	128·7	120·0	140·7
% population in different age groups						
Under 15						
1900	32·5	34·3	25·7[a]	32·8	34·4[a]	33·5[f]
1920	28·2	31·7	22·4[b]	23·7[d]	31·1[b]	36·5
1938	21·9	25·6	24·4[c]	21·6[e]	30·7[c]	36·9[g]
1950	22·4	26·8	22·7	21·8	26·7	35·4
1980	21·1	22·5	22·3	18·2	20·5	23·5
15–64						
1900	62·8	61·5	65·8[a]	62·3	59·6[a]	61·3[f]
1920	65·8	63·6	68·4[b]	70·5[d]	61·7[b]	58·3
1938	69·4	67·8	65·5[c]	70·6[c]	61·9[c]	58·4[g]
1950	67·0	64·7	65·9	68·9	66·0	59·7
1980	64·0	66·2	63·8	66·3	66·7	67·4
65 and over						
1900	4·8	4·1	8·4[a]	4·9	6·1[a]	5·2[f]
1920	6·0	4·6	9·2[b]	5·8[d]	7·2[b]	5·2
1938	8·6	6·5	10·0[c]	7·8[e]	7·5[c]	4·7[g]
1950	10·7	8·1	11·4	9·3	8·1	4·9
1980	14·9	11·3	14·0	15·5	12·8	9·1

a 1901.   b 1921.   c 1936.   d 1925.   e 1939.   f 1903.   g 1935.

Notes:
Germany refers to the whole of Germany before 1950 and then to the Federal Republic of Germany. UK includes Southern Ireland in 1900.
Age distribution: figures for Germany are for those under 14 years and 14–64 years for 1900–50; figures for Italy are for those under 14 years and 14–64 years in 1980.

Chart IV.9   Age distribution, 1900, 1938 and 1980

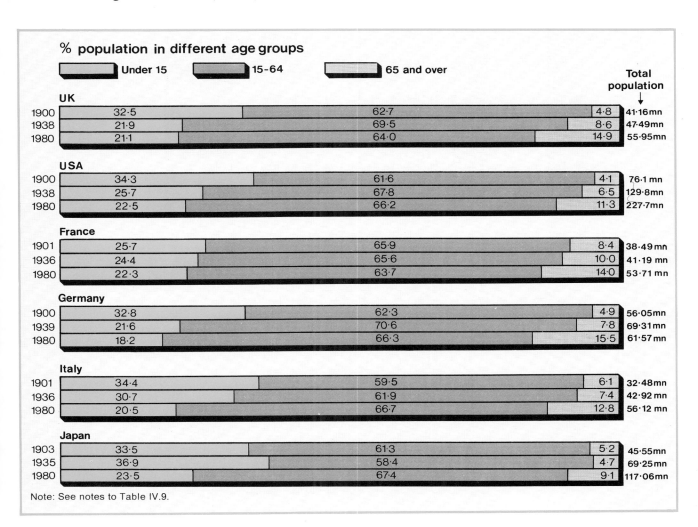

Note: See notes to Table IV.9.

***Table* IV.10** Rates of growth of consumer prices, six countries, 1900–83

	UK	USA	France	Germany	Italy	Japan
	Annual averages, per cent					
1900–13	0·75	1·33	0·62	2·05	1·41	...
1920–29	− 4·41	− 1·71	5·64	3·81[a]	3·00	− 4·03[b]
1929–38	− 0·63	− 2·22	1·49	− 2·23	− 0·38	1·02
1950–60	4·11	2·09	5·89	1·76	2·94	4·03
1960–73	5·05	3·18	4·20	3·41	4·71	5·58
1973–83	13·60	8·37	11·28	4·73	16·97	8·39
1900–38	1·47	1·38	5·38	1·31	4·73	...
1950–83	7·28	4·39	6·82	3·30	7·72	5·95

a   1924–29.
b   1922–29.

Chart IV.10   *Rates of growth of consumer prices*

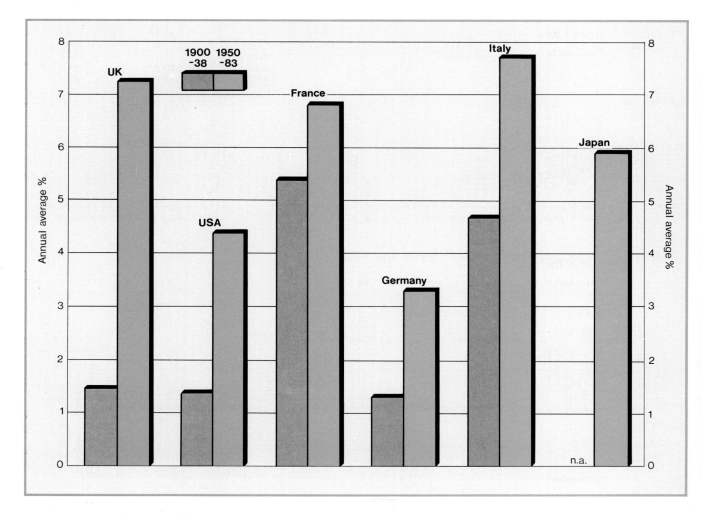

***Table* IV.11** Rates of growth of earnings in manufacturing, six countries, 1950–83

	UK	USA	France[b]	Germany	Italy	Japan
	Annual averages, per cent					
1950–60	6·81	4·41	9·89	7·43	4·96	7·86
1960–73	8·29	4·87	9·65	9·00	11·60	13·43
1973–83	14·37	7·92[a]	14·80	6·55	23·88	9·14
1950–83	9·50	5·57[a]	11·15	7·77	12·74	10·42

a   1973–82 and 1950–82.
b   Wage rates.

***Table* IV.12**   Commodity composition, external trade, UK, selected periods, 1900–83

	% share of total imports of:				% share of total exports[a] of:			
	Food, drink & tobacco	Basic materials	Fuels	Finished manufact.	Non-manufact.	Fuels	Manufact.	Machinery & transport equipment
1900	42·1	31·7	1·3	24·3[b]	18·6	11·0	69·8	8·8
1920	39·3	37·0	3·7	5·3	18·4	8·0	72·7	4·6
1938	46·5	26·1	5·2	7·1	18·2	8·8	70·7	22·0
1960	33·1	23·2	10·3	11·1	10·4	3·4	82·8	40·7
1980	12·4	8·1	13·8	35·6	9·9	13·6	73·5	34·4
1983	11·9	7·2	10·7	42·3	9·6	21·7	65·9	30·3

a   These rows do not add up to 100% because miscellaneous items (e g parcel post) have been included in the total but not in the categories.
b   Includes semi-manufactures.

Chart* IV.12   *Commodity composition, external trade, UK, 1900, 1938 and 1980

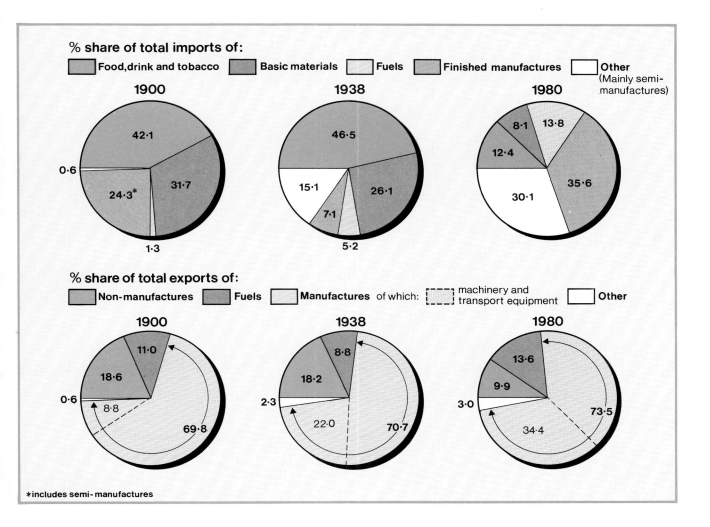

	% share of total imports of:				% share of total exports of:			
	Food, feeds & beverages	Industrial materials & supplies	Petroleum & products	Consumer[a] goods (incl. autos)	Food, feeds & beverages	Industr. materials & supplies	Fuels & lubricants	Consumer[a] goods (incl. autos)
1900	27·2	48·9	—	23·9	39·2	35·4	7·5	23·8
1920	34·4	49·0	0·6	16·6	24·7	34·5	11·6	38·9
1940	21·2	67·7	2·7	6·4	6·1	50·8	9·9	12·3
1960	21·8	52·3	10·2	16·8	15·4	38·5	4·1	12·9
1980	7·4	52·7	32·2	25·5	16·0	31·8	4·0	14·7
1983	7·0	41·0	20·8	33·7	15·4	28·2	4·9	15·2

a   Including capital goods, 1900 and 1920.

Chart IV.13   *Commodity composition, external trade, USA, 1920, 1960 and 1980*

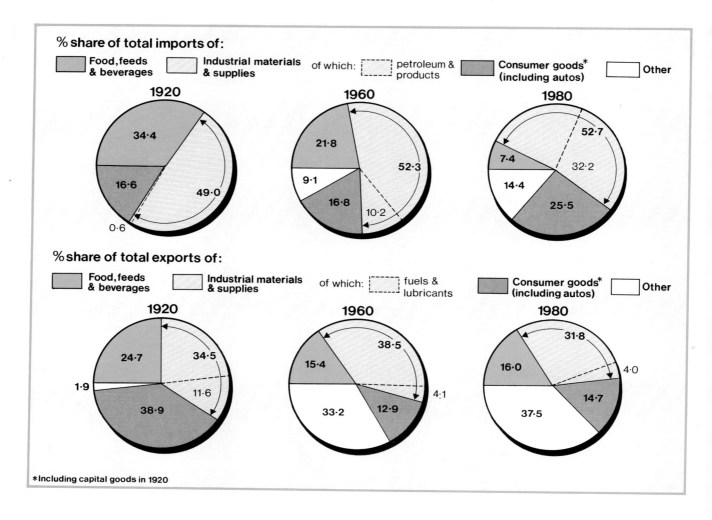

*Including capital goods in 1920

Table IV.14   External trade by area, UK, selected periods, 1900–83

	% imports from:			% exports to:		
	European Community	North America	Japan	European Community	North America	Japan
1900	30·4	31·2	0·4	30·8	13·6	2·8
1910	25·4	22·0	0·6	27·3	16·0	1·9
1920	12·7	17·6	1·6	28·9	11·6	1·8
1930	29·4	13·4	0·8	31·5	10·8	1·2
1938	18·7	21·7	1·0	24·8	10·0	0·4
1950	19·1	15·1	0·3	20·0	11·4	0·1
1960	20·4	20·4	0·9	21·1	15·7	0·8
1970	27·0	20·6	1·5	29·9	15·2	1·8
1980	41·3	15·0	3·4	43·4	11·3	1·3
1983	45·6	13·7	5·1	43·8	15·4	1·3

Chart IV.14   *External trade by area, UK, 1900, 1938 and 1980*

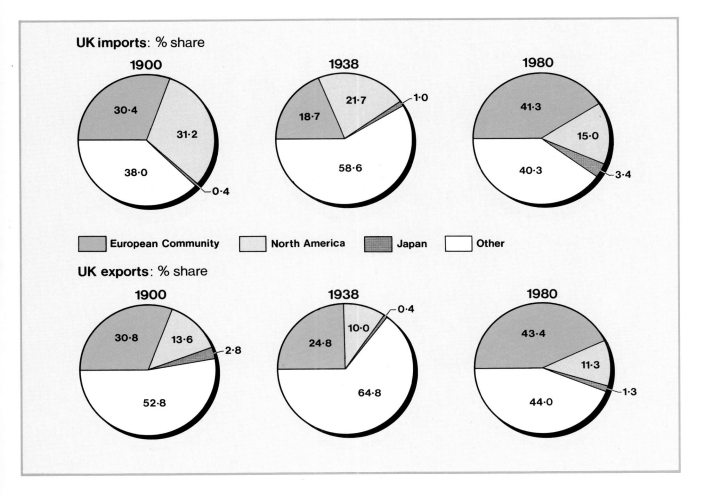

137

***Table* IV.15** External trade by area, USA, selected periods, 1900–83

	% imports from:			% exports to:		
	UK	Germany[a]	Japan	UK	Germany[a]	Japan
1900	18·8	11·4	3·9	38·3	13·4	2·0
1910	17·4	10·9	4·2	29·0	14·3	1·3
1920	9·7	1·7	7·9	22·2	3·8	4·6
1930	6·9	5·8	9·1	17·6	7·2	4·3
1940	5·9	—	6·0	25·1	—	5·6
1950	3·7	1·2	2·0	5·3	4·3	4·1
1960	6·6	6·0	7·6	7·2	6·2	7·0
1970	5·4	7·7	14·6	5·9	6·3	10·8
1980	4·0	4·8	12·5	5·7	5·0	9·4
1983	4·8	4·9	16·0	5·3	4·4	10·9

a Federal Republic of Germany from 1950.

Chart* IV.15   *External trade by area, USA, 1900, 1940 and 1980

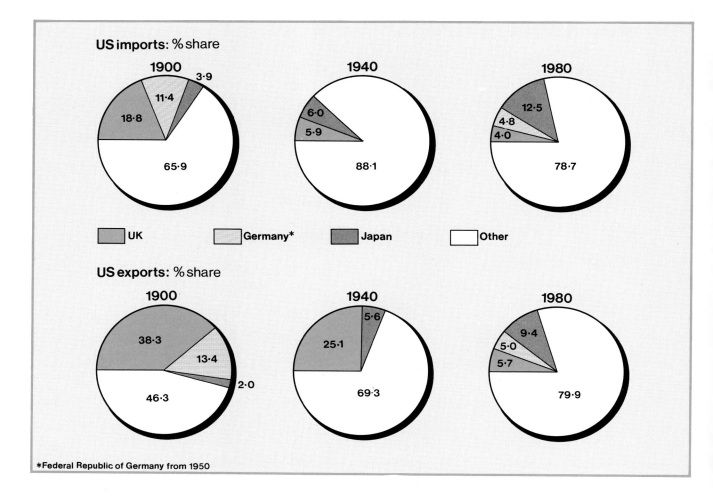

*Federal Republic of Germany from 1950

138

Table IV.16 UK share of trade with France, Germany, Italy and Japan, selected periods, 1900–80

	% total exports to UK from:				% total imports from UK in:			
	France	Germany	Italy	Japan	France	Germany	Italy	Japan
1900	29·9	18·6	11·2	5·3	14·5	12·5	21·2	24·5
1910	20·5	14·7	10·1	5·1	13·0	8·6	14·8	18·2
1920	15·8	9·2	11·9	4·4	20·7	16·6	17·2	8·8
1930	16·1	10·1	9·8	3·3	10·1	6·2	9·7	4·6
1938	11·6	7·0	5·6	3·4	7·0	5·7	6·5	1·7
1950	9·2	4·3	11·4	3·1	3·7	4·3	5·5	0·7
1960	5·0	4·5	6·9	3·0	3·6	4·6	5·1	2·2
1970	3·9	3·6	3·8	2·5	4·6	3·9	3·8	2·1
1980	7·0	6·5	6·1	2·9	5·4	6·7	4·4	1·4

INDEX TO TABLES